PERSONALITY AND SOCIAL NORMS

About the Authors

Dr. Anita Sharma, received her M.A. (Psychology) and Ph.D. from Himachal Pradesh University, Shimla. She has also received Master's degree in History and Education from Himachal Pradesh University. She started her teaching career in 1997 as a school lecturer (Psychology), Shimla and joined the Department of Psychology, Himachal Pradesh University in September, 2005 as an Asstt. Professor. She has presented papers in National and Internationl Seminars and has over 10 articles to her credit published in national and international journals. Presently, she is engaged in the project entitled "Enhancement Scholastic Attainment through Motivational training among tribal students of Kinnaur district in Himachal Pradesh."

Professor (Dr.) Dalip Malhotra received his M.A. (Psychology) and Ph.D. from Panjab University, Chandigarh. He began his teaching career in 1976 at the Himachal Pradesh University, Shimla as an Assistant Professor. He visited U.S.A. in 1990 as a Fulbright Scholar at the West Virginia University. He has about 80 research publications in national and international journals. He completed a major research project on the productivity in public and private sector enterprises funded by the U.G.C. in 2002. Presently he is engaged in the project entitled Enhancement of Achievement Motivation and Scholastic Attainment in tribal students of Himachal Pradesh. He became professor of Psychology in June 1995 and currently is the Chairperson of the Deptt. of Psychology at the Himachal Pradesh University, Shimla (India). He has also remained Dean of the Faculty of Social Sciences between 2001-2003.

Personality and Social Norms

Anita Sharma
Asstt. Professor
Deptt. of Psychology, H.P. University, Shimla
and
Dalip Malhotra
Chairman
Deptt. of Psychology, H.P. University, Shimla

CONCEPT PUBLISHING COMPANY, NEW DELHI-110059

Cataloging in Publication Data—DK
Courtesy: D.K. Agencies (P) Ltd. <docinfo@dkagencies.com>

Sharma, Anita.
Personality and social norms / Anita Sharma and Dalip Malhotra.
p. cm.
Study conducted among the 500 students of Himachal Pradesh University, Shimla, India.
Includes bibliographical references (p.)
Includes index.
ISBN 13: 9788180694844
ISBN 10: 8180694844

1. Social norms. 2. Personality development India—Himachal Pradesh. 3. Social psychology—India—Himachal Pradesh. I. Malhotra, Dalip, joint author. II. Title.

DDC 155.250 954 52 22

ISBN-13: 978-81-8069-484-4
ISBN-10: 81-8069-484-4

First Published 2007

Published and Printed at
Ashok Kumar Mittal
Concept Publishing Company
A/15-16, Commercial Block, Mohan Garden
New Delhi (INDIA)

Phones : 25351460, 25351794
Fax : 091-11-25357103
Email : publishing@conceptpub.com

Foreword

The focus of the book is on Development of Social Norms among different Personality and Gender groups. Social norms are the essence of social interaction, which serve as the basis for organized social system without which social relationships would be full of chaos, and possibly even leading to destruction. This book is an outgrowth of Eysenck's parenthetical statement (Dimensions of Personality, 1947) that introverts learn the social norms early and faster as compared to the extraverts because of their higher cortical arousal and good conditioning. But it remained in that realm only and was purely theoretical without any empirical evidence. The authors have attempted to put these contentions empirical test. This book deals with the contentious issues of crime, aggression, violence and all sorts of anti-social activities as time and again question is being asked as to who are the adherents of social norms and why do they behave so? This book serves an important purpose in solving the queries of the people in this regard.

The authors Dr. Anita Sharma and Dr. Dalip Malhotra of the Department of Psychology, HP University, Shimla have attempted to settle and encourage this psychodynamic process. The main thrust of the study has been on the youngsters through the lab studies of Sherif and Asch. It has been found that introverts because of their socialized structure learn social norms and expectations faster and retain them as long as the social norm is in vogue. Introverts also come under pressure more often as compared to their counterparts due to high susceptibility to punishment.

Similarly, in the case of gender groups, females have been found to follow the social norms closely and the retention power is greater as compared to the males who not only drift away from the norms but also thwart due to their casual disposition, pesonality and genetic make-up. Females also yield to group pressure for the fear of rejection by the group and are relationship-oriented as compared to their counterparts because of their early socialization practices, which produces a gender schema. These findings were borne out of the significant interactions.

Hence, the present book serves a fruitful purpose to the students, researchers and to the common man at large. The efforts of the researchers are laudable and the practical implications of the research should be tried as well as applied for the welfare of all segments of the society.

(Virbhadra Singh)

Former Chief Minister of Himachal Pradesh

Preface

Deviation or breach of the social norms is a burning topic of today or you can say the order of the day. May it be anything! As the aim of our present study revolves round the central topic of 'Social Norms' because the question in social psychology is perpetually asked time and again that who are the persons who adhere to the social norms and who are the ones who violate these; so we have mainly focused our research on this topic.

The problem of social norms like many other borderline issues fall within the province called social psychology. The present society is facing all sorts of ills especially the challenge of breakdown of norms and values that is threatening the stability of our society. The many ills that our society is facing today are mainly due to the crisis of norms. Norms in public life seem to be at the cross-roads. The people are losing ground in cherished values and norms for which this nation or world as a whole stood for in the ancient past. There is an erosion of social, moral, cultural, economic and political norms at all levels. This has led to the spread of callous selfishness, unlimited greed, bribery, corruption, parochialism, rowdyism, hooliganism, violence, destruction, frustration and crisis of character.

With the emergence of materialism, man has become so money-minded that he is discarding the values such as honesty, social service, patience, truth etc. and hence is offing towards crime and finally destruction by becoming sociopath. It is the psychopathic family pattern which is primarily responsible for the present state of affairs—may it be anything. Man is becoming slave to instincts, drives, urges, impulses, desires and motives etc. and thus is losing touch with the existing values and there is a gross violation of social norms leading to social indiscipline. Therefore educationists, parents, teachers and elderly people condemn this ever-growing tendency among the students and youth who have become a regular source of bother for them. Students of today are the leaders of tomorrow. It is out of them that the nation will have leaders in the areas of scholarship, sciences, army and politics and industry. But if they who are the backbone of the society indulge in undesirable activities, the society as a whole will terribly suffer.

It is rightly said that the youth community is a dynamic force. Given a purposeful direction, its tremendous energy, enthusiasm and ideas can do wonders for the betterment of society. In the absence of proper guidance, the energy of youth either withers away fighting for petty causes or moves into wrong channels and creates law and order problem manifesting itself in strikes, violence, clashes and danger to property because they do not form the proper conditioned responses.

The disease of violation of norms has become so widespread that they could be termed as antisocial in the public such as columns of the newspapers deal with youth strikes, their violent and ugly demonstrations and other acts of rowdyism. Their studies suffer, but they do not mind. They rather treat strike as a pastime, a fun, an excitement and adventure, which gives them an outlet for their surplus physical energy and an escape from their academic boredom.

As the fundamental prerequisite of individual existence is the freedom of thought and action, the fabric of society is built on free individual, his actions, choices and rights. Consequently, society is an aggregation of individuals with substantial liberties and rights: "Freedom being the prerequisite to normal life in the individual, equal freedom becomes the primary need to normal life in society." Propelled by such impulses of individual freedom, individuals establish relationships of "attraction" as well as of 'repulsion' with the result that the 'due-balance' between these two becomes the ultimate basis of 'social-stability'. More important for our discussion is that society's emergence and persistence are contingent upon observing certain social norms and values by the individuals. This is because so long as members of the group do not combine their energies to achieve some common end, there is little to keep them together. Hence, the general order of society into which individual's actions are integrated results from concrete purposes which individuals pursue, but from their observing rules that limit the range of their actions.

Thus, social norms are the standards of behaviour that exert a powerful influence on social behaviour. They are the essence of social interaction which serve as the basis for organized social system among humans. A society without norms is like a ship without a rudder. Indeed it can readily be seen that without norms social relationships would be haphazard, chaotic and possibly even dangerous. It is the norms therefore that give order, stability and predictability to social life. Hence, where there are no norms, there is also no society.

Social norms are learned through the process of socialization by which an individual learns the rules and norms of appropriate behaviour. In the framework of society, individual has to adapt and learn these norms and values. Social norms are the building blocks of society and a society can function in a healthy manner only if the inhabitants of society follow these norms. But today the very members of the society are shattering these norms. Hence, the question remains to be answered as "why do some people follow these norms more closely than others even when the imparting agencies of socialization are the same"? The answer lies in "personality and genetic make-up". Some people learn social norms not only quickly but retain them too and, on the other hand, there are people who lack in learning these norms adequately and do not adhere to these norms but deviate due to which they become antisocial. This is mainly due to personality disposition. In this context Eysenck has observed that introverts because of their greater conditionability and higher arousal leading to increased behaviour restraint learn social norms faster and retain them too as compared to extraverts whose conditionability is poor and fail to learn the norms and thus violate the same because of lack of behavioural control. Eysenck traces the origin of differences to Pavlov's conditioning that not all dogs condition alike. Hull's reactive inhibition, Sokolov's and Teplov's weak and strong nervous system confirmed that introverts condition faster than extraverts. Gray has also stated that introverts have more reactive hippocampal "stop system" and extraverts are more reactive in the medial forebrain bundle and lateral hypothalamic areas (the "go system"). Hence, introverts condition faster and learn social norms earlier than the extraverts. There is a high susceptibility to punishment in introverts than extraverts in whom psychopathic behaviour is easily regarded as a tendency to take a reward by say stealing, lying or sexual gratification without thought for the consequences and even fail to learn from the consequences. They fail to learn because of short-term memory. Brebner and Cooper and Kumar et al have also confirmed the findings that extraverts are stimulus hungry and are geared to respond. Introverts as they opt for accuracy, learning will be good and is followed in the case of norms by learning social norms early, accurately and retaining them due to higher discriminatory power, greater long-term memory and serious disposition as compared to extraverts who not only fail to learn these norms but violate these too because of greater excitement, impulsivity, lower arousal, low discrimination and poor memory. Hence, socialization is mediated by conditioning and who condition faster are likely to adhere to norms and conform to social pressure.

Thus, our attempt is to put these contentions to test as these have been hardly attempted before. Similarly, there are also gender differences in learning of social norms due to socialization practices at the very onset of life that produces a gender schema. Boys and girls are taught differently and are rewarded for performing behaviour that are thought by society to be appropriate for man and woman respectively. Females due to social expectations follow social norms seriously as compared to males who consider themselves superior and break the norms as being their prerogative.

We owe special thanks to the above-mentioned researchers for their esteemed work which inspired us to work on this particular field. Also the critical condition of today's society propelled us to work in this area. We express our gratitude to colleagues, friends and to all who encouraged us time and again for writing this book. We do not want to weaken the bond by merely mentioning their names. In short, the existing gaps in the knowledge may be bridged by combining personality with gender and development of social norms in the present research. Thus, the present research/study is designed to uncover the psychodynamic processes of learning of social norms and expectations among different personality groups and gender groups.

Anita Sharma
Asstt. Professor, Deptt. of Psychology

Himachal Pradesh University
Shimla.

Dalip Malhotra
Chairman, Deptt. of Psychology

Contents

List of Tables

List of Figures

1

Introduction

The paradox of human society—that it has a unity and continuity of its own and yet exists solely in the minds and actions of its members—can be resolved only by understanding how the member individual is moulded into a social being. Without this process of moulding, which we call "socialization", the society could not perpetuate itself beyond a single generation and culture could not exist. Nor could the individual become a person; for without the ever repeated renewal of culture within him there could be no human mentality, no human personality. Both the person and the society are alike dependent on this unique process of psychic amalgamation whereby the sentiments and ideas of the culture are somehow joined to the capacities and needs of the organism. No one understands the process thoroughly. It is still as mysterious as photosynthesis or organic aging.

Society, Culture and Personality

It is said that "society" teaches its values, beliefs and attitudes during the socialization process.

Society refers to the unity of individuals. Culture refers to the learned and shared behaviour patterns characteristic of a society. In 1924 E.B. Tylor gave a descriptive definition of culture which still holds its own: "... that complex whole which include knowledge, belief, art, morals, law, custom and other capabilities and habits acquired by man as a member of society." But both the concept of society and culture are abstract—abstracted from concrete human behaviour. This is important to keep in mind. After all, a person does not look at human behaviour through 'magic' glasses and somehow see society and culture. Like every one else, he sees clusters of people working, playing, loving, living-busy striving to get what they consider to be the necessary and desirable things of life. It is only from the regularities of this multifarious behaviour that the concepts of society and culture are abstracted. Similarly, the term personality is abstracted from the same concrete reality—individuals and their behaviour and hence the three concepts society, culture and personality have important interrelationships (Linton, 1957). Society gives rise to culture and culture develops one's personality. It is rightly said that personality is the mirror of one's culture. This interrelationship may be diagramatically conceptualized as shown in the following figure:

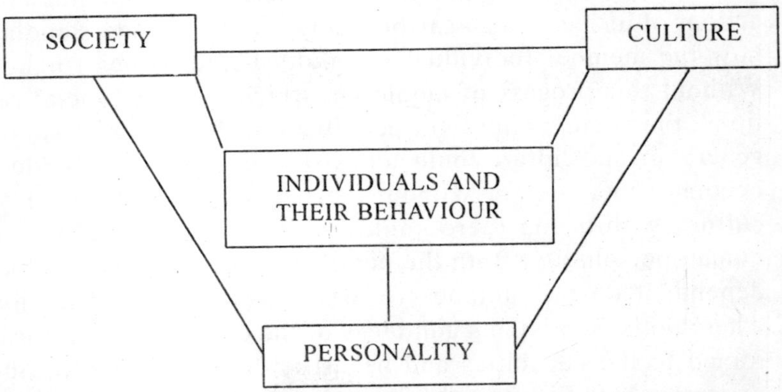

Figure 1: Interrelationship between Society, Culture and Personality.

The role of culture in personality formation is dramatized in the following photograph of "Culture Turnabouts" (See Figure 2).

Thus, individual cannot become a personality without contact with his fellows and the very concept of society implies interaction of individuals. Society depends essentially on what George H. Mead called the 'social act'. That is, a social configuration is present whenever any given action tendency is modified by or is not completed without the intercession of another human being. Equipped with his organic constitution, the newborn baby comes into the world of his fellows, and from relations with them and with their more or less fixed patterns or culture, his personality emerges. The child is not born human or social. He is at the outset an organism belonging to an animal species. It is only through his interplay with his fellows that he gets his "human nature" and that combination of acts and thoughts,

Figure 2: Role of Culture in Personality Formation.

[Paul Fung, Jr. (left) who is completely American in culture and Joseph Rhinehart (Fung Kwok-Keung) who is a white American by birth but who was reared in a Chinese family in China and was completely Chinese in his culture when he first returned to America as a young man. Brought together by Amram Scheinfeld, they were photographed in his studio (February, 1950) just after Paul Fung, Jr., a professional cartoonist, had drawn a sketch of Joseph Rhinehart, below which the latter had written his name in Chinese. For a further description of the two men, see Amram Scheinfeld, The New You and Heredity, pages 505-506. (From Amram Scheinfeld, The New You and Heredity, 1950. Reproduced by permission of the author and J.B. Lippincott Company. Photograph by M. Lasser)].

which we label the personality. Personality is the mirror of one's culture as has been stated earlier. From birth on, the individual is under the influence of culture at the hands of his fellows (society). Just as we may say that the group is antecedent to any given individual, so, too, we may state that there is always a body of culture which gives content and direction to the society in which an individual will develop as a person.

An infant enters the world without knowledge of rules, roles or relationships among people. Between infancy and adolescence society's basic expectations and limitations are imparted to the child in a complex series of processes generally referred to as socialization.

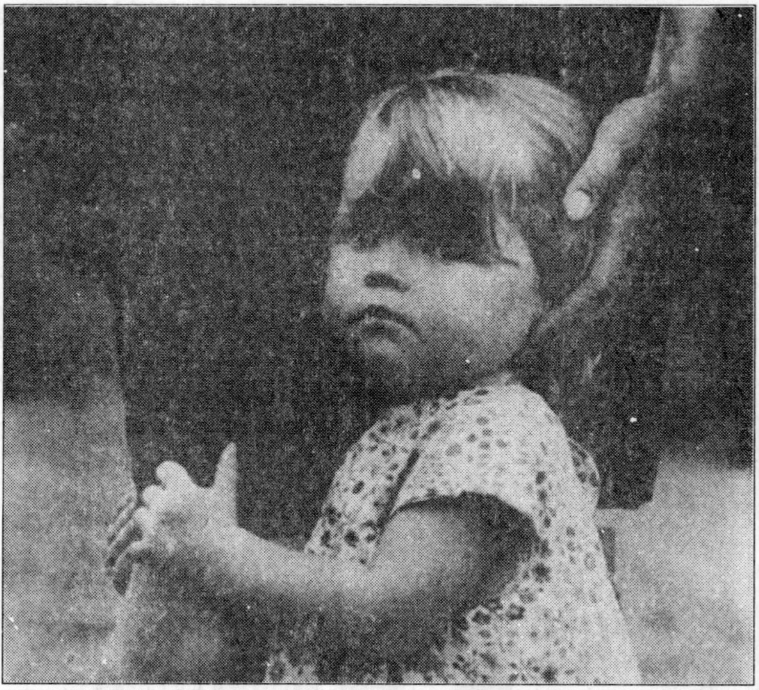

Figure 3: The prolonged helplessness and dependency of humans makes possible a long period of socialization.

Socialization is a process that continues throughout life. Through socialization an individual learns to behave in accordance with social traditions and mores. The human child possesses a tendency towards imitation. The child develops according to the environment in which he lives. The individual tries to win the praise of the group in which he lives. Man is a social being. He of his own nature tries to adopt the culture of society. Man becomes what he is by socialization and it is by virtue of this that he is believed to be superior to animals. Socialization brings balance to his personality because the social aspect of personality is extremely important. The prolonged helplessness and dependency of humans makes possible a long period of socialisation (See Figure 3).

Mechanisms of Socialization

There are several mechanisms of socialization by which transmission of such training of acquisition of behaviour takes place in human beings. Following are the three main mechanisms of socialization.

(i) Reward and Punishment: Actions which repetitively culminate in rewarding experiences are generally retained or learnt and those which result in painful consequences are gradually eliminated or rejected. Most parents are aware that rewarding a child for certain behaviour reinforces that behaviour. Parents generally use some form of punishment to reduce or completely eliminate undesirable behaviour. Teachers in the classroom also use this method of rewarding any type of accomplishment in curricular or co-curricular activities and punishing unwanted behaviour like indiscipline etc.

(ii) Imitation and Modelling: Much of the human behaviour is transmitted either deliberately or inadvertently through the behaviour examples provided by the other people. This process of learning through observation of others is designated as modelling. In many situations the person may be uncertain about how to act. The easiest way is to copy someone's behaviour in the similar situations. Children are hero worshippers. Heroes or models are generally successful persons and children see their achievements as possible goals in their own lives. Models provide direction and children feel proud to act accordingly. Children don't choose their models at random. Selection of model depends upon actions of the model and satisfaction obtained by imitating the model's behaviour. Children in families generally imitate their older siblings, parents or neighbouring persons as their models (See Figure 4). The model need

not be a person in real life form. Even pictorial or symbolic presentation of a model like film or television personalities, sports persons, artists, politicians and other historical persons and their actions are good enough for modelling.

Figure 4: Children often learn by "modelling" parents' behaviour. The human child possesses a tendency towards imitation.

(iii) Identification and Internalization: In many social situations persons imitate others to achieve success. As a result of satisfying relationship or some special characteristics a child tries to shape his/her behaviour according to his/her model. This is called identification. It is the process by which an individual comes to define himself/herself in terms of his nation, social class, religious group etc. Identification can result in imitation or conforming to the expectations of admired persons. When such expectations become one's own standards of behaviour or characteristics and mannerisms of another person are incorporated into one's own behavioural repertoire, such an influence is referred to as internalization. It is the process by which an individual accepts attitudes and values of his/her model as his/her own. But a person may not be able to internalize or even accept all attitudes and values of his/her model.

Acculturation

Acculturation refers to the cultural and psychological changes that are brought about by contact with other people belonging to different cultures and exhibiting different behaviours. Also, cultural contact takes place in the socio-political context of one's group. Historical and contemporary experiences, colonial experience, international trade, invasion, and migration often lead to cultural contact and, therefore, change in the original culture. For instance many groups in India became acculturated to aspects of British life-style during the British rule. This lead to many changes in social structure education, and economy. Such changes are obvious in the domains of language, dress and religion. Acculturation can take place at any time in one's life. It requires relearning or resocialization conciliation. It leads to new problems and offers new opportunities to people. Thus, contact with a new culture leads to changes in the original culture's behavioural patterns.

People experience a variety of psychological changes as a result of membership in a changing cultural group. The experience of immigration to a new country is an interesting example of acculturation. The differences in language, climate, work habits, religion, and dress etc. pose important challenges before the immigrants. Similarly, changes are required in case of the colonised countries. The case of tribal people coming into contact with the people of non-tribal culture is another example of acculturation. The contact with a different culture may result in many kinds of reactions. Some may happily embrace the new culture, others may not like it. People may selectively engage and, some may merge the new culture with the old or original culture.

Acculturation often brings with it many things. It may lead to population expansion, cultural diversification, attitudinal reaction, and formulation of new policies, Thus, people in any culture differ in the degree of involvement in the process of acculturation. The degree of contact and participation is assessed with the help of indicators such as level of schooling, urbanisation, mass media, political participation, language, changes in daily practices, and social relations etc.

There are many ways in which an acculturating individual (or group) wishes to relate to the dominant society. They are known as acculturative strategies. They include:

(i) Assimilation: When people absorb into the existing system. People incorporate new information into their own existing knowledge i.e. they merge the new culture with the old or culture.

(ii) Separation: When the original culture is maintained by the people i.e. they do not embrace the new culture.

(iii) Integration: When people interact with new culture and integrate with the old one.

(iv) Marginalisation: When there is little possibility or interest in cultural maintenance.

Agents of Socialization

In human socialization, the child is trained intentionally by agents of the society who relay to him its value, beliefs and conventional standards, preparing him for assimilation into the society as an adult. It is individual members of a society who are responsible for passing on the culture to children and most studies have focused on the chief agents of socialization e.g. parents, teachers, and associates or peers (see Figure 5).

Parents

Parents are the primary socialization agents. The child's earliest encounter with other members of his society normally involve his parents and they are the first significant agents of that society in his experience. Early parent-child interactions are especially crucial in socialization. The family embodies a network of relationships and interactions marked by continuity, cooperation and emotionality perhaps not duplicated in any other system. Major functions of the family are to serve as a culture carrier, to interpret and simplify this complex world by giving the child freedom to explore, to solve problems, to provide pleasant group living conditions and protection thus developing his/her all-round personality. This is the only stable group with which a young child can identify himself/herself. The family plays perhaps the most important and most dominant role in

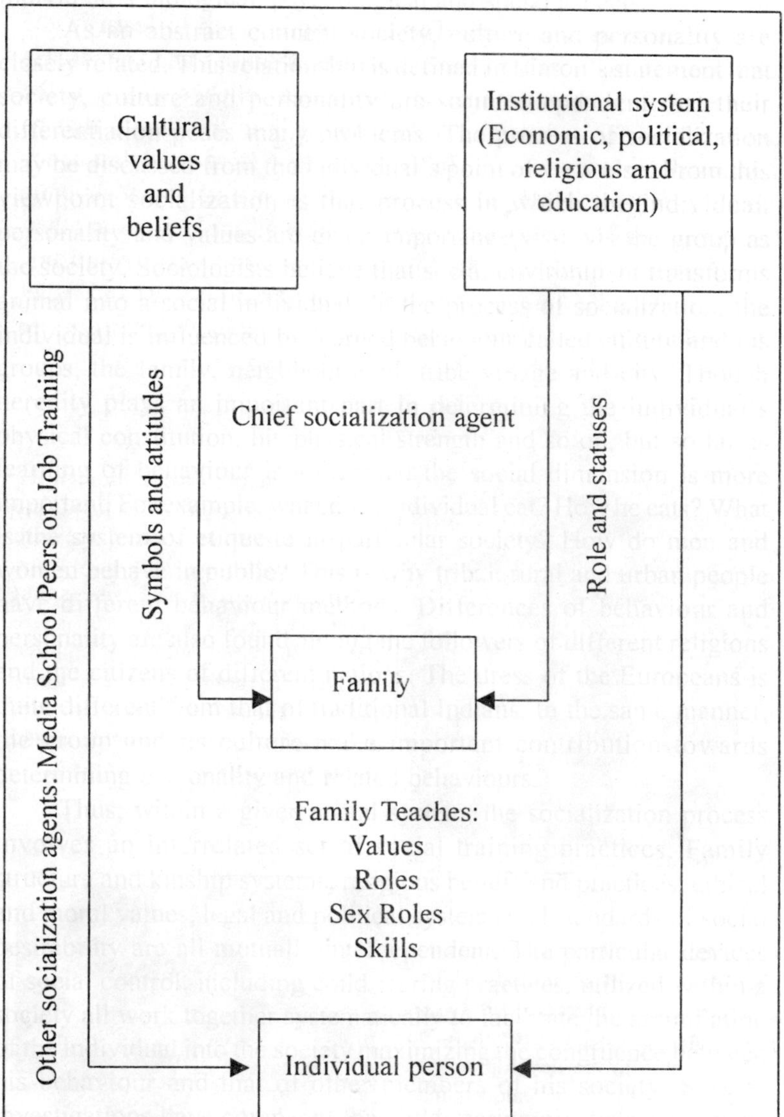

Figure 5: Showing the process of socialization.

the individuals socialization. The child finds much to learn in the behaviours of his family members, parents, relations and friends. He imitates them in their mannerism, behaviour, cliches, etc. It is the family which forms his good habits and it is in the family that he acquires deviant tendencies. In the book new light on delinquency and its treatment, Healy and Bruner have contended that juvenile delinquents mostly hail from families which at one time or another, have suffered hindrance in the fulfilment of social relations. Psychoanalysts, prominent among them are Freud (1922) and Adler (1927), have proved that a man behaves in society according to whatever he has become in the family. (See Figure 6a & b).

(a) While taking a walk through the woods, the members of this family are socializing with each other. They are teaching each other how they value nature recreation and time spent together. Parents who do not share outdoor activities with their children will teach them something quite different about their values, attitudes and beliefs regarding the outdoors and use of leisure time.

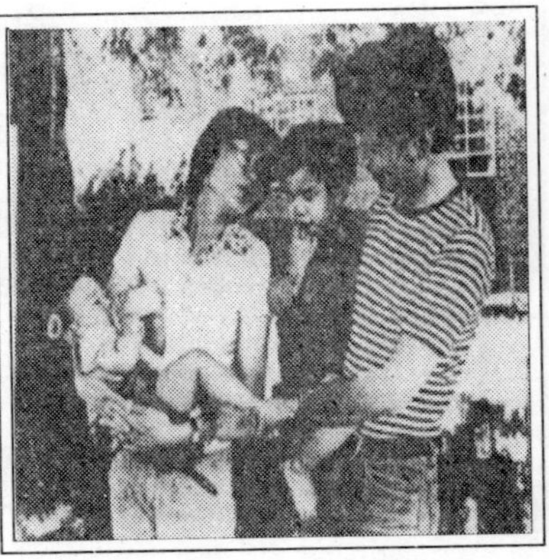

(b) A universal function of families is that of nurturant socialization. The primary group interaction between parent and child has proven to be indispensable to the development of mentally and physically healthy human beings. The role of the father is important in this process and it appears that an increasing number of fathers are becoming more in world in performing nontraditional child rearing tasks.

Figure 6 (a & b): Family as an Agent of Socialization

Teachers

Teachers then begin to exert an influence on the child and with school and playmates become largely responsible for socialization. The most important person in school is the teacher. He/she is a central figure in the classroom. The role of the teacher with his/her authority and knowledge is crucial in the child's school life. The teacher influences behaviour of his/her students in every class. In lower classes children take every word of the teacher as command and try to imitate his/her behaviour. The teacher through his/her behaviour may influence the behaviour of his/her students as follows:

(a) Teaching Values: The first and perhaps the most important impression which the teacher has on the child is about honesty, fairness and justice; (b) respect for competence; (c) self-discipline; (d) hard work; and (e) self-understanding.

School does not denote the structure or building only. It consists of all organized activities systematically arranged to cater to all-round growth and development of its students. It provides environment for learning new skills and this process of teaching learning helps in development of all aspects of a child's personality. Classroom is an important unit of the system. It is a place where teaching-learning of the child takes place. Compulsory attendance and maintenance of discipline is required in the classroom. Child is expected to behave according to set norms. Rules, routine and regularity govern his/her life which are uniformly enforced in the school. He/she finds that his/her needs and interests are not of much concern to anyone else. He/she has to control his/her whims, moods and wishes. He/she has a special place to sit and can stand or walk only with permission and may not leave the room at his/her sweet will. In addition, he/she is accepted to acquire certain skills and keep his/her achievement upto the expected level. For the child the school is society and it is within its boundary that he is socialized, his abilities find expressions and he gets the opportunity of developing his personality. The personality and character of the teacher are ever present before him as ideals that continuously influence his own personality. Schools are charged with teaching young people the skills and knowledge they will need to be useful citizens. The school also introduces children, usually for the first time, to the impersonal rules and regulations of the formal organization. Thus, schools and especially the teachers are officially designated as agents of socialization (Epperson, 1988) (See Figure 7).

Figure 7: Teacher as an Agent of Socialization.

Neighbourhood

The term neighbourhood implies nearness in locality. A neighbourhood is one who lives nearby. Although the neighbourhood relationship seems to be very important, it tends to be less emotionally intense and sometimes the two neighbours are barely on speaking terms or they may even be antagonistic to each other. When a child grows, he/she comes into contact with the children of his/her immediate neighbourhood. He/she enjoys their company because they are different from his/her siblings. The child generally behaves towards the neighbours and their children according to relationship of his/her parents (See Figure 8). These experiences involve transmission of new ideas and information to the child. In many situations friends and neighbours have great influence upon children. But it depends whether a person is living in a multi-storied building wherein he/she can even hear the quarrels in his/her neighbourhood or is a big bungalow where there is virtually no communication. The behaviour in slum neighbourhood is also different from those of semi-urban or town neighbourhood. People sharing common facilities like water, toilet etc., behave differently as compared to those enjoying these facilities in their homes. The neighbourhood in rural areas evokes different responses from those of urban areas.

Figure 8: Neighbours help one another. They share joys and sorrows of one another. They exchange things. They co-operate with one another when it is needed. Hence, Neighbourhood plays a vital role in socialization.

Peer Group

As the child grows older his/her contacts increase and he/she develops friendship with his/her age-mates from neighbourhood having different social and cultural backgrounds. Children are responsive to their peers from the very beginning. Most of the social interactions of peer occur in the setting of play. Chasing each other around the school grounds, swinging on swings, climbing trees or enjoying in other such games give children plenty of time to be with their friends. An adolescent's peer group has greater appeal to him/her than his/her parents, teachers and other elders because this group is similar, more interesting and easily available to the adolescent. They engage in lively and interesting activities.

In the process of socializing with peer groups, the adolescent learns social interactions. Peer group activity is usually an enjoyable one. The adolescent acquires information, values, attitudes and develops skills of competing, contending and matching his/her wits which contribute towards his/her growth and development. He/she understands that with his/her equals he/she is not bound to obey and he/she perhaps enjoys it. He/she often takes more interest in his/her own peers and may choose his/her role and group activities. Sometimes this group may involve in adventurous activities Association with this group gives the adolescent a broader point of view about life in general. Many of their ideals may differ from his/her ideas and if impressed he/she may change his/her own stand. He/she learns to give and take, to share, to be a good sport, to be sympathetic with them when they are in trouble. These groups set and enforce standards of conduct and behaviour. The adolescent gives attention and approval to the activities of his/her group members. He/she learns to praise, offer help, give affection and acceptance to his/her peers, which is important in socializing behaviour. Submission to other's ideas with pleasure, cooperation, compromise and sharing things are important behaviour, which an adolescent learns in his/her peer's company. Friendliness, adjustment a reasonable level of self-esteem and sensitivity to the needs and feelings of other members are important personality characteristics which emerge out in his/her interaction with peers.

Peers influence one another primarily through interaction, particularly during play. And of course, children are also motivated to learn things on their own. After childhood, social interaction takes place increasingly in peer groups—equal in age, sex, occupational level and so on. Members of peer groups tend to become friends because of their equal status and mutual interests. Friends do not intentionally set out to change each other, but friendship leads to shared opinions and values. Peers influence each other and become significant others in socialization process (See Figure 9a & b).

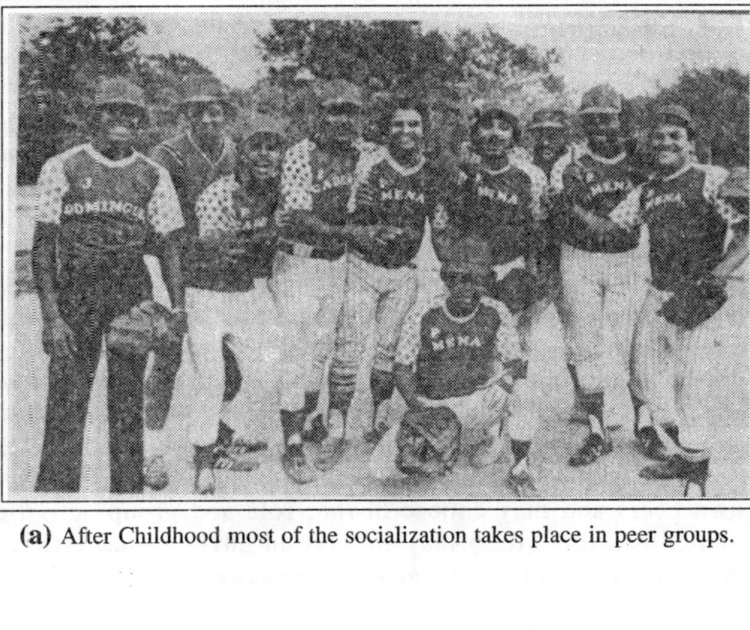

(a) After Childhood most of the socialization takes place in peer groups.

(b) Students who spend a great deal of time together socialize each other. These students have all learned appropriate dress and hairstyles from other members of their peer group. The styles they have agreed on are not necessarily those encouraged by parents or school officials.

Figure 9 (a & b): Peer-Group as an Agent of Socialization.

Mass Media

The media is also an important agent of socialization. The media provide not only formal instructions but valuable information and cultural enrichment. Mass media have the potential of affecting over all behaviour of children. Books, magazines, novels, comic strips, newspapers, radio, video, television, drama shows and cinema expose children to information ranging from reality to fantasy and from education to entertainment. This encounter with the world of knowledge stimulates curiosity, communication and verbal skills. The communication imparted through mass media inculcates in children the social norms, cultural values, national pride and other important aspects of personality. Mass media has given continuity to cultural heritage. Through folk songs, folk tales and folk dances, children continue to enjoy the tradition as well as social ideals. The role of myths, legends and festivals is highlighted through mass media which helps in discovering common features of contemporary religions, their importance in modern context and above all one's own identity through self discovery.

The available evidence indicates that they can and do affect social behaviours and attitudes. In addition to being our principal sources of information and entertainment, the mass media are important agents of socialization (McNeil, 1975; Jennings, Geis and Brown, 1980 and Morgan, 1982). A major concern shown is about the violence caused by TV viewing. Studies indicate that frequent TV viewing is related to overt aggression in children. Cinema is also working as a power influence on shaping the minds of people especially children exposing them to life like experiences and providing vicarious satisfaction (Reiss and Roth 1993) (See Figure 10).

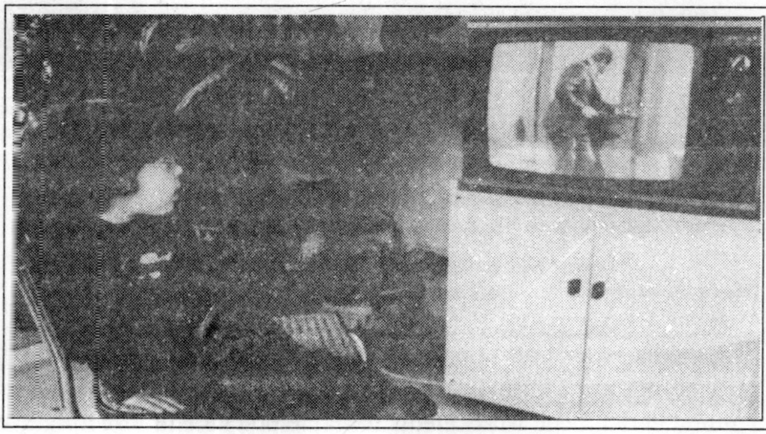

Figure 10: Mass Media as an Agent of Socialization.

Religious Groups

Religion has some fundamental principles which ultimately lead to the goodness toward humanity. But each religion elicit different behaviour in its followers depending on its philosophy. For example Hinduism believes in the theory of Karma and rebirth. Certain rituals are supposed to be regularly followed by Muslims. Jains and Budhists give more stress on renunciation and abstention from certain things. This means when a person is born in a certain religious group his/her behaviour to some extent is determined by that group. Religious ceremonies are a part of daily fabric of societal life which give children an opportunity to participate, observe and imitate their elders. Each religion is propagated through its priests and places of worship (See Figure 11a, b, c & d). Children tend to follow the religious philosophies of their parents without question in childhood. If parents are anti-religious in some form, their children acquire familiarity with this point of view. If parents are in favour of a particular religious system this also becomes the lasting experience for children. If children develop religious convictions they tend to continue their religious ideas. But if they are unconvinced or unprepared, religious dedication dies with each generation. Although different religions have played important role in the acculturation through inculcation of higher human values, sometimes tolerance for other religious groups takes a back seat and community clashes occur which harm wider interests of national unity and harmony.

(a) Sikhism: The Sikhs worship in Gurudwaras. They bow before the "Guru Granth Sahib" which is their holy book.

(b) Islam: The Muslims go to a mosque to pray. They pray to Allah. They offer prayers (namaz) five times a day. The name of their holy book is "Quran".

(c) Hinduism: Hindus go to a temple to worship. The Vedas, Upanishads, Bhagwad Gita and Ramayana are the holy books of Hindus.

(d) Christianity: The holy book of the Christians is the Bible. They worship in a church.

Figure 11 (a, b, c & d): All religions teach us that God is one. We must speak the truth and respect our elders.

Thus, religions provide occasions to shape the belief system of their adherents and are socialized accordingly.

Caste Groups

In arranging and sustaining marriages of their children older generation transmits the caste identity to younger generation. Children inculcate caste values through observation of familial patterns of interaction, communication and adoption of prescribed occupations. The caste system also determines behaviour of the individual. Sometimes children resent their caste barriers and try to break away from these chains but bonds of the caste and community are still going strong and sometimes cause tension between individuals and groups. Although in big cities caste system seems to be breaking but its identity is not completely lost because even now the parents or kin take responsibility of arranging marriage of their sons and daughters within their own caste and communities. But children of today are violating the norms of marriage and are doing inter-caste marriages.

Day Care

In today's world when both parents go to work and there is no one to look after the young kids at home, day care centers provide alternate arrangements for parenting. Such centres supervise the upbringing of children when parents are not available. They are of various types. There are family day care arrangements in which kids go to the home of some one in the vicinity, who is not a family member. These centres offer various types of learning experiences. If it is of good quality the day care contributes to the social and intellectual development of children. Nursery schools or pre-schools are also coming up in a big way. They are arranged to foster development of children between 2 to 6 years (See Figure 12). The Aganwadis under the programme of

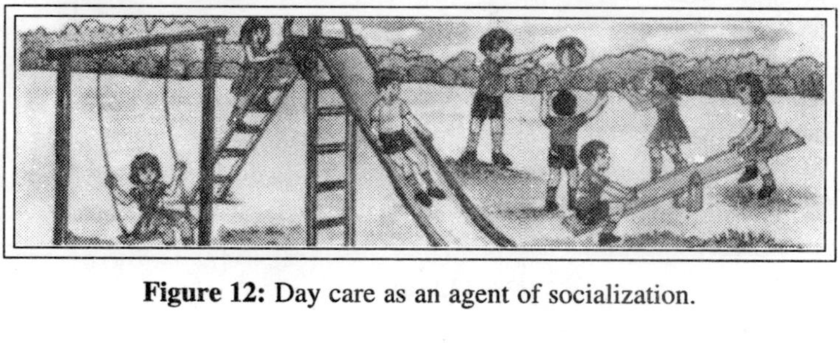

Figure 12: Day care as an agent of socialization.

Integrated Child Development Services (ICDS) provide day care to the children from poor and deprived background (Broota, Misra, Sibia and Srivastava, 2002).

Thus, through the process of socialization one learns norms and values. Social norm is defined as a standard or better as a scale consisting of categories that define a range of objectionable attitude and behaviour for members of a social unit (Kretch, Crutchfield and Ballachhey, 1962). Thus, social norms is a concept that can be used generally in social psychology to refer to all those regularities in social life that can embody evaluation of objects, persons, actions and ideas.

An adequate theory of socialization or social learning has to deal with the child's acquisition of the norms upheld by "significant other" people. These significant others are typically members of a group to which he/she belongs or aspires to belong.

Thus, family is the main agent of socialization. And it is in the family that the child learns to behave as a male or a female. According to Sandra Bem (1987), socialization produces a gender schema, a cognitive framework that organizes and guides a child's understanding of information relevant to gender. On the basis of what their schemas are regarding what is or is not appropriate for being a male or female, children begin to behave in ways that reflect society's gender role (See Figure 13a & b). Broadly speaking we can divide the various forms of family into two main categories, the patriarchal and matriarchal. All types of family organizations—ancient as well as modern, fall within one category or the other represent a combination of both.

Children are socialized from early childhood to behave in masculine or feminine ways.

13 (a)

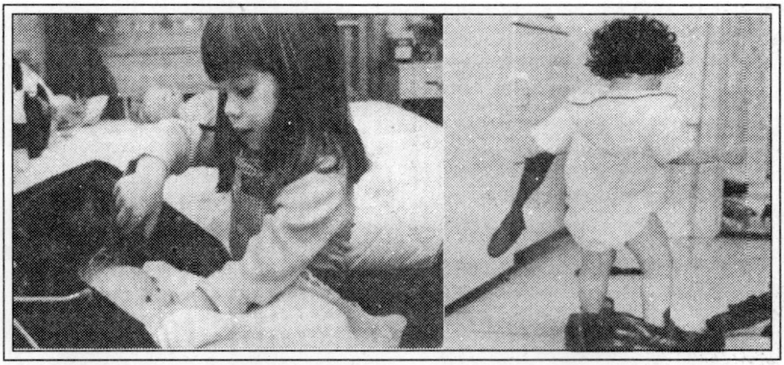

13 (b) Children are more likely to imitate the behaviours of the parent of the same gender than a parent of the opposite gender.

Figure 13 (a & b): Development of Gender Schema due to Socialization.

The Matriarchal family is that type in which the control of the family is centered around some women member. (See Figure 14). In these families name, status and material inheritance are transmitted through the female line. The main features of this type are: (i) descent is traced through mother, (ii) and in most cases, the family resides at the home of mother, husband has only a secondary position in the home and often that is regarded as below the position enjoyed by brothers of his wife along, (iii) due to above, authority in maternal family frequently belongs to some male representative of wife's kin. In this system, child's system is determined by the mother, and the father has little authority. As a result children are more closely tied to their maternal uncles.

But, in the patriarchal family which has been the most prevalent type in both ancient as well as modern civilization, the male of the family plays the dominant role as compared to the position of womenfolk. Societies which follow the patriarchal system of family organization place the women on a lower level of social status than that of men. The usual way to trace descent is through the male line which is known a patrilineal descent system. Under this system a man gets his name, his social identity from his father, his paternal grandfather, and so on. A woman marries into her husband's family and takes his name. In advanced industrial societies patriarchal arrangements tend to break down in fact, although they may still persist in theory. Decision-making is rarely left entirely to the male head of the family.

The Trobriand Islanders, about 200 miles off the north-east coast of New Guinea, have a matrilineal descent system. While some powers and functions, such as that of village chief, are vested in the male, these hereditary offices or social positions are passed on exclusively through the mother line. The Trobriand Islanders do not consider a child to be biologically related to its father, for they believe the father has no procreative function. Thus, the important males for children are not their fathers but their mothers' brothers.

Figure 14: Role of Matriarchical Family System in Socialization

In modern type of family, the woman has been placed on equal footings with man but her status as a whole continues as inferior to that of male. Thus, the type of family in which the children are reared gives rise to sexual differences.

Culture plays a vital role in the process of socialization. Roles of men and women are dramatically different from culture to culture. Margaret Mead, one of the most widely read researchers in this area studied island societies in the pacific cultures to see whether important behaviour patterns differed in various cultures. She reported that adolescents on Somoa did not experience emotional upheavals similar to those often reported in many western societies (1939). She interpreted this as evidence for the idea that cultural pressures and not simply glandular changes are involved in the emotional aspects of adolescence. She also studied sex differences in social behaviour in three New Guinea Cultures. In her early work on sex and temperament in three principle societies (just published in 1935), Mead noted sharp variation among in the roles played by the sexes. Among the Arapesh, sex differentiation was minimal. Both sexes were gentle, nurturant and cooperative. In contrast among the Mundugumor, who had been cannibalistic, in that both sexes were aggressive, indisciplined and ruthless. In these two societies there was little sex differentiation, but in the third, the Tchambuli, sex differences were prominent. Contrary to western culture, the women of the lake-dwelling people were the dominant sex. They procured the food as fisherwomen and were impersonal and directive in social relations, while the men adorned themselves physically and were involved in the decorative aspects of the culture (carving, dancing and painting).

From her study on cultural influences on sex role behaviour, Mead concluded : "standardized personality differences between the sexes are: cultural creations to which each generation, male and female is trained to conform".

As we might expect, stereotypes and beliefs about gender roles or expected behaviour of males and females, differ greatly from one culture to another as well as groups and across time within a given culture. For example, in the United States, African American culture, children often hold less stereotyped views of women than do white children perhaps because African American children have been exposed to more women as heads of households and as principal family wage earners (Benedict, 1942).

Enculturation and Socialization

Apart from the agencies of socialization, the learning of social expectations and norms is through the process of enculturation. Enculturation, as this complex process is called, prepares the individual, from infancy through adulthood, to orient himself to his group, adjust itself to its demands and expectations, and acquire skill in interpersonal relationships. When therefore, we wish to define learning by what is learnt, we call the process enculturation : the assimilation by a human organism of the customs and traditions of his group. Rokeach (1960, 1961) has shown and demonstrated that our feelings towards other people are affected more profoundly by the degree to which we think they share our attitudes and values than by any other social categorization, including their race or ethnic grouping. According to this view if a poor white farmer in Mississippi is prejudiced against blacks, he is not responding to their race as such. Rather the former supposedly assumes that the values and beliefs of black people are very different from his own and he dislikes blacks because of this. Thus, social expectations becomes the norms. In short, in social learning the individual is conditioned to respond in prescribed ways, to "internalize" the social world of customs and modes of behaviours into his own action system. The content of social learning consists of the body of ideas, values, and traditions which we call the culture of the group. Thus, while we come into the world with fundamental biological mechanism of behaviour, the direction our behaviour will take and the meaning it will have are determined by the norms of the society comprising family and larger groups.

Socialization and Personality

The process of socialization has two aspects. According to the first aspect the individual internalizes the social values under the influence of social and cultural influences. The second aspect develops his personality. Thus, through socialization the aims of social responsibility and individual autonomy are achieved. The role of socialization is very important in individuals life from two points of view. The individual's self develops through socialization. Socialization develops his personality and the process of mental interaction. By socialization the individual learns to distinguish among 'I', 'You' and 'they'. First of all, socialization stands for the unity of personality and interaction of personalities. For the existence of society, it is necessary that there are more than one individual and there are mutual relations among them. Culture is the system of common behaviour learnt in a particular 'society'. Society and culture are abstract ideas. A question may be raised here, what is personality? Defining personality, Newcomb says, that personality indicates the individual's organized tendency of working, seeing, thinking and feeling. The unification of individual's socio-psychological behaviour is reflected in personality. It is expressed through the habits, tendencies and thinking of the individual. Personality develops through contact with other individuals. Therefore, it has a social as well as a psychological aspect. Personality is formed by putting together the individual's biological, psychological and social aspects.

As an abstract concept society, culture and personality are closely related. This relationship is defined in Linton's statement that society, culture and personality are so interdependent that their differentiation poses many problems. The process of socialization may be discussed from the individual's point of view also. From this viewpoint socialization is that process in which the individual, personality and values are given importance vis-à-vis the group as the society. Sociologists believe that social environment transforms animal into a social individual. In the process of socialization, the individual is influenced by learned behaviour called culture and his groups, the family, neighbourhood, tribe village and city. Though heredity plays an important part in determining the individual's physical constitution, his physical strength and so on, but so far as learning of behaviour is concerned the social dimension is more important. For example, what does individual eat? How he eats? What is the system of etiquette in particular society? How do men and women behave in public? This is why tribal, rural and urban people have different behaviour methods. Differences of behaviour and personality are also found among the followers of different religions and the citizens of different nations. The dress of the Europeans is quite different from that of traditional Indians. In the same manner, the group and its culture make important contribution towards determining personality and related behaviours.

Thus, within a given social system, the socialization process involves an interrelated set of social training practices. Family structure and kinship systems, religious beliefs and practices, ethical and moral values, legal and political systems and standards of social desirability are all mutually interdependent. The particular devices of social control, including child rearing practices, utilized within a society all work together systematically to facilitate the assimilation of the individual into the society maximizing the congruence between his behaviour and that of other members of his society. Several investigations have compared the child-rearing practices of various societies which are as under:

Socialization in six societies. A group of social scientists from Harvard, Yale, and Cornell Universities conducted a series of investigations on child-rearing practices, ecological background, economic systems and political organizations in various cultures. Six relatively unknown cultural samples were studied. New Englanders in Orchard Town, USA (America); the Gusu community of Nyasango in eastern Kenya; the Rajputs of Khalapur, in northern India; the village of Taira, in north eastern Okinawa; the Mixtecan Indians of Juxthahuaca, in south-western Mexico; and the Liocos of Tarong, in the northern Philippines. Observations of child-rearing practices in each society (see Table 1) were compared to behaviour patterns in the adult samples in order to support the investigator's hypothesis that different patterns of child-rearing will lead to differences in the personality of children and thus to differences in adult personality. This assumption was schematically conceptualized as shown in Figure 15.

Table 1: Child-rearing attitude and practices in six societies

Child Rearing Practices	*Society*					
	America	*Kenya*	*India*	*Okinawa*	*Mexico*	*Philippines*
Infancy: upto age 2						
Parental view of infant	Potential for future development	Instrumental to household	Pure and "God's gift"	Pitiable and helpless	"empty state" no awareness	Charming and helpless
Parental response to infant's crying (hunger)	Demand feeding (most families)	Demand feeding	Demand feeding	Demand feeding	Demand feeding	Demand feeding
Parental response to infant's crying (discomfort)	Ignoring, regarded as inevitable, "good for character and lungs"	Annoyance, threat, derision, physical punishment	Pacification by distraction or use of opium	Pacification by distraction or petting	Annoyance, scolding, physical punishment	Pacification by distraction or petting
Infant's toilet	Strict, praise of scolding	Strict, physical punishment	Lax	Lax	Lax	Lax

(contd.)

Child Rearing Practices	*Society*					
	America	*Kenya*	*India*	*Okinawa*	*Mexico*	*Philippines*
Early Childhood: age 2 to 5						
Availability of peers	Minimum	Minimum	Average	Maximum	Minimum	Minimum
Expected attitude toward adult	Politeness, no rudeness, no aggression	Blandness, no aggression, no sex-play, little initiative	Obedience	Adequacy but without excelling	Obedience	No demands no expectations
Enforcement of socially desirable behaviour	Strict, praise of scolding	Strict, physical punishment	Lax	Lax	Strict, physical punishment	Lax
Sex-appropriate behaviour	Encouraged	Discouraged	Indifference	Encouraged	Indifference	Encouraged

(After B.B. Whiting, ed., Six cultures, rev. ed., Wiley, 1966).

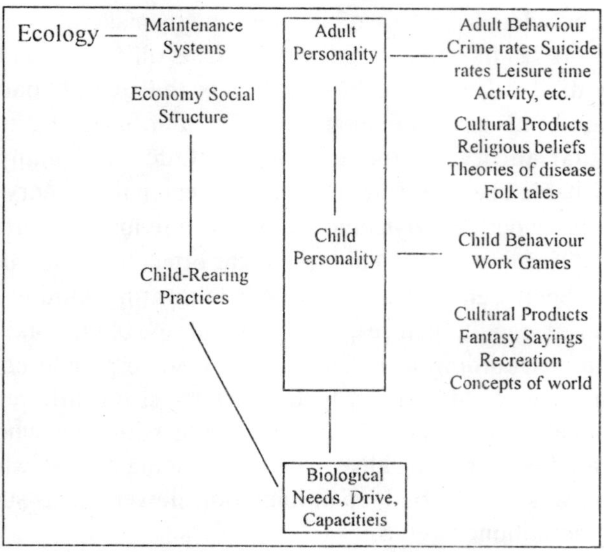

Figure 15: A conceptual scheme for relationships between socialisation and personality, (After B.B. Whiting, ed., Six cultures, rev. ed., Wiley, 1966).

Learning of social norms is through social influence. Social influence refers to the change in an individual that occurs because of contact with other people. Conformity is a major source of social influence for adherence to social norms. Social conformity facilitates social interaction. Crutchfield (1955) assesses that the essence of conformity is the yielding to social pressure.

The fact of behaviour as well as the factors that enhance its occurrence have been demonstrated in literally by laboratory and field studies. Muzafer Sherif, (1935) conducted his classical study on the development of social norms. Social norms are patterns of behaviour typical of a particular group and sanctioned by that group. In effect they become standards of reference by which the behaviour of individuals can be judged. Utilizing the autokinetic effect, Sherif showed that individual judgements could be made to converge to a group norm in the micro society of the laboratory. According to Sherif social interaction brings about conformity.

According to Asch (1951, 1956) conformity to social norms is through social influence, who observed this by conducting conformity experiments in visual perception of line drawing with seven to nine person groups who were confederates and one naive subject. But the process of learning of social norms and expectations is different in different individuals because of their personality make-up. According to Brody (1972) the study of personality rests ultimately on the fact of individual differences. Personality is the overall pattern of integration of his structure, modes of behaviour, interests, attitudes, intellectual ability, temperaments, aptitudes and many other distinguishable characteristics. Eysenck's personality theory throws light on the underlying dynamic factors of individual differences in the area of learning of social norms and the effect of social influence. This has been demonstrated through laboratory studies of the formation of conditioned responses through eyeblink conditioning in humans. According to Eysenck (1947), some people condition better and some condition slowly. Eysenck traces this differentiation in individuals to Pavlov's (1927) experiments with dogs who found that not all dogs condition alike. There were some dogs in whom the excitation was quicker built up of inhibition slower and as such they could be conditioned better.

Franks (1954) conducted an experiment on eyeblink conditioning with matched groups of hysterics, dysthymics and normals and found that dysthymics condition more quickly than hysterics.The crucial experiments conducted by Field and Branglemann (1961) with eyeblink conditioning, Vogel (1961) with measures of GSR conditioning, Quay and Hunt (1965) with conditioning gave conclusive evidence that conditioning was related to introversion mainly.

Eysenck has attempted to relate his biological theory to social behaviour. His notion of socialization to his personality theory by organizing that introverts by virtue of their greater capacity to form conditioned responses than extraverts would be more socialized than extraverts who are undersocialized due to their relatively poor capacity to form conditioned responses. The greater conditionability of the introverts is attributed by Eysenck to a higher level of cortical arousal in the ascending reticular activating system (Gray, 1972).

Not only this, the relation of Introverts and Extraverts (I/E) with academic success is also an established fact. Eysenck (1955, 1957) has emphasized time and again that the learning and performance are related to extraversion because of individual differences in level of cortical excitation and inhibition. EEG Studies have provided evidence that there is a lower level of cortical arousal in extraverts (Gale, Coles and Blaydon, 1969 and Shagaas and Canter, 1971) Eysenck (1967) attributes better performance of introverts to higher arousal and poorer performance of extraverts to their poor arousal plus quicker cortical excitation and slower accumulation of Ir (reactive inhibition) and its faster dissipation in Introverts. Himmelweit (1946) has found that hysterics have a bad vocabulary in relation to their intelligence. Broadbent (1958) and Furneaux (1956) have found that students who do well in the University examinations have a lower score on extraversion. Dennis Child (1964, 1966) too obtained that the promoted children were significantly more introverted than the demoted ones. Similar results were reported by Savage (1962), Mehta and Kumar (1985). Mehta, Kumar and Jerath (1989, 1990) obtained positive and significant relation between introversion and academic achievement among school and college subjects. In this regard it would be plausible to state that two implications may be drawn from this that introverts in educational and other psychomotor tasks opt for accuracy and extraverts for speed (Eysenck, 1947). Brebner and Cooper (1974) later elaborated that introverts are geared to inspect and extraverts are geared to respond. Introverts are stimulus hungry and extraverts are response hungry. Later, Kumar, Malhotra and Jerath (1986, 1989) also did experiments on speed and accuracy of introverts and extraverts on Choice Reaction Time and Visual Selection Task among 60 University male and female students. On Choice Reaction Time an indices of performance in terms of RT and errors committed, and on Visual Detection Task, the indices of performance were the number of digits detected and errors committed. In visual detection task, extraverts showed superiority initially but committed more errors in the process. But gradually, the speed of extraverts decreased and the errors increased in comparison to those of introverts. Similarly in choice reaction time, the results show the superiority of introverts over extraverts in terms of speed. Thus, from the above studies it can be concluded that introverts gradually due to their steady arousal maintain the speed as well as accuracy. The contentious issue is that in the society we find that individuals differ in terms of learning of social norms and expectations i.e. some uphold the norms and behave in accordance with the expected standards of behaviour. The present endeavour undertakes to study the difference in learning of social norms and expectations through the personality differences within the framework of Eysenck's model, because Eysenck (1947) stated that introverts learn social norms and expectations better than extraverts who are poor in forming conditioned responses (CRs). But the statement regarding norms remained in the realm of uncertanity because no systematic laboratory study was conducted to test his contentions and it remained only an observational affair. The present investigation undertakes to study the differences in introverts and extraverts and males and females through Sherif's experiment of autokinesis as how the two groups learn to adjust and retain the norm through interaction with a group of 3 to 4 comprising of introverts and extraverts and the two genders. Secondly, in the Asch's study it would be seen that how the introverts and extraverts behave under social pressure of the confederates in the line drawing experiment in the two sexes.

Apart from these experiments of social norms, it would also be tested that how introverts and extraverts differ in their performance through two learning tasks.

Conclusion

To conclude, personality is the outcome of culture and socialization. Even in the same culture diversity in the socialization practices occur due to subcultures which affect both the sexes but females are affected more as compared to their counterparts called males.

The Present Research Work

The present endeavour is designed to uncover the psychodynamic process of learning of social norms and expectations through the autokinetic effect and perceptual line drawing task in the genders and personality groups as no direct attempt seemingly has been made.

2

Conceptual Framework and Review of Literature

In the previous chapter the present problem has been delineated in the form of social norms and social expectations being learnt separately i.e. simply and normally in different personality groups.

The focus of the present chapter would be on providing a theoretical foundation of the variables used along with the review of related literature in the light of which the hypotheses of the present investigation would be formulated. The review of related literature is presented in the following sections:

(1) Social Norms
(2) Gender and Social Norms
(3) Personality and Social Norms.

SOCIAL NORMS

In Every Society a man wishes to stand well with his fellows, to win their respect and approbation, to have relations with them that will make it possible for him to carry out those activities with which he is concerned. Therefore, he acts in conformity with the customs, traditions, values, and the like prevailing in the society. A Brahmin in an orthodox community must rise early, take his bath and sit down to worship. In large towns people waiting for a bus must stand in a queue and await their turn. In England a 'gentleman' must take off his hat on entering a room, must let ladies enter first, must express regret by saying 'sorry' when he brushes past a stranger, and the like. In some Indian communities Hindu widows shave their heads, in "Others" they only cover their heads. The Hopi look down upon all striving for personal power and prestige, and the Kwakiutl commend competition and struggle for status and rank. Thus, each cultural group has specific characteristics expressed in customs, traditions, values and the like. They represent their social norms or standards. A Hindu is surprised that there are people who eat frogs and beef just as a Red Indian is surprised that among some oriental communities all the work is done by men and women sit behind *purdah*. A man should have only one wife, a woman should have only one husband; people should work only five days in a week; infants should be breast-fed for two years; all are examples of social norms obtaining in anyone cultural group.

A. HISTORY OF SOCIAL NORMS

The history of social norms is as old as the history of civilization. Social norms develop due to needs and also due to joint effort more precisely due to individuals of the group through social dependence on others interaction. Norms develop due to social interaction. Because people are profoundly influenced by other's ideas and actions, interaction causes group members' thoughts, feelings and behaviours to become more alike. Norms reflect the group's generally accepted way of thinking, feeling or acting. A recurrent question has often been raised by philosophers throughout the intellectual history of Western civilization—How and why did organized social systems among men arise? The opinions and points of view have been manifold. Plato, more than centuries before the time of Christ, suggested in "The Republic" that states originate because man, the individual, is not self sufficient. Plato argued that each man in order to satisfy his own essential goals needed the conjoint effort of others. Thus, his proposed answer to the question is a utilitarian one. He suggested that man is committed to be a social organism because of pragmatic, presumably reasonable, voluntary entry into cooperative organization.

Somewhat in contrast to Plato, Aristotle (also, some few centuries before Christ) in his Treatise on Politics posited an instinctual basis for man's entry into the organized social system. Like Plato, Aristotle conceived man to be clearly committed to social participation, but he suggested that man is bound by his inherent nature to be gregarious and affiliative with others. Aristotle's arguments like many that have followed, even into the twentieth century unfortunately tend to dismiss the most provocative aspect of the question by simply ascribing the basis of man's participation in societies to "human nature".

Recovery from the intellectual stagnation of the "dark" Middle Ages led eventually to a late—Renaissance burst of intellectual and philosophical concern with the same old problems. The seventeenth century represents a phenomenal peak of intellectual focus on social and political questions. A number of philosophers who have profoundly influenced the evolution of western political social thought wrote during this period, and perhaps not merely as coincidence, several crucial social movements followed with in the century: the Protestant Reformation, the French Revolution, the settlement of the New World, and the origin of new focus of government in the New World. All of these carried the dominant theme of the dignity of the individuals with in the framework of a social system. Rousseau, in the middle of the seventeenth century wrote the social contract as an exposition and extended development of the utilitarian notion that man's entry into organized social systems was essentially an act of compromise for his own eventual benefit.

John Locke, during the latter part of the seventeenth century, reiterated much of Rousseau's point of view, stressing particularly man's rationality. Locke, with rather strong convictions about the dominance of man's intellect over his emotions, found his attention on the argument that man is basically a rational and logical creature, and that his intellect underlies his practical and utilitarian decision to participate in social organizations.

Also during the seventeenth century, Hobbes wrote an intellectual fantasy about the origins of a hypothetical state, the Leviathan, which is essentially congruent with the ideas of Locke and Rousseau in arguing that man voluntarily enters into social organization and thus evolves complex social systems. Although the many interpreters of Rousseau have difficulty in selecting his quotations to determine exactly how "good" or "bad" he thought society was for man, there is little doubt that Hobbes conceived social systems as highly ameliorative (become better) and ennobling (making noble). Rousseau referred in his writings to "the noble savage", implying that man in his preorganized state was essentially a noble and beneficent creature, and also to the fact that social organization was sometimes a set of "shackles" in which man is "enchained". Thus, there is some reason to argue that Rousseau regarded social organization as a "compromise" at best and as a "necessary evil" at worst.

Hobbes (1651 A.D.), in contrast, characterized the natural and presocial states of man as solitary, crude, and savage, and argued that it is through social organization that he is able to rise to something better. Locke (1689 A.D.), more of a neutralist in the matter, simply held that man is reasonable, and that he arrived at the logical conclusion that social organization is to his advantage. Bentham (1789 A.D.), stressed collective practicality and implied that man realizes, rationally, that societies provide "the greatest good for the greatest number."

*There are certain prescientific notions of man and his fellow man regarding the basis of social interaction from which social norms develop. Following are these notions:

(1) *Confucius (520 B.C.), in "the Analects"* said that the word shu serves as the principle of life (it means) do not do unto others what you do not want others to do you (social contract). (2) *Plato (360 B.C.), in "The Republic"* said that A state arises out of the needs of mankind. No one is self sufficing, but all of us have many wants (utilitarianism) (3) *Aristotle (350 B.C.), in "Treatise on Politics"*, said that to live alone, one must be either an animal or god. Thus, he referred to the suggestions instinct. (4) *Mathew (100 A.D.) in "The New Testament"* said that, As ye would men should do to you, do ye also to them likewise. Thus, he emphasized the social contract. (5) *IBN—Khaldun (1378 A.D.) in 'Prolegomens'* said that it is evident that men are by nature in contact with and tied to each other. Such contact may produce solidarity nearly as powerful as that produced by kinship. Thus, he referred to gregarious instinct. (6) *Hobbes (1651 A.D.) in 'The Leurathan'* by emphasizing on beneficial social contract said that without social interaction, the life of man is solitary, poor, nasty, brutish and short. (7) *Locke (1689 A.D.) in an "Essay on Human Understanding"* emphasized on rational social contract by saying

* These have not been seen in original but are taken from John V., McDavid and Herbert Harari, (1967) Social Psychology, Individual groups and societies. A Harper International edition. New York: London; Tohyd.

that, for God having joined virtue and public happiness together, and made the practice thereof necessary to the preservation of society, it is no wonder that everyone should not only allow, but recommend and magnify those rules to others, from whose observance of them he is sure to reap advantage to himself. (8) *Rousseau (1762 A.D.) in "The Social Contract"* said that all men are created free. Society takes from man his native individual powers and equips him with other powers, which he cannot use without the assistance of others (men). (9) *Bentham (1789 A.D.) in the "Introduction to Principals of Morals and Legislation"* said that social interaction is guided by the principle of utility; the greatest possible number of members of society.

Thus, the above quotations suggest that man participates in organized social systems voluntarily, by choice, and presumably for some purposive end which is the basis of social interaction. When the human interacts with others then only he learns to behave in the society. Hence, dependence and interaction play a vital role in learning social expectations. This is the first stage of the development of social norms.

Another set of ideas, developed during the latter part of the 19th Century, had a profound effect upon virtually all of the life sciences especially Darwin's theory of evolution and the survival of better adapted forms of life. Although Darwin's theories were primarily addressed to biological evolution and accounted for the apparent phylogenetic continuity of the world's variety of living organisms, they contained implications for social adaptation as well. Herbert Spencer (1855) and; Lecomte de Nuoy (1947) articulated these implications in the argument that social evolution seemed to proceed also as though a principle of "survival of the fittest" were in operation.

Just as biologically well adapted forms of life were more likely to survive and reproduce their own kind, so also were socially well adapted organisms more likely to survive and perpetuate their forms of social adaptation. Thus, the utilitarian aspects of man's purposive entry into organized social systems were further emphasized by the claim that social organization has survival value and contributes directly to the maintenance of man as socially participating organism.

Thus, social norms are the essence of social interaction which serve as the basis for organized social system among humans.

Concept of Social Norms/Conceptualization of Social Norms

A norm is a rule, standard, or pattern for action (from the Latin "norms", a carpenter's square or rule). Social norms are rules of conduct. The norms are the standards by reference to which behaviour is judged and approved or disapproved. A norm in this sense is not a statistical average of actual behaviour but rather a cultural (shared) definition of desirable behaviours.

Norms are mental models or guidelines by which, ideally we control and evaluate our action and that of others. Normative order is control because upon it largely depends the possibility of mutual cooperation, which should be taken here to include mutual non-interference of action units that are engaged in distinct activities.

The Computational vs. The Sociological Concept of Norms

The computational concept of Norms:

In recent years, the computational study of norms through simulation has grown in importance (Shoham and Tenneholtz 1992a, Shoham and Tenneholtz 1992b, Conte and Castelfranchi 1995a, Conte and Castelfranchi 1995b, Walker and Wooldridge 1995, Castelfranchi, Conte and Paolucci 1998).

In the Artificial Intelligence Literature a norm is operationalised as a behavioural constraint on agents which interact with each other in a multiagent society. According to Ullman-Margalit 1977, there are three different conceptualizations of norms within a game theory.

(1) Norms as solutions to problems of coordination

Here, norms are seen essentially as conventions, behavioural conformatives, that do not presuppose explicit agreements among agents. They emerge from the individual interests of the agents. (Schelling 1960, Lewis, 1969), but do not presuppose explicit agreements among them. Lewis example is that of two persons unexpectedly cut off in a telephone conversation. Each has to choose whether to call back or wait. Norms of coordination emerge gradually from interactional practice. There is no conflict of utility because both participants want to resume their conversation.

(2) Norms as solution to conflicts of utility

In case of social dilemmas the conflict structure calls for norms whenever the agents' choices tend to produce a state of affairs that is both individually and socially undesirable.

(3) Norms as solutions to problems of inequality

In this case norms aim at maintaining a state of affairs in which one party is favoured or privileged at the expense of another.

Following Ullman-Margalit (1977), Conte and Castelfranchi (1995b) refer to the moral philosopher Hart (1961) who defines norms as a prescribed guide for conduct or action which is generally complied with by the members of a society. They emphasized three features of norms: their perspective force, their expected necessity for social life and expected clashes between norms on one hand and interests and desires of the agents who owe the duty, on the other. Conte and Castelfranchi (1993, 1995a, 1995b) and Castelfranchi, Conte and Paolucci (1998) account for norms as prescriptions represented in the minds of self-interested agents. They propose a model in which norms are seen as both macro and micro objects, social objects and mental constructs. Two concepts of normative behaviour are introduced. Norm abiding behaviour, which appears to correspond to some norms and norm governed (fully normative, Conte and Castelfranchi, 1995b) behaviours, which results from cognitive processing of norms and implies a mental representation of norms. They discuss the relative advantages of three different architectures of norm-abiding behaviour: norms as built-in constraints, goals or obligations. These differ in reliability, learning, novelty, faculty to change and repair and social control and make the representation of norms increasingly demanding leading up to norm-governed behaviour (see Table 2).

Table 2: Alternative representations of norms inside the agents' architectures (norms-abiding system)

Norms as	*Built in constraints:*	*Build-in ends (goals):*	*Built-in obligations:*
	Norms are seen as constraints on the agents' action repertoires (behavioural action); no truly normative choice.	Cognitive agents are allowed to choose among competing goals (instead of simply applying procedure and routines) but they treat norms like any other of their goals.	Explicit and specific mental object; differs from a constraint since it does not automatically reduce the set of actions available to the agents; and from a goal since it is not immediately transformed into a goal.
Reliability	*High reliability:* The constraints will always be executed.	*Low reliability:* Goals may be abandoned when they clash with more urgent needs.	*Average reliability:* Agents may give up normative goals, but this will cost them more than abandoning ordinary goals.
Learning	*No learning:* New constraints are implemented when the system is off-line.	*Average learning:* Build-in ends should be added when the system if off-line.	*Normative:* Goals are automatically produced on the grounds of normative beliefs and in principle beliefs may be acquired when the system is on-line.
Novelty	*No novelty:* Constraints reduce available actions; only prescriptions that is, prohibitions	*Build-in ends:* May correspond to prescriptions and not only to prohibitions; but since learning is not granted, there ought	*Normative:* Beliefs may be formulated as prescriptions, and not as mere prohibitions.

(contd.)

(contd.)

Novelty	*No novelty:*	*Build-in ends:*	*Normative:*
	(Don't ...) can be represented but not prescription ('Do....').	to be one-to-one correspondence between social norms and internal goals with a consequent high computational complexity.	
Repair	*No repair:* Agents are not endowed with the capacity for modifying unsuccessful constraints.	*Goal oriented:* Systems ought to be able to try out sexual solutions and choose those that achieve their goals to the highest degree, before giving up their goals.	*Change and repair:* As with any other kind of goal, plans for normative goals are subject to change and repair.
Social control	*No need:*	*No social control:* Agents may have preferences corresponding to norms or not; they may cling to these or abandon them as a function of circumstances.	*Need of control:* Since normative goals are a special type of goals, and normative actions have specific costs, agents can be shown to be interested in some monitoring of norms.

Sociological Concept of Norms

The sociological study of norms has developed from different conceptualizations of norms (Nonner and Winkler 1984) including even an overall suspension of the concept of norms itself.

(1) The statistical conceptualization of norms originates in behaviourism. A behavioural pattern becomes a norm if the majority of actors infact behave due to this pattern. Thus, norms are objectively observable and measurable. From this perspective any regular behaviour becomes a norm. One cannot distinguish between regular

and rule obeying behaviour. Examples of this approach are the theories of the formation of social norms by Geiger (1962) and Sherif (1967).

(2) The theories of action of Durkheim, Weber and Parsons represent the 'sociological' conceptualization of norms. According to Durkheim (1965) norms are social facts which can be identified through the mere existence of certain sanctions. The sanction does not constitute the norm, it is the symbol of it and 'as this symbol has the great advantage of being objective, accessible to observation and even to measurement, it is a good method to prefer it to the thing it represents' (Durkheim 1966). Durkheim does not deny the reality of a subjective perspective on norms, but he promotes the methodological principle that scientists should choose the perspective of an objective observer. It was Weber (1960) who made explicit the difference between objectively observed behaviour and subjectively intended action. There are behavioural regularities which are based on practice (Customs or traditions), on similar interest (market behaviour), and on notions of legitimate order. It is constitutive of normative action that the actor perceives behavioural rules as obliging or representative. In Parson's theory (1964) norms represent institutionalized role expectations. The objective character of norms is guaranteed by the integration of role expectations into the cultural system, its subjective character by internalization.

(3) Ethnomethodologists deny the overall relevance of sociological conceptualization of norms. According to Garfinkel (1967) there is not such a thing as a general norm which is independent of concrete context conditions. There are only situation specific expectations of concrete interaction partners which are actively negotiated by both sides. It is then the question how individuals constitute a common world. Ethnomethodologists have discovered several basic rules which have a pseudo-normative character. They are seen as obliging and deviations are sanctioned. But they are not equivalent to sociological norms: they are far more deeply rooted in society, and are not amenable to reflection. Deviation from these basic rules is judged in clinical, not moral categories. Furthermore, 'a society's members know the moral order as perceivably normal courses of action' (Garfinkel 1967), i.e. in concrete interactions actors resort to the statistical conceptualization of norms.

(4) Finally, developmental psychologists have put forward an ethical conceptualization of norms. Kohlberg (1969, 1971) reconstructed the development of the moral consciousness of man. At any time, a subject is actively structuring and reflecting his/her social environment. Throughout his/her moral development three main stages can be distinguished: at the first stage of preconventional morality a child conforms to norms in order to avoid punishment—this corresponds to behaviourism; at the second stage of conventional morality a subject conforms to norms because he/she has internalized the norms of his family, peer group or society—this corresponds to Parson's view; at the third, and final stage of post conventional morality a subject conforms to norms because of insight into abstract principles that allow for the foundation and justification of norms—this corresponds to the ethical conceptualization of norms.

Haferkamp (1980) defines norms as conceptions which are internalized by the majority of members of a social situation.

Henri Jules, defines the social norms as the "law" (the rule or the principle) intended to orientate the behaviour in keeping with the values. We then call "norms", the rules of collective behaviour which, without our continuously assuming consciousness of them inspire our actions.

A norm is a standard which prescribes the performance or characteristics of a large group of people against which other individuals can be compared. There are, for example, norms of intelligence or infant motor development. Some psychologists draw a distinction between norms and standards. The word standard, according to them, implies a goal to be achieved or objective to be reached, but a norm is not a measure of what ought to be, but of what actually is. Such a distinction may hold good in psychological measurement, but in social psychology a norm indicates a standard of behaviour as defined by a group, society or culture. The term social norm was first introduced by Sherif to denote the accepted customs, rules, traditions, attitudes and values found in every established group. These norms provide frames of reference, which guide the judgements, feelings and actions of members of that group. Thus, respect for the aged mother, worshipful regard for the cow, taking breakfast after bath are accepted social norms among Hindus though they are occasionally violated. They regulate behaviour within the group.

Social norms are being constantly built in the course of social interaction in everyday life. For example till recently railway porters in India used to rush to the compartments when any train arrived and snatch luggage from passengers. Now they all stand in a row and instead of rushing about await to be called by passengers of the compartment halting just in front of them. A social norm has been built up and every railway porter is expected to conform to it. Thus a social norm refers to any criterion of experience and behaviour in social interaction which regulates the behaviour of group members. It is a generalization covering behaviour in a number of similar social situations by a number of members.

Social norms involve judgements of value. An act of behaviour is either approved or disapproved according as it conforms or does not conform to a social norm. Thus social norms denote patterns of behaviour expected or demanded of members of a group, how they should or ought to behave, whether they actually behave that way or not. In fact at any time a number of members may not conform to them or the same member may sometimes conform and sometimes ignore them.

Social norms have a high emotional tone. Hindus abstain from beef and condemn those who do not. Sikhs hate smoking, and Muslims prescribe *purdah* for women. These norms have emotional tinge and their violations are strongly resented by members. Even then they are generalizations which now and then permit exceptions and variations. Very young girls may not observe *purdah*, old women too may do without it, and lack of *purdah* among highly educated ladies is not objected to.

Social norms are transmitted from one generation to another and in some ancient cultures some of them can be traced to several centuries back. Folding hands to greet people, taking off shoes before entering the kitchen or cleaning one's mouth after meals are very ancient social norms among Hindus though they are changing under the impact of foreign culture. That social heritage influences the behaviour of the present generation is too true in India. Some social norms are short-lived like fads and fashions but others endure through centuries and are woven into life of the people. Dhoti and kurta have been replaced by bush-shirt and pant and guests are entertained with tea or coffee instead of milk and curd.

It may seem that the effect of social norms is to make society static and uniform so that each generation repeats what the previous generation did. But this is not so. In the first place they allow variations and are not rigid. Secondly, some of them are based on universal values which may be interpreted in new constructive ways. In fact our great social reformers in India like Raja Ram Mohan Roy, Swami Dayanand and Mahatma Gandhi have helped to change and reconstruct social life in India by interpreting traditional social values in new contexts so that change and reform is rooted in the past for which masses have a great reverence. Mahatma Gandhi's political programme of civil disobedience and non-co-operation was based on the ancient social norms of ahimsa and truth and was thus made readily acceptable to the masses.

Social norm is a very wide term and includes all types of social expectations and demands in the form of customs, traditions, folkways, rules of conduct, etiquette, values and the like. Naturally therefore social norms cannot be rigid, must make allowances for individual variations and latitude in action. They do not specify single courses of action but cover a wide range of behaviour which is permitted or tolerated. This is particularly so when the type of behaviour covered by them is less important. In the case of very significant and important matters, social norms are less elastic and impose a narrow range of permissive behaviour. Secondly, group norms may be established about anything and everything, real or imagined. In Hinduism for example, there are norms about such abstract things as *Maya* or *Pralaya* (doomsday). Then there are norms about such concrete things as food, water or making presents to daughters and sisters.

An important thing about group norms is that they enable members to communicate with each other. People can interact without any common body of norms; a mother and an infant can interact but they cannot communicate, that is, share each others meanings unless they have common norms. Communication implies similar experiences and similar meanings of those experiences. This is possible if they share the same frames of reference. Social norms therefore imply standard meanings and not standard behaviour. Group members often behave in very much the same manner; for example, they all enjoy a festival match, they may enjoy it in very much the same manner, their behaviour will have the same standard meaning of enjoyment, but they may also enjoy in slightly different ways. This means that social norms may lead to different types of behaviour but continue to have the same standard meaning for all members, that is, all members will understand the common meanings of different kinds of behaviour. Thus mutual understanding is made possible by common standard meanings. Such understanding is not always perfect depending on whether common meanings are precise or vague.

Though social norms tend to change and there is nothing fixed or absolute about them they are absolutely necessary for the stability of social structures and the perpetuation of culture. They provide it with relatively fixed and limited standards of judgement by means of which we interact or give meaning to particular events. Without such standards of judgements, which have been called frames of reference, an individual would lose his moorings and would not know what to do in this complex and complicated world. It is not possible for every individual to spend endless time and energy in thinking everything out and arrive at some opinion about everything. So most of us accept them uncritically as guide posts till such time they fail us or need revision and change.

Social norms and values of a society are not usually codified though attempts have been made to do so. Manu Smriti is one such attempt, and laws of a state, penal codes, lists of religious commandments and the like have tried to list social norms. In modern life an individual belongs to several groups which may have different or even conflicting norms. A grown-up person may belong to several social and religious organizations because his family has always done so. He has professional associations, merchants' chamber, bar association, doctors' club, bankmen's union and the like. If he is rich he may belong to a night club where he drinks, dances and lets himself go. He may be manager or president of an educational institution or an informal group of bridge players. Each of these groups has its own social norms. Some of them may be similar, others may differ and leads to conflict. He may be compelled to give up membership of certain groups because of this difference or he may adjust by behaving differently or even in contradictory ways in different groups.

Some groups are all-pervasive and affect every area and aspect of life and work. A member of the Congress has not only to hold certain definite views on political and social work and change but also to wear *khadi*, to spin and do constructive work in villages, to abstain from smoking and drinking, to work for the uplift of the depressed and suppressed classes and so on. But some groups have a narrow range of work. Porters at a railway station put on red uniforms and stand in a line when a train arrives. The norms of the two groups will accordingly vary in range. Social norms of the former group will affect every important aspect of life while those of the latter will be limited to the time and place of work.

Groups may be formally organized or just informally got together. In formal groups social norms are codified into rules and laws. A legislative assembly has written rules and regulations for the conduct of its proceedings. Formal clubs, organized games of cricket and hockey and the like have standardized ways and written rules, but rural assemblies, community meetings or groups of working women have no such formal rules. They just improvise rules of work on the spot. If a group of children are given a rubber ball they devise games and formulate rules for them, and a little later pass on to another game and make rules to manage that. But on that account it cannot be said that they have no group norms. They punish those who violate their unwritten rules by depriving them of play and accord recognition and praise to those who play according to rules. Professional conduct among teachers, doctors or lawyers is regulated by social norms though there is no written code of do's and don'ts. If a new entrant to the profession tries his new-fangled methods of approach he is frowned upon and soon falls in line.

Lastly, social norms are in a way social stimulus situation. The individual does not react to the abstract value or ideal implicit in the norm but to its concrete forms. We do not react to 'law' when we stop at the traffic signal; we react to the danger involved in it and to the policeman who bars the way and may pull us up. We shout 'Jai Hind' or salute the flag because others are doing, and not doing it would mark us out in a crowd, but all the time we are learning the abstract value of love of our country. Children salute their teachers because it is done and expected in the school and they are learning the social norm of respect for teachers.

Law and Social Norms

Sociologists have long incorporated the concept of norms into their analyses of human behaviour. More recently, however, the idea of norms has come to the attention of the legal academy as well (Ellickson 2001 and Richard, H., McAdams, 2001). In the past decade, these prominent legal scholars have published articles how social norms interact with formal law in regulating human behaviour. According to these legal scholars, norms are rules of behaviour that are enforced primarily not by courts but by other forces. For example, in the United States there are norms prescribing that one ought to wear shoes in the office and to ask permission before smoking in another's house. People perceive such norms as serious constraints on day to day behaviour. This is true even though it is extremely unlikely that a decision to take off one's shoes at work, or to "light up" at a dinner party, would trigger a criminal investigation or a civil suit for damages. Thus, law and norms go side by side and where the law differs from norms, crime is more. In Britain, law is based on unwritten social norms. It goes with the traditions, customs and conventions i.e. why laws are different from state to state in Britain and America.

Norms are prescriptions serving as common guidelines for social action. Culture provides with a set of guide posts readymade definitions of situations by which we align our individual actions to create social or joint actions, these guide posts are norms. Norms are rules that specify appropriate and inappropriate behaviour. Norms are expectations—consumption of ideal behaviours—that are shared by the members of a society at large or by the members of particular group within a society.

Human behaviour exhibits certain regularities, which are the product of adherence to common expectations or norms. In this sense human action is 'rule governed'. A social norm is not necessarily actual behaviour and normative behaviour is not simply the most frequently occurring pattern. Since the term refers to social expectations about 'correct' or 'proper' behaviour, norms imply the presence to legitimacy, consent and prescription while deviation from norms is punished by sanctions—norms are acquired by internalization and socialization.

Social norms play an important role in the regulation of social behaviour. Through social norm we distinguish between accepted and deviant behaviour. Social norms are nothing but those laws and values that have grown and developed for controlling social behaviour of the humans i.e. the social interactions which regulate activities. It is these norms that determine the ideals of behaviour and society. Generally most of the members of the society accept them and their social behaviour is guided by them. These social norms determine and guide the status of different individuals.

Social norms are standards of behaviour that are agreed upon by group members and exert a powerful influence on social behaviour. They are thus considered to have agent characteristics, even though no actual person need be present when their influence occurs. At a minimum, it is only necessary for the focal person to be aware of the norm to be subject to its presence.

Social norms regulate the performance of the group as an organized unit. Social norms are those accepted criterion developed by the group that regulate the behaviour of the members of the group. Like other aspects of social organization, norms may be either formal as in the case of written constitution, bye-laws or recorded laws governing conduct, or informal as in the case of unstated, more or less "intuitively" accepted conventions that bind participants in a society or group. Group norms specify not merely a "straight and narrow path" of prescribed behaviour, but a range of acceptable variability in behaviour.

Society and Social Norms

Social norms develop due to society. Groups cannot exist without rules that regulate the member's behaviour. The chief advantage of rules or norms has been discussed by Thibaut and Kelley (1959), who note that rules serve to coordinate behaviour, that is rules are established to avoid conflicts i.e. between a member's self-interest and the groups interest or conflicts between group members and non-group members.

The term "society" or "social group" can be applied to no animals other than humans for the ties that bind a human group are abstract social relations and not merely biological needs. Human beings depend upon each other from birth not only for physical and economic survival, but they also rely on each other socially and for personal development. Human beings alone live in true social groups. Although most animals, like humans, form groups, with even prolonged association, mutual dependence, and cooperation toward biologically common goals, only human social groups share sets of common meanings or symbols and social systems of mutual obligation. Although some people may say that certain human counterparts characterize the lives of other animals, human beings alone have such social institutions as a political state, an economic system, and a religion. Only humans have laws and moral judgements, and only humans experience recurring and repeated social interaction leading to complex social relations. In this process of social interaction each individual, by his actions, takes into account what he considers to be the expectation of others, in turn his behaviour shows that he expects others to act toward him in a certain manner.

As a result of group experiences, a human being becomes dependent upon others for human associations, conversation, and social interaction. The importance of this dependence on groups can be demonstrated in situations where group contacts are removed e.g., prison officials have learned that solitary confinement, with its almost complete isolation from human association, is one of the most severe forms of punishment for any human being. A few days of this type of treatment will usually render the most defiant prisoner tractable. Admiral Byrd, the famous explorer of the Antarctic, voluntarily isolated himself for several months in uninhabited polar regions more than a hundred miles from the nearest human being of his expedition. He described his experiences of being alone and vividly showed how dependent the individual is on social groups when such contacts are removed.

Seeing interaction among individuals in pursuits of life and its betterment a group structure takes shape. The individuals take on different functions. Each acquires a relative status. A routine and rules for the conduct of affairs are stabilized. Routines, rules, standards of conduct, values to uphold are thus by-products of group interaction. Such a superstructure of rules, standards and values is referred to generically as the social norms of the group.

It is hardly possible to discuss group formation and functioning without discussing their products. Therefore, group norms figured prominently in our dealing with status relationships, leadership, and group functioning. When individuals with common motives or problems interact over a sufficient time span, a group structure evolves. Concomitant with differentiation of group structure, by-products of the interaction process are stabilized in the form of catchwords, nicknames. jargon, slogans, customs, traditions, values and the like. Most of the by-products thus stabilized may be referred to under the genesis term social norms.

Social norms refer to any criteria of experience and behaviours formed in group interaction which regulate the behaviour of individual members of relevant stimulus situations. Thus, norms represent standardized generalizations concerned with expected modes of behaviours in any matter of consequence to the group. Human social relations and behaviours are regulated through social norms. As standardized generalizations, norms are concepts. They are concepts which are evaluative by nature. They not only encompass the given ranges of behaviour in relation to persons, objects and situations, but incorporate value judgements concerning them. Therefore, norms denote expected behaviour or even ideal behaviour. Social values or norms seldom specify just one point or a one single way of behaving like all concepts, norms encompass, a range of behaviour which is tolerable (permissible) to the group. The range of tolerable behaviour varies in extent, specificity, or permissiveness both in terms of the importance of the position of a particular member in the group hierarchy.

Through participation in the formation of group norms, individual members take part in the production of new values, new goals, new ideals. The individual acquires personally experienced motives which are truly social in origin. To the new group member, social norms are initially external. No matter what urgent pursuits brought individuals into interaction or led them into an existing group, they form new motives as they become functioning members of a group structure with particular norms. Men come into industrial plants primarily to earn a living form themselves and their families. If they are paid rates for each piece of work with a bonus for production above a certain level, it would seem that they would work and strive to produce as much as possible, within limits of their physical capacity and health. However, the worker in this situation finds himself in an informal work group. He soon learns from the others that one does not produce above a certain amount even if he can. There is a social norm governing production output, the good member of the group keeps his production within a certain range as governed by the norms. If he does not, he will receive notice from others in the form of comments, warnings, standardized physical annoyance or ostracism by the group members. Those who persist in ignoring the group norms for production, are the ones who do not relate themselves to the informal work group.

The fact that the production norm is informal working group may be below a feasible ceiling, for production does not indicate that the group norms usually bring a "levelling effect". In the case of this norm; there are reasons why adherence may result in lower production than is feasible for some individuals.

The social norms of the group make explicit a bottom and a ceiling for aspirations of individual members. They constitute a reference scale for the aspirations and experience of failure or success of individual members. Social norms provide one of the most important mechanisms of social control of the behaviour of individuals within a society. M. Sherif and Carolyn (1936) have defined social norms in the following terms: "Super structure rules, standards and values is referred to generally as the 'social norms' of the group. In fact it is a social expectation."

Group norms regulate both diversity and uniformity within the group by prescribing rules of conduct for individual members of the group. Uniformity of individual behaviours within a group stem from variety of sources. For one thing, individuals who participate in a group are usually exposed simultaneously to the same general patterns of stimulation from events that confront the group and the environmental context of the group. Members of Boy Scout troop, for example, tend to be influenced by the same agents of socialization, by the same kinds of activities and by the same kinds of presentations of information about the world. Homogeneity of behaviour among individual members of the troop develops in part because each member is individually influenced by the same kinds of forces surrounding the group, and not necessarily because of the factors within the group. Members of delinquent adolescent street gangs tend also to be homogeneous, although quite differently from Boy Scouts, because they too experience the same kinds of activities and are presented the same kinds of information about the world and certain patterns of stimulation that might be common for delinquents may be quite rare for the average Boy Scout.

However, group norms also account for a great deal of uniformity among members of a group. There are atleast two important ways in which group norms operate to induce uniformity of behaviour: *First*, group standards may provide information and guidance to the individual with respect to matters he cannot handle independently. One may act like others in a group simply because he is uncertain as to how he might otherwise behave, he may merely look to others for information about possible actions that will be effective in meeting the circumstances. Thus, the influence of group norms on the individual may stem from his quest for information from other members of the group. *Second*, group norms may be a key to the individual's acceptance by others in the group. One may adhere to group norms because he sees direct values in uniformity and simply feels that some kind of advantage is to be gained by behaving as others expect. This advantage may be some instrumental means to satisfy his own personal goals, or it may be the reward of social acceptance and membership in the group or of interpersonal approval and nurturance. Thus, the influence of social norms on the individual may also stem from his quest for agreement with the group for its own sake.

Characteristics of Social Norms

Following are the essential characteristics of social norms:

(1) Norms are standards of group behaviour: An essential characteristic of group life is that it is possessed by a set of values which regulate the behaviour of individual members. When a number of individuals interact, a set of standards develop that regulate their relationships and modes of behaviour. These standards of group behaviour are called social norms.

(2) Norms incorporate value judgements: Secord and Backman (1965) say "A norm is a standard of behavioural expectations shared by group members against which the validity of perceptions is judged and the appropriateness of feeling and behaviour is evaluated." Members of a group exhibit certain regularities in their behaviour. Such regularities in behaviour have been explained in terms of social norms. Norms represents "standardized generalizations" concerning expected modes of behaviour. It may be said that norms are based on social values which are justified by moral standards or aesthetic judgements. A norm is a pattern, setting limits on individual behaviour, as defined by Broom and Sclznick, "The norms are blueprints for behaviour, setting limits within which individuals may seek alternate ways to achieve their goals."

(3) Norms are related to factual world: It may not however, be presumed that norms are abstract representing imaginary construct. Sociologists are interested mainly in 'operative norms', that is, norms that are sanctioned in such a way that violater suffers penalties in the group. Norms in order to be effective, must represent correctly the relations between real events. They must take into account the factual situation. Normative system, since it is meant to achieve results in the factual world should be related to the events in the real world.

(4) Norms are both generalized and generalizable: Norms are always to some extent both generalizable. They may refer to all human beings at all times and in all places or they may refer only to a specific category of persons in specific type of situation. A norm calls for "right action" and implies a generalizable reason for the rightness of the indicated conduct. Ultimately this propriety or rightness traces back to some standard of value that is taken without further justification as valid by the individual or group in question.

(5) Norms are more than an idiosyncratic expression: Norms are more than an idiosyncratic expression of the wants or desires of a particular person. Even quite specific norms imply a basis for assent by someone other than the norm sender himself. At the same time, norms actually can guide conduct only if they prescribe or proscribe identifiable courses of action; therefore norms are more specific and socially imperative than values or ideals. For example, "honesty" is a generalized value (a conception of desirability) but it is still found socially necessary to have specific rules for concrete situations such as student's behaviour in examination or the financial responsibility of banking officials.

(6) Norms are learned: Norms are learned by individuals in social intercourse with others—that is, in the process of socialization. By definition, then norms are shared by two or more individuals. Some norms are particular to quite small groups, such as a husband-wife pair or a clique of friends, while other norms may be held by a large collectively that is one of several existing in one nation. Still other norms may be shared by most adult members of a nation or of an entire civilization.

(7) Norms may arise in relation to any aspect of human activity: Norms may arise in relation to any aspect to human activity and expectancy that comes to be regarded as of any importance or consequence. There are norms for perceiving, feeling, thinking,

judging, evaluating and acting. Thus, there are cognitive and logical norms for carrying out scientific investigations, aesthetic norms for judging music etc. There are the norms of moral conduct which guide direct social interaction. The term "social norm" may refer to any of these but most commonly is used to designate rules for social interaction.

(8) Norms are diverse: Norms are exceedingly diverse not only in their objects but in respect to their important properties in different societies and in different historical periods. Some norms are widely known, accepted and followed where as others are characterized by law consensus and only partial conformity. Some norms are learned early in life through identification and socialization. Others are acquired in later life through secondary social relations. To understand any particular norm it is important to know whether it has been "internalized" so as to become part of the conscience of self-ideal of the individuals in question, if so, there will be much conformity even if there is no external surveillance of conduct or punishment for deviant behaviour. Norms not thus internalized can be enforced only through external rewards and penalties. Those norms that are primarily enforced through punishment and threat contrast with standards that are maintained by a flow of the social rewards such as wealth, prestige or social approval. Great variations exist in consistency of enforcement, source of authority, degree of allowable variation in conformity, extent of deviance, and type of enforcing agency.

Legitimization of Social Norms

Social norms are supported by some form of legitimization, that is, an explanation of why the rule should be obeyed. In some cases the legitimization is fairly obvious; there is little need to justify the rules against murder, robbery and physical attack. In other case, however, there is little rational reason for the rule; there is no known biological reason why adultery should be outlawed, why gentleman should shake hands, or why people should not smoke marijuana. In these cases the legitimization is usually based on appeals to Gods (Adultery is wrong because the Ten Commandents forbid it), or tradition ("well, we've always greeted others with a handshake"), or the good of the society ("what if everybody decided to smoke pot—nobody would work") often the legitimization makes no sense to the outsider, but to the people of the culture it provides adequate justification for the norms (see Figure 16).

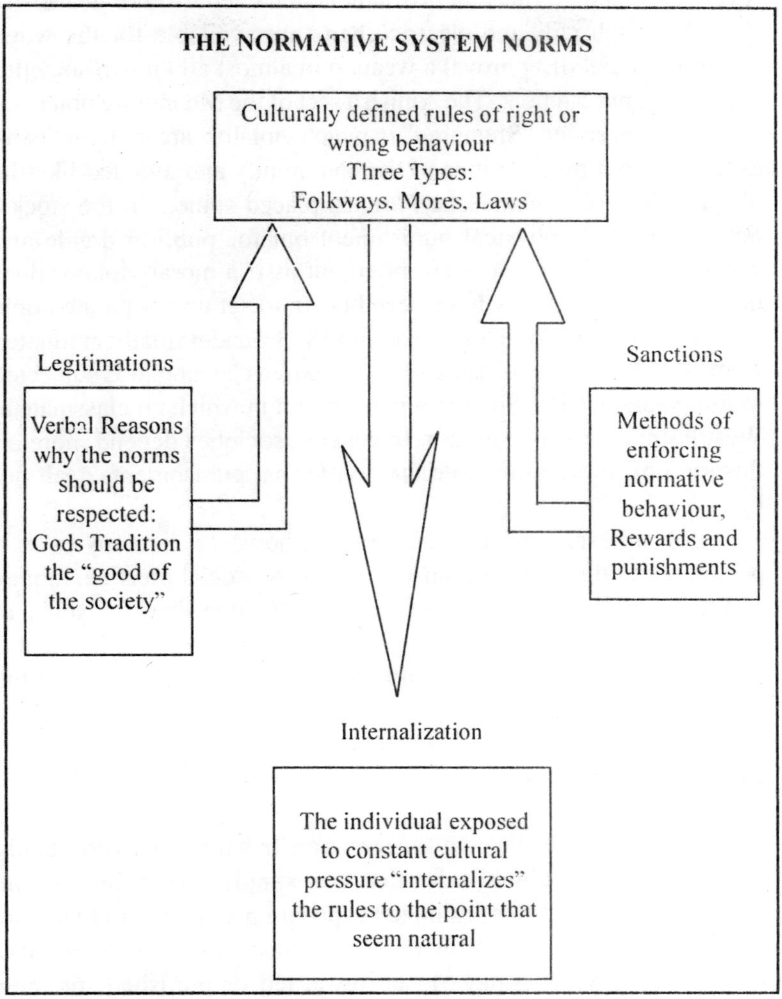

Figure 16: Model of Normative System
Sharma, A. (2000) Development of Social Norms among different Personality Groups. Unpublished Doctoral Thesis H.P.U. India.

Sanctions: In addition to legitimization, norms are backed up by sanctions, either punishments or rewards; that literally "force" people to obey them. Sanctions for some norms are very minor. Using the wrong spoon or belching in public draws only frowns of disapproval at worst. Sanctions for major norms, however, are quite severe and include fines, imprisonment and even exile or death.

Although jails and electric chairs are available for the worst violators, social disapproval a weapon in almost all known societies is the usual punishment. The Amish a sect of the Mennonite practiced a punishment called "Shunning" in which violators are systematically excluded from the activities of the community and avoided like the plague. In New England, the Puritans placed sinners in the stocks, not so much for physical punishment but for public ridicule and harassment, Eskimo tribes are often out as if a moral violator does not even exist, and they have been known to set up a separate home in which the offender lives in exile; in 1973 a cadet finally graduated from West Point who, because of his supposed cheating, was subjected to four years of "The Silence: a punishment in which no classmate at West Point ever spoke to him. In general, societies depend more on this kind of informal ridicule than on formal punishments dealt put by courts".

Not all sanctions are punishments, however, in many cases a person obeys the norms because of rewards—social prestige, money and power. Usually, the carrot is more effective than the stick. In effect people are rewarded if they obey the norms and punishment if they disobey them. Rewards and punishments are two sides of the same sanction coin.

Internalization of Norms

The final reasons people obey the norms are that they are so constantly exposed to these cultural rules that they simply accept them as the natural way to act. After prolonged exposure people literally take the cultural rules and make them a part of themselves—they internalize them. People seldom have to be rewarded or punished for their behaviour, they are so socially brainwashed that they rarely think of doing anything to violate the norms. In most cases people literally do not realize that it is possible to violate the norms. The few obvious violations such as murder and other crimes cover up the fact that most of the time people simply cannot violate the norms because they do not know of alternatives. They obey the norms simply because they have been culturally taught that no civilized human would act otherwise (see Figure 16).

There are three types of norms

Folkways

Not all norms have the same seriousness; committing murder and violating etiquette are hardly on the same level. They are the most usual and least serious types of norms which are the customary patterns of behaviour that Sumner (1906) called folkways. The most obvious way to determine the importance of a norm for the society is to observe how severely they punish who violate it. Norms which are not looked upon as extremely important or to state it another way, norms which can be violated without severe punishment—are called folkways. Adult males should wear coat and tie to church. People should be on time for appointments. Professors should not serve whisky in their offices. These are some of the folkways which refer to the old customs whose origins are lost in antiquity but continues to be followed (see Figure 17).

Mores

Whereas, folkways are relatively minor regulations for social conduct, mores are serious social rules, people believe that if the mores are violated, the society may actually fall apart. Examples of American mores include protection of young, helpless children, patriotism to the nation, monogamy and sexual fidelity to one's mate, male leadership in dating, respect for elderly people, and reverence in church. The legitimization for mores come from people's sincere belief that if they are violated, reasonable social life would be impossible. Of course this legitimization is not necessarily valid. Bigamy might very well alter the present family structure, but would it destroy the society? Would female leadership in dating cause society to crumble? The objective facts do not justify people's fears about violating mores, but since people firmly believe them, they obey them. Sanctions for violating norms can be severe (see Figure 17).

Figure 17: Comparison for 3 kinds of Norms.

	Folkways	*Mores*	*Laws*
Definition	Minor rules about social conduct.	Major rules of conduct deemed essential by society.	Formally enacted norms enforced by police power, codified into documents and sanctioned by specific penalties.
Examples	Dress, patterns, dating table manners.	Adultery rules. Incest taboo patriotism.	Laws against murder, stealing, using drugs or fixing prices.
Legitimization	Tradition: "That's just the way we have always done it.	Religious obser-vances.	Official enactment by the state "for the good of the people."
Negative Sanction	Minor social gossip and ridicule.	Severe ridicule shunning, break in social relationship physical attack.	Enforcement by police and courts: fines, imprisonment and death.

Laws

Some norms, considered so important that their enforcement cannot be left to chance, are made into law. Laws are norms with several special characteristics:

(1) Laws are formally enacted by the states. The legitimization for law is an official enactment.

(2) Laws are not left open to informal public understanding; they are codified into written documents that are precise and subject to legal interpretation.

(3) Laws have special enforcement agents: police, judges, district attorneys, lawyers and so forth.

(4) Laws have definite, specified sanctions. Whereas the penalty or reward for less serious norms may vary considerably, the penalty for disobeying a specific law is clearly stated in the law itself. If you rob a bank, you get 20 years in jail; if you murder your landlord, you get life prisonment or death (see Figure 17).

Advantages of norm-governed system: The advantages of norm-governed system are avoiding useless, stupid and self-destructive behaviour favoured by the right execution of routines, as well as the spreading of errors and deviations produced by pure imitations. Therefore, it is promising to construct autonomous artificial agents with a capacity for applying norms.

Importance of Social Norms

A normless society is an impossibility. Norms are of great importance to society. It is impossible to imagine a normless society, because without norms behaviour would be unpredictable. The standards of behaviour contained in the norms give order to social relations. Interaction goes smoothly if the individuals follow the group norms. The normative order makes the factual order of human society possible. If there were no normative order, there could be no human society. Man needs a normative order to live in society because human organism is not sufficiently comprehensive or integrated to give automatic responses that are functionally adequate for society. Man is incapable of existing alone. His dependence on society is not derived from fixed innate response to mechanical social stimuli but rather from learned responses to meaningful stimuli. Hence his dependence on society is ultimately a dependence upon a normative order. Importance of norms can be made clear through its functions which have been stated under the separate heading of norms.

Functions of Social Norms

From the beginning, the functions of norms in society as a whole have been a central field of research in sociology. There are two positions in this area. First, norms have been analyzed as solutions to social problems (Marx, Durkheim, Parsons). According to Marx (1936) norms are dependent on the economic foundation of society. Hence, the functions of norms follow the interests of the ruling class. Following Durkheim 'society cannot exist if its parts are not solidary, morality consists in, being solidary' (Durkheim 1966). In Parsons' L—I—G—A or A—G—I—L scheme norms fulfil the I—(Integration) function of social systems. Solidarity is produced primarily at the level of values, which are shared by more or less everyone in society. Children are socialized by their parents so that the basic values and norms of society are 'internalized' as parts of their personalities. As a result, individuals need and want to do what society demands of them. Second, norms have been analyzed as generating social problems themselves. Dahrendorf (1962) states that wherever behaviour is regulated by and measured in terms of established norms, and wherever these norms are backed by sanctions, a rank order of social status is bound to emerge.

Social norms have six major functions

(1) *Group Maintenance:* Norms help groups to maintain themselves as a group.

(2) *Group Locomotion:* Norms help groups to accomplish their goals.

(3) *Social Reality:* Norms help the groups to create and maintain a commonly shared frame of reference which seems as a social reality.

(4) *Defining relationship to social surroundings:* Norms help group members to define their relationship to social surroundings such as other groups, organization, institutions and other components of the society.

(5) *Gives cohesion to society:* We can hardly think of a human group apart from norms. A group without norms would be to use the words of Hobbes, "solitary, poor, nasty, brutish and short". The human organisation in order to maintain itself must live in a normatively regulated social system. The normative system gives to society a cohesion without which social life is not possible. Those groups which cannot evolve a normative order and maintain normative control over their members fail to survive because of the lack of internal cooperation.

(6) *Norms influence individual's attitudes:* Norms influence an individual's attitudes and his motives. They impinge directly upon a person's self-conception. They are specific demands to act made by his group. They are much more stable. They have the power to silence any previously accepted abstract sentiment which they oppose. They take precedence over abstract sentiments. Becoming a member of a group implies forming attitudes in relation to group norms. The individual becomes a

> good member to the extent he abides by the norms. The norms determine and guide his intuitive judgement of others and his intuitive judgments of himself. They lead to the phenomena of conscience, of guilt feelings, of elation and depression. They are deeper than consciousness. Becoming a member of a group consists of internalizing the norms of the group. Through internalization they become a part of himself automatically expressed in his behaviour.

Implemented computational studies of norms have explored two different functions of norms (1) to permit or improve coordination among agents (Shoham and Tenneholtz, 1992a, 1992b) and to control aggression between them (Conte and Castelfranchi 1995a, Castelfranchi Conte and Paolucci, 1998 and Walker and Wooldridge, 1995).

Conte and Castelfranchi state that the finder-keeper norm, while controlling aggression efficaciously, also reduces the variance of strength among the agents i.e., their inequality (Conte and Castelfranchi 1995a). They point out that this norm is not truly a norm of property, since the possession are not ascribed exclusively on the grounds of the 'right of birth', but may be acquired over the course of each agent's life. They investigate distributive rationality which leads, in the long run, to the best possible outcome or the least possible harm, for all agents and collective rationality which leads in the long run to the best possible outcome for a collective entity even though it does not imply the best outcomes for all its sub-components, (Conte and Castelfranchi, 1995b). Refusing to those norms that control aggression they state: 'Norms seem to play an equalizing role (Conte and Castelfranchi, 1995b).

Group norms are social products

A necessary condition for the formation of group norms is interaction of individuals with common motives or problems over a time span. One person cannot form a social norm. Since group norms are products of interaction, the concept is a sociological designation. Social norms refer to any criteria of experience and behaviour formed through group interaction which regulate the behaviour of individual members in relevant stimulus situation. Since social norms are formed by individuals interacting in groups, the terms, "said norm" and group norm may be used interchangeably. Some use the term group standard. At some time in past, or recent history—social norms evolved in specific group interaction. When that group and its membership can be specified, group norm is the more accurate term since it makes explicit the relationship between behavioural criteria and group membership. Characterized here, group norm is a generic term, concerning a host of products of past and contemporary group interaction. Among these are social values, standards, customs, mores folkways, rules, fads and fashions. However, referring to these various social products generically does not imply that they are identical.

Social norms of any description represent standardized generalization concerning expected behaviour in matters of consequences to the group or groups in question. In other words, social norms represent one particular kind of concept. Like all concepts, norms refer to groupings or classes of items. They do not usually refer to just one behaviour for one specific situation. A concept denotes a generalization encompassing a range of items with more or less clear limits.

The feature distinguishing norms from concepts in general is their evaluative nature as evident in the examples. Social norms incorporate value judgements pertaining to a range of items. They imply evaluations of modes of behaviour relative to persons, objects or situations. Specifically norms refer to the expected or even ideal behaviour in matters of some importance to the group.

Norms are not formed by all groups in relation to every kind of behaviour and every possible situation. They are formed in matters of consequence to the group in question. Ordinarily, the relationships among members and the unity and continued existence of the group as a social unit are consequential to any group.

The scope of behaviour regulated by norms varies considerably in different groups. For example, the norms of most Protestant Churches in America today pertain chiefly to ethical matters. However, some sections like certain memonite groups have norms concerning a much broader area of life, including apparel, modes of transportation, forms of entertainment, schools and so on.

The average behaviour of members in a group may or may not coincide with that denoted by its norms at any given period in its history. In fact, certain norms may set such a high level for desirable conduct that average behaviour of members could approach it only at exceptional times. Nevertheless, the degree of adherence to major group norms by members is one index of solidarity in the group.

When the behaviour of member begins to diverge consistently from the bounds implied by group norms, it is safe to predict significant changes in group functioning. The nature of such change depends of course on other factors. It may be that as a result of external conditions or internal frictions, the group is in the process of disintegration or changed conditions facing a group may lead to weakening its norms and to the formation of new norms more congruent with the new conditions. In modern differentiated societies, the degree of adherence to norms in a particular group is affected by the fact that members frequently belong to a number of groups. These various groups may have conflicting or even contradictory norms. Therefore, the degree of adherence to norms in one group may in part a function of the extent to which norms of other reference groups of the membership are congruent with them.

When informally organized groups function once a period of time, norms become formalized and may even be written down as rules, regulations and laws. Analysis of formalized norms and legal regulations in large social organization has to begin in by specifying the different groups functioning within the larger structure, their norms and the power relations among those groups which are most influential in establishing the laws and in enforcing them. Large organizations today are seldom composed of just one group encompassing all individuals, although this might still be the case in relatively small, isolated societies. As a recent analysis for French governmental structure indicates, persons with in such structure may be members of groups with widely differing norms and interests.

Norms as Effective Guides for Social Behaviour

Kurt Lewin (1943) was one of the first social psychologists to demonstrate the powerful effect of group norms on behaviour. During the second world war, traditional cuts of meat like steaks and chops were scarce and when available, were very expensive. To keep the civilian population healthy, the U. S. Government wanted people to consume more liver, kidneys and other unfamiliar organ meats. Commendable as this goal was, U.S. citizens found it hard to swallow at the dinner table. Pamphlets extolling the nutritional value of these meats, newspaper stories appealing to patriotism even public lectures by expert nutritionists had little impact on well entrenched food buying and eating habits. Lewin believed that changes in such habits could be accomplished only by changing the prevailing norms governing what was appropriate to eat. To test this idea, he brought home-makers together in small groups to discuss in depth such questions as how to cook the new cuts and how to overcome family members' resistance. In the course of these discussions, group members' willingness to try the new foods increased, and this produced a shift in norms. A follow-up survey showed that over 30 per cent of the discussion group members actually tried the unusual goods, compared with only 3 per cent of home-makers who listed to a lecture advocating the same course of action but had no idea how other people in the audience would react. Norms had an impact that information alone could not achieve. But the question is how do norms come to influence behaviour, and why are they so effective?

How Norms Guide Behaviour

Norms must be brought to mind before they can guide behaviour. They can be activated by deliberate reminders or by subtle cues, such as observations of people's behaviour (Baron, 1988).

No norm, attitude, or other cognitive representation can influence behaviour unless it comes to mind. Norms, like attitudes can be activated either by deliberate reminders or by subtle cues. Deliberate reminders of appropriate norms are all around us. The sign in the library requests "quiet please". The reluctant child is instructed "Do as you are told". And the announcement at baseball game states, "Please rise for the playing of the national anthem." Not surprisingly this direct approach pays off in norm-based behaviour. In one demonstration of this effect, Robert Cialdini and his colleagues (1990) placed handbills on the windshields of cars parked at their campus library. Some handbills activated antilittering norms in a straight forward way, announcing, "April is keep Arizona Beautiful Month. Please do not litter." Others, delivered a message irrelevant to littering "April is Arizona's fine Arts Month. Please visit your local art Museum." Unobtrusive observance counted the handbills thrown to the ground. Twenty-five per cent of those receiving the irrelevant message discarded it before getting into the car, compared with only 10 per cent of those receiving the direct reminder about antilittering norms.

Although deliberate reminders effectively bring norms to mind, our behaviour is usually influenced less directly. More often, people, places or proceedings provide subtle cues that activate norms which in turn guide behaviour, the silence of others in libraries and in churches keeps our own voices hushed; the raucous cheering of basketball and football fans lets us its fine to yell. We slow down at the sight of flashing lights and pull over at the sound of a siren. The first few notes of the national anthem bring us to one feet, and the dimming of lights at a concert settles us down.

Norms and the Environment: Most of us have had the experience of having someone drop trash on the floor or the ground near us. When this happens, probably the first things that spring to mind are norms about such action: littering acceptable behaviour or not? Direct reminders—like a sign posting the fines for littering—offer an easy guide, but your surroundings may also offer clues about the prevailing norm. Heaps of discarded trash suggest that other people have found it acceptable to litter, whereas a pristine environment implies norms against such behaviour. Researchers have found that people are more likely to litter in messy environments than in surroundings that are clean and free from trash (Krauss et al., 1978). And the more salient the reminder of the norm is, the greater its impact will be.

One study demonstrating this point placed subjects in one of two settings: one was littered, the other was clean (Cialdini et al., 1990). The researchers found that more subjects littered the dirty environment than the clean one. These actions are evidence that prevailing norms have a big impact on behaviour. For other subjects in the same environments, researchers drew attention to the norms regarding littering by having a confederate walk by and drop a piece of trash. Subjects who saw the confederate litter the clean environment littered even less than the subjects in the same environment with no confederate. In contrast, the confederates littering made subjects throw even more trash into the dirty environment (see Figure 18).

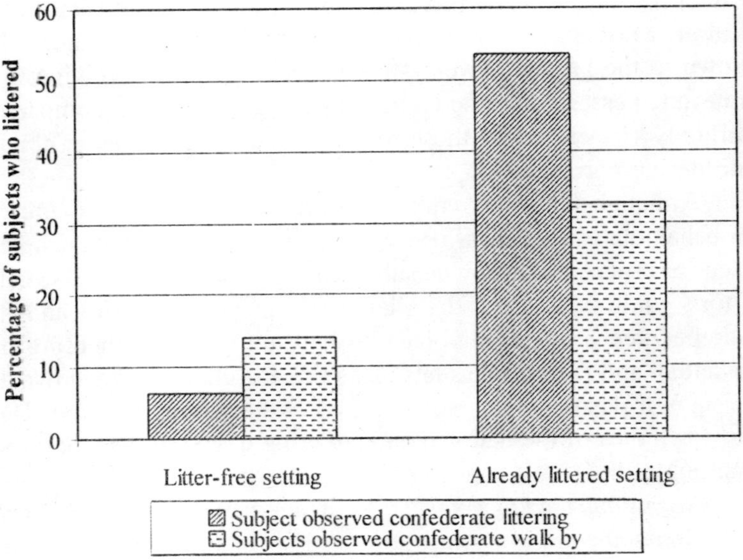

Figure 18: Effect of Activited Norms on Littering.

Explanation: In this study, people littered least when they observed someone sullying a clean environment, and they littered most when they saw trash being thrown into an already dirty environment. Researchers explain this paradox in terms of norm accessibility: the litterer's behaviour called attention to the prevailing norm, whether cleanliness or messiness, and the norms in turn influenced behaviour.(Data from Cialdini and others, 1990).

Evidently, the confederate's behaviour made the norm implied by the state of the environment—whether neatness or messiness—even more accessible, and in doing so, it increased behaviour consistent with the norms.

Why Norms Guide Behaviour So Effectively

Norms are sometimes enforced by rewards and punishments. More often, however, people follow norms because they seem right, because they are endorsed by the behaviour of other group members, because they are frequently activated and because they offer solutions to problems.

Why do we resist the impulse to deviate the norm? and why do people adhere to social norms at all? The answer lies in the following reasons:

(a) Enforcement: Do it, or Else: The most obvious reason we conform to social norms is that groups sometimes use a carrot-and-stick approach—rewards and punishments—to motivate people to adhere to group standards. Norms are important, often vital, to the smooth functioning of groups, and groups take quite seriously their need to identify and stop norm violators. In fact, people are better at detecting violation of social norms than they are at detecting violations of logic (Cosmides, 1989), you soon notice the colleague who never puts money into the office coffee fund while you dutifully pay for your daily mug of Java.

Groups handle norm violations by embodying their norms in legal statutes—by specifying behaviours that are legitimate and those that are not. Society takes this action not only out of concern for any particular wronged individual but to reinforce the importance of the norm to the group as a whole. And groups often attempt to maintain conformity to social norms by withdrawing social acceptance and support from norm violators. Building social conventions can be both a lonely and a painful activity.

Using rewards and punishment may be the most obvious way groups can establish and maintain norm—consistent behaviour, but it is also the least effective. First, the carrot—and stick approach may produce public compliance, but it is less likely to bring about private acceptance of norms. When those who are merely complying publicly with group norms escape group surveillance, watch out! Second, no society can afford enough monitors to enforce all appropriate norms on all its citizens all of the time—to say nothing of the problem of who will monitor the monitors.

(b) Internalization: It's right, so I do it. Although reward and punishments are effective, behaviours often matches norms for a much more powerful reason, most norms are internalized and they seem right. People accept group consensus as true reflecting reality, and norm-based actions are a way of maintaining a shared reality and expressing group identity. As any parent can testify, it takes considerable time and effort to teach new group members which behaviours are appropriate and why. Children are taught to ask before

they borrow someone else's property, to show respect toward people in authority and a seemingly endless list of other do's and don'ts. Luckily for parents, rules that benefit the group usually benefit the individual which makes persuasion a lot easier. The new North American immigrant in England, for example accepts with little resistance the norm that he must drive on the left side of the road to avoid injuring himself and others. Of course, the individual benefits of social rules are not always so immediately clear. Nevertheless, these norms of obedience for example, or the norm of social responsibility—became deeply ingrained through the process of socialization. Part of the process of learning what it means to be a group member is accepting and following group norms. Adhering to such norms not only feels like the right and proper thing to do but also makes people feel respected by others whose opinions they value.

Consensus and Support

You are Doing it, so I'll Do it Too. Because other members of our groups endorse the same norms, their presence promotes rather than interferes with normative behaviour. Our intentions to act in line with our attitudes are sometimes undermined by others who do not share our convictions. We may intend to be cooperative but a persistently aggressive opponent may make it difficult to carry out that intention. Some activities inherently require the participation of others, and almost any behaviour can be undermined if others actively oppose it. With normative behaviours, this is not a problem—those around you are likely to be openly supportive, either because they share the same set of norms or because they are likely to be engaged in the same behaviours themselves. All of your fellow Sierra club members will clean up the camp-site before leaving, and they expect similar behaviour from you.

Frequent Activation

Sometimes Made Me Think About It, So I Do It. As we interact with other members of our group, we are often reminded of its norms. The more often cognitive representation come to mind, the more impact it can have on behaviour. No wonder, then, that norms influence a lot of behaviour: because norms are associated with groups, any reminders of belonging to the group can bring its norms to mind. The presence of fellow group members, hearing the group's language or seeing its symbols, and then the presence of out-group members can activate group norms and increase norm-consistent behaviour. Put the average college sophomore in team colours by the side of classmates on a seat in a basketball arena, for example, and watch for behavioural signs of increased school spirit! And note what happens when the opposition team takes the court! Because people are so often reminded of their group memberships by choice or circumstances, norms have lots of opportunities to influence behaviour.

Action Heuristics

I do it because it makes my life easier. Like other cognitive representations, norms helps make decisions or decide on actions when the relevant information is very complicated or our emotions are running very high. If deciding how to distribute resources is particularly difficult, for example, people might rely on the norm of equality—"everyone gets an equal share"—to come to a decision without further thought.

Classification of Norms

Norms may be classified according to the degree of their acceptance, the mode of any given norms enforcement, the way any norm is transmitted, and the amount of conformity required by the norm. Some norms are fairly stable in nature, others are more localized. Some social norms may require considerable force to ensure compliance, others may require little or none. Rarely are individuals in a society consciously aware of the often arbitrary nature of the social norms of a culture or sub-culture, since they have been introduced to them in the ongoing process of living. They have been learned in this process and transmitted through groups from generation to generation; in this way each individual has incorporated into his own life organization the language, the ideas, and the beliefs of the groups to which he belongs. In the maintenance of order, norms are crucial. They may be regarded as cultural ideals, or they may be considered in terms of actual behaviour in a statistical sense: for example sexual norms can be examined as cultural ideals or in terms of actual practices. Ideal cultural norms can be inferred from what people say or by observing what they support through their sanctions in the form of rewards or penalties.

Norms may emerge in a variety of situations/ways: institutions may prescribe behaviour (institutional norm formation), they may be created by a social contract (voluntary norm formation) or they may gradually emerge without either bargaining or the involvement of norm making institution (evolutionary norm formation). There are three types of norm formation—

***(1) Institutional Norm Formation*:** Especially in industrial societies, either certain individuals (for example owners of firms, heads of departments, kings or dictators) or institutions (example parliaments or bureaucracies, boards of films or of voluntary organizations) may be authorized to form and enforce norms, and thereby regulate the behaviour of certain groups of individuals. Since institutions or persons occupying certain positions in institutions state the norms, we may speak of institutional norm formation.

***(2) Voluntary Norm Formation*:** Norms may also emerge because groups i.e. two or more persons reach a voluntary agreement that some of their actions are on the one hand, compulsory, or on the other hand forbidden. A collective decision may also operate to enforce a norm. Such voluntary norm formation may effect only two people (example neighbours agreeing to take it in turns to meet the border between their gardens) or it may occur among all the citizens of a country (as in the case of a referendum). A characteristic of voluntary norm formation is that only those who participate in the decision are actually affected by it.

Evolutionary Norm Formation

Unlike institutional or voluntary norm formation, in the case of evolutionary norm formation, norms and or measures for their enforcement are not explicitly stated or planned. This is the critical difference between this and the two previously discussed types of norm formation. Thus, norms are the unreflected result of social development according to Megner. They develop as a result of trial and error (Thibaut and Kelley, 1959) in an unplanned and obscure manner rather than by deliberate inauguration (Davis, 1966), in a process of gradual change according to Demsetz, or they develop spontaneously or in an evolutionary way according to Von Hayek. These writers in all, in their own terms are referring to evolutionary norm formation.

"Conformity" and Deviation Imply the Existence of Norms

The existence of norms is inferred from the general sorts of behaviour: conforming behaviour on one hand and deviation or non-conformity on the other (Berg and Bass, 1961).

The terms "conformity" and deviation (non-conformity) imply two definite conditions. *First* they both imply the existence of some standard or norm in terms of which particular behaviour is evaluated. *Second,* they both imply membership in a social group which possesses the norm in question.

It is obvious that an individual's behaviour can be characterized as "conforming" or "non-conforming" only in relation to a relevant standard or norm for the behaviour in question. Furthermore, "conformity" and "deviation" are meaningful characterizations of behaviour only when the individual whose behaviour is in question is a member of a group possessing the norm. It would be observed to speak of a Methodist who refrains from dipping his fingers in holy water at a Catholic Church as a "non-conformist" or "deviate". Therefore, it is seldom feasible to refer in an overall way to the conformity or deviation of a large population for a particular social norm. Most large populations, like modern nations are composed of diverse groups with different or even contradictory norms in some respects. Of course, some norms will be common to all groups in the general culture. But the meaningful analysis of conformity to social norms in such large population starts by referring specific norms to membership in specific groups. What appears at fight sight, to be deviation by large sections of a population or "patterned evasion" may in fact be conformity to other norms by members of groups who are at an advantage in the power structure at the time. For example, a legal regulation exists in the state of Oklahoma today prohibiting the sale of intoxicating beverages. "Patterned evasion" or deviation from this legal norm exists. However, a recent referendum and continuing agitation for enforcement indicate that the law in question represents a functioning norm for a considerable portion of the population. This part of the population has identifiable group memberships. Certain other organized groups support the law for reasons related to their own interests. Widespread and continuing deviation from legal norms becomes possible when groups within the population do not possess the norm and when the membership of these groups is in position to influence enforcement processes. Thus, deviance is the recognised violation of cultural norms (see Figures 19 and 20).

Figure 19: Each and every normative pattern creates the possibility for deviance. Many societies retain traditional norms that women should be soft and submissive; in this context, women who develop their physical strength or those who are assertive may be viewed as deviant.

Typical examples of conforming behaviour which reveal a group norm may be observed in functioning group units. Members of Youthful gangs in New York City in the 19th century were identifiable through their conformity in matters of dress (see Figure 20). The "Shirt Tails"; all wore their shirts outside of their trousers. The "Plug Uglies" adopted large plug hats which they stuffed with wool and leather and drew down over their ears during fights. Some gangs wore stripes of a certain colour on their trousers. The recent zoot-suit styles and their modifications are well known. When workers taking part in a strike refuse to participate in the services of their church because a non-striker is present or when "strike breakers" are ignored by people they have known for years, it can be inferred that a group norm formed in previous or current strikes is regulating behaviour toward those who do not take part.

Figure 20: Sutherland, in his differential association theory of deviance, suggested that criminal and deviant behaviours are learned in group interaction. Members of ganges, for example, socialize one another as to what type of behaviour are appropriate or inappropriate and what norms and laws can be violated.

A norm is not always a prescription for a single act: it is, more typically, a set of categories defining classes of acceptable and objectionable behaviour. It follows that in assessing norms, the norm cannot be represented as a point or as a single value. This deduction is particularly important in determining whether an action is conforming or represents a case of deviation.

Groups everywhere recognize individual differences within an acceptable range. It follows that a social norm is best represented as a class of behaviour that are acceptable or permissible and a class of behaviour that are objectionable and punishable. Social norms define a latitude of acceptance and a latitude of rejection.

What kinds of data are needed to characterize a norm, hence to provide the baseline for assessing conformity or deviation by single members? Research has included the following observations:

(1) Observed similarities and regularities (over time) in attitudes and behaviour among one set of persons that are not evident in another set and that vary within more or less definite limits.
(2) Increasing similarity or convergence toward a range and mode of behaviour during interaction overtime. For example,

the entrance of a new member into a group or confrontation by a new problem situation provides an opportunity to detect the existence of a norm.

(3) Sanctions (correctives) for certain behaviours and praise or regards for other behaviours. Reactions to deviations and to idealized behaviour are among the best indicators of the existence of norm and its limits. Sanctions may range from disapproval, frowns, a silent treatment, to threats and actual punishment.

Social Norms and Individual Behaviour

From the very birth every individual is surrounded by and subjected to social norms. They are given to him in the learning process in the home by parents and in the school by teachers; art, music, drama, films, means of transport, communication, production and distribution, food habits, dress, etiquette, and numerous other institutions and influences of socialization impress upon him values, standards, and norms of society. They serve to control and regulate the behaviour of an individual in a group. Rules of etiquette, manners, mores, conventions, laws reflect some of the major norms of the group. They bring about regular and recurrent responses in an individual and it is because of such regulations that we can predict an individual's behaviour in any social situation.

We are frequently admonished by our elders and our teachers to think about what we are doing. The late philosopher Alfred North Whitehead once remarked that this advice is nuisance if it is meant to apply to the ordinary affairs of life. As a matter of fact, he continued, the more things we can do without thinking, the better off we are. If we had to reflect and deliberate and think about what we are going to do when we enter a store, classroom, cafeteria, or ticket line and meet a clerk, teacher, cashier or ticket seller, we should be able to accomplish only a very small number of our objectives in the course of a day. The principal function of the norms for the individual is thus to reduce the necessity for decision in the innumeral social situations that he confronts and in which he participates. Without them, we should be faced from moment to moment with an almost intolerable burden of decisions. One can only imagine the confusion that would result in the absence of norms.

Indeed it can readily be seen that without norms social relations would be haphazard, chaotic and possibly even dangerous. It is the norms therefore that give order, stability and predictability to social life and that in consequence, all exceedingly important elements of the social structure. A situation of complete normlessness, or anomaly, as Durkheim (1915) called it would be intolerable, and no normless or anomie society could long endure. As anarchy is the contradiction of government, so anomaly is the contradiction of society. Where there are no norms, there is also no society. Thus, it is the norms that make possible the orderly social intercourse of people in societies and thus serve the individual as guides to conduct.

Social Norms are Initially External to the Individual

To a growing child, or a new member of an organized group, norms are at first external and are revealed through the actions and words of other people. Awareness of knowledge of norms does not lead automatically to regulation of behaviour by them.

But mere knowledge of them is not enough to regulate his behaviour. In the beginning children may not respond to them or even ignore or resent them. But through constant presentation of these norms in social interaction children come to understand their meaning and scope, and learn to adopt them as their own. What they did from external pressure is now done of their own free will. Norms are social stimulus situations and their effects are found in the enduring dispositions, and the ways in which these dispositions affect behaviour. Through learning, these social norms are 'internalized', that is, the individual adopts them as his own and learns to conform to them. His implicit habits of thinking and attitudes, as well as his outer mannerisms and skills become organized according to the social norms. A soldier not only learns soldiering, but he learns to think and feel like a soldier. Thus social norms ensure conformity, solidarity, and continuity of a group, community or culture.

Studies of children by Piaget (1932) and others have shown that young children first respond to the dicta (formal sayings) of adults and rules of play set by elder children in much the same way that they respond to physical restraints. Moral dicta and rules are external stimuli which the child responds to and regards in a rather absolute fashion. Although he falls away from them under the firm hold of momentary desire or in the flow of fantasy, they tend to be regarded as final and inflexible, resting on the authority of Mommy or Daddy. However, as the child matures, he interacts with other children and grasps the notion of reciprocity with others. In the process of reciprocal interaction, the child comes to see rules or norms as based on mutual agreement. He finds that they can be changed and that new rules can be made. When he begins to take part in the process of changing and making rules himself, they truly become his "own" rules by which he abides through inner autonomy. Thus, the crucial condition for willing, autonomous, and even enthusiastic internalization of social norms is participation in reciprocal interactions with other people.

Properties of Social Norms

Social norms have a variety of properties:

(1) They shape behaviour in the direction of shared values or desirable states of affairs.
(2) They vary in degree to which they are functionally related to important values.
(3) They are enforced by the behaviour of other persons.
(4) They vary in how widely they are shared; they may be society wise, or they may belong to groups of varying sizes, even as small as a two person group.
(5) They vary in the range of permissible behaviour; some norms set more stringent limits on behaviour than others.

Social Differentiation and Sub-cultural Norms

In complex modern societies, group norms may differ radically or only slightly from one another; in other cases the norms simply differ in emphasis. As a result persons who belong to a number of groups, with each group having either different norms or emphasizing them differently, may experience much personal conflict. The norms and social roles a person acquires from the family group do not necessarily always agree with the norms and social roles of the play group, the age or the peer group, work group or political group. Certain groups may become more important to an individual's life organization than others, and he may as a result, tend to conform more closely to the norms of the groups with which he feels more closely identified. Although the family group is important, it is only one of the many groups related to a person's behaviour, whether deviant or non-deviant. Many other sources of norms and social relationships in modern societies are important: social class, occupation, neighbourhood, school, church, and the gang or clique (Robert Edgerton, 1976).

The sub-cultural norms of most large societies, because of the degree of social differentiation, are so diverse that in all probability only a few norms are accepted as binding on all persons. Sometimes the social groups that have arisen in the manner described here may develop and share a set of values and meanings shared by society of which they are a part. When this occurs, such a group may be called a sub-culture. Simply speaking, a sub-culture is a "culture within a culture". The social norms and behaviour of social classes in the United States vary greatly with respect to many attitudes and values. The norms of Longshoremen differ from those of doctors and professors; construction workers display markedly different attitudes than do college students. Child-rearing patterns have been shown to differ significantly. Lower class parents, for example, tend to use corporal punishment more often as a disciplinary measure than do middle-class families. Nearly all crimes of violence, such as murder and forcible rape are committed by lower class persons. Prostitution appears to be more prevalent among the lower classes. The more ordinary, overt type of crime, such as burglary, are rare among members of the middle and upper classes; members of these groups are more involved in types of crimes termed white collar crimes. Such crimes of a different type, involving more sophisticated fraud and deception, are committed by white collar persons in the middle and upper classes, such as government officials, people in business, labour union leaders, doctors and lawyers. Neighbourhoods in large U.S. cities are often characterized by distinct behavioural norms and values. Those of one neighbourhood may contribute to the development of stealing among teenaged boys who regard it as a form of recreation or the means to gain social status, in another neighbourhood the social norms and values may encourage teenage participation in scouting programs or other community directed programs/activities more conducive to nondelinquent behaviour. The neighbourhood norms of one area may define policemen as "enemies", while in another they are defined as symbols of respect for law.

Thus, in modern complex societies there may be almost as pronounced differences among the groups within the society in respect to the norms of accepted behaviour as there are differences between large cultures themselves.

Norms in the western countries and in the eastern countries are entirely different. People in western countries live an independent life from the very beginning. Parents adopt permissive approach in the development of their children. Thus, the more the freedom, the more is the aggressiveness which leads to violation of norms and thus indulge in crimes (See Figure 21).

Figure 21: In Saudi Arabia, Women cannot vote, drive a car, or appear in public without being veiled. Given this rigid regulation, crimes by women are rare. In the United States, women have much more freedom over what they do and how they dress. This greater freedom is reflected in crime rates that are steadily moving closer to those of men. Even so, women have less power and remain subject to more extensive social control than men.

That is why crime rate in western countries is much higher as compared to those of eastern countries for example in Britain which is just based on norms and there is no written code. But by and by as they are offing towards materialism, the written constitution is heading.

Cultural Norms and Personality

What is Culture?

Before we discuss how culture influences personality, let us try to understand what culture is. The term 'culture' has been used in various meanings. People commonly define culture as 'good manners and good taste'. Social scientists use the term in a more specific and more inclusive sense. It is that complex whole which includes knowledge, beliefs, art, morals, law, customs, techniques, ideas and values which man acquires as a member of society. It is our social heritage and includes institutions like state, church, community and family, mores and customs of all sorts, and ideas of right and wrong, techniques of food production and use, crafts and modes of recreation, ways of thinking and living, and modes of communication. Each society is distinguished from others by the ways of doing things which are peculiar to that society. The ways of meeting the needs of human nature which are common to the members of a given society constitute the culture of that society. Culture includes all of man's acquired power of control over nature and himself.

A distinction is often made between the material and non-material elements or aspects of culture. The whole of man's material civilization, tools, crafts, industry, weapons, clothing, means of transport, and other physical objects man has produced for his use constitutes the material aspect of culture. On the other hand, art, religion, moral codes, literature, political ideas, institutions and systems are a part of the spiritual heritage of non-material culture. But the two elements or aspects are not independent or separate. They interact, depend on each other and develop together. It is an essential characteristic of culture that it is passed on from one generation to another. It is transmitted by teaching and learning, both formal and informal. But it is not static and changes in the very process of transmission. These changes are slow and gradual, but they are constant. However, certain basic features of the cultural pattern persist for a considerable time. In conservative societies like those of Hindus, Tibetans or Afghans a number of basic elements of their culture have survived the numerous changes in history.

We become conscious of the peculiarities of our culture only when we come in contact with people of different culture. Orthodox Hindus are shocked to see Western people in their uninhibited ways of living and dressing. Usually common people attribute such differences to heredity, climate or geographical conditions, but they are due to social heredity and culture.

Personality and Culture

Personality varies with the kind of culture in which it develops. The cultural and social environment in which an individual is brought up exercises a powerful influence on personality traits. Broadly speaking, an American is different from a Hindu as is a Chinese from an Arab. Primitive people are different from civilized people, an orthodox Hindu is different from the one who returns to 'India after ten years' stay in the West, an Englishman who has spent most part of his life in Hong Kong will be different from one who has lived mostly in London. Such differences are due to the cultural backgrounds which have affected their ways of doing and behaving, their personality traits. 'That individuals living in societies with cultures different from our own show quite distinctive personality characteristics is evident even from slight acquaintance with persons from other societies'.*

Earlier personality has been described as 'the subjective aspect of culture'. In every society there is a 'basic personality type' or a 'basic personality structure' consisting of certain personality characteristics which are in harmony with the type of institutions provided in that culture. These characteristics the individual has in common with his fellows, and they distinguish him and his fellows from the members of a different culture. This, however, does not rule out individual differences but refers to these attitudes and beliefs which result from the cultural influences of any social structure and which are common to a large majority of people of that group or society. Culture allows and makes for individual differences but there are similarities too which mark off individuals of one group from those of others. These imply the peculiar imprint of culture on

---

* K. Young, *Handbook of Social Psychology* (London: Routledge and Kegan Paul Ltd.), p. 136.

personality. There are certain personal habits, traits, attitudes or beliefs which every individual acquires in the course of his own experience with his environment, and these provide individual differences.

Just as culture is a growing changing phenomenon so also basic personality characteristics grow and change. Indian culture has passed through several phases in history involving corresponding changes in basic personality characteristics. Broadly speaking Muslim and British influences on Indian culture were reflected in the personality pattern of an Indian in those periods.

Anthropologists have always been interested in the customs, institutions, and behaviour of primitive people, but recently they have dealt with personality differences. M. Mead's studies of the inhabitants of Samoa and New Guinea are now very well known. Samoans lived in large families, their attitude to sex was very liberal, there were very few taboos and inhibitions, and they were very well adjusted. Adolescence among them was not a period of stress and strain. On the other hand the Manus of New Guinea are very aggressive and self-assertive, they are more industrious and physically stronger, and they have greater respect for authority. Sex is surrounded by taboos and is repressed. Naturally, therefore, adolescence is a difficult period of great strain.

In another study Mead investigated cultural differences in sex roles. No characteristic of a person is more immediately and clearly perceived than sex and all societies assign more or less distinctive roles to men and women. That such roles make a difference to the personality of men and women is quite obvious. Among Hindus and Muslims women are submissive, responsive and cooperative, the traits prized most among them are obedience, loyalty, devotion, service and self-effacement. Among Americans women are less inhibited, more independent and aggressive, dominating and assertive. Mead (1935) studied three primitive groups of the New Guinea island, viz. the Arapesh, the Mundugumor and the Tchambuli.

The Arapesh make no distinction between men and women. Both are considered equally human and both have the same object in life to grow children and food. Both take a motherly interest in their children, are gentle, cooperative and unaggressive. Both may take positions of leadership just for the sake at sharing labour and responsibility. But their personality characteristics are individual ones. Most of the Arapesh are trusting, gentle and cooperative because these characteristics are stamped into the child's early experiences with his parents.

The Tchambuli people have clearly defined roles for men and women. Men are mostly concerned about ceremonial activities. They are artists skilled in painting, carving, plaiting, dancing and the like. Their chief role is on the stage and they are busy making masks and costumes. They are the centre of social appreciation and recognition. But women have the real power, for they control economic affairs like trade, fishing, gardening or food supply. They look after the household and bring up children. Men cannot spend without the permission of women. In love women take the initiative and appreciate the performance of men in games and arts. Men keep to themselves and are sly and quarrelsome.

The Mundugumor people are rough and violent, and admire violence, aggressiveness, and physical power in others. They are very strict with their children and bring them up very roughly. This pattern and ideal of life is the same for both men and women. Meekness, gentleness or softness are looked down upon, and competition, jealousy, revengefulness, fighting and violence are highly prized in both the sexes. Instead of a feeling of joy at the prospect of the birth of a child, and the anticipation of working together to love and protect him, the Mundugumor man and wife feel resentment. Hostility is pronounced between husband and wife and this attitude is carried over into parent child relationships. The infant receives poor maternal care. There are no warm bodily contacts with the mother. His feeding is short and hurried. Same is the case with father. He does not bother about his child, rather hates the child for it is responsible for cessation of intercourse with his wife.

Thus, practically every Mundugumor is a hostile and aggressive individual because he was socialized by harsh and aggressive parents. The personality is said to be of competitive, jealous, aggressively sexed and violent.

Thus, in these three tribes living in the same island and having the same geographical conditions and racial heredity, different personality characteristics are appreciated and developed because of the distinctive cultural tradition and climate.

Individual differences in personality are partly due to heredity, neuro-muscular and glandular make-up, and partly due to maturation, nutrition, sex, age. Each individual grows and develops according to his own biological pattern but the content and direction of this growth is provided by culture as he interacts with it. Culture is often described as social heredity made up of traditions, customs, mores, institutions, beliefs, arts and sciences, luxuries and necessities provided by industrial plants. This is common to all members of the society and provides common experiences for all of them, thus giving rise to common characteristics of a basic personality. A general personality type is found in different culture patterns and reference has already been made to 'basic personality'. This concept was proposed by Abram Kardiner (1939) and Ralph Linton (1945) and has been found useful.

These two authors also emphasized that cultural influences are exerted through ways and methods of child upbringing and training in the home and the school. Though Freudians were the first to lay great stress on the value and importance of early childhood experiences on the subsequent growth and development of adult personality there is general agreement that early training is very significant. If the pattern of cultural training is similar there is similarity in personality structure also. What care and affection mothers are able to give their children, what affectionate relations obtain between parents and children and between parents themselves, the nature of discipline to which children are subjected in the home and the school–it may be too strict or too lax, and what relations are found among brothers and sisters, these and the like influence children's attitudes and their social development.

Parents in India are very much child-minded. The mother in India feeds her child at her breasts much longer than does a Western mother. Children are generally accepted and welcomed. There is little systematic toilet training and children are not punished for toilet irregularities. Children are not left alone for long and are mostly carried by one member of the family or the other. In the early years infants learn mostly by imitation and their training is not forced. This is in strange contrast to child upbringing in the West where infants are put on the bottle early, are left alone for most part of the day, sleep in a separate crib, or start receiving training in toilet, sitting, standing or walking very early, where parents are too busy with their own life outside the home. Psychoanalysts hold that much of widespread neurosis in the West may be due to forced weaning and training in early years.

Many psychiatrists and psychoanalysts have studied the relation of culture and personality from their own angle. Karen Horney held that neurosis is rooted in the cultural pattern in the contradictions in the demands and the values of our culture. She mentions three types of contradictions: (1) between competition and success on the one hand, and brotherly love on the other; (2) between stimulation of our needs and our frustrations in satisfying them; and (3) between alleged freedom of the individual and his numerous limitations. All these factors result psychologically in the individual's feeling that he is isolated and helpless. Such contradictions in American life today breed neurosis. Conflicts are readymade by the American way of life and these culturally determined conflicts when experienced in intensity lead to neurotic trends in basic personality.

Let us study some examples of personality structure from primitive tribes as also from modern nations.

Personality in Some Primitive Cultures

The Hopi are an American Indian group living in northern Arizona. The climate of the region is mild, vegetation scanty and the number of the tribe less than four thousand. Their chief occupation is farming and hunting. They are divided into clans and exercise social control through gossip and ridicule. Women are the centre of the household and all the property is vested in them. Land is passed on from mother to daughter and the position of women is quite high and dominant. There is no trace of aggressiveness and prestige-seeking in their social life, and the economic system is co-operative. Personal striving is regarded as abnormal due to witchcraft and is socially disapproved. Hopi children find greater pleasure in meeting social demands of co-operation than in personal achievement. Although they are found quite intelligent on the performance scale due to tribal tradition they are afraid of supernatural powers. They become angry at aggression and do not like any tendency to stand out separate from the group. Hopi personality is markedly co-operative. Though there is much indulgence in early life, the strong help the weak and social dependence is emphasized. Pride and selfish wishes are not permitted, any expression and self-assertion is absent. Personal ambition has no place and group goals motivate life and behaviour. The severest punishment is denial of social support and participation. A Hopi is a quiet and passive person and is completely socialized. According to modern thinking it may be said that his ego or self is suppressed. There is great stress on shame and the fear of shame is the basis of social security. Children are hurried from childhood to adulthood and there are no problems of adolescence. There is greater freedom in sex.

In sharp contrast to the Hopi the Kwakiutl of the Pacific North-west coast have a highly developed system of social ranking. There are high nobles consisting of the first born of the families of high rank. The younger people like others belong to the lower rank. There is another class of slaves. The region is rich and there are reserved places for fishing and hunting. The chief provides for the needy. Every member of the tribe is obsessed with the ideas of rank and strives for prestige. In fact rank and prestige are considered more important than property. There are various titles and crests given to individuals on the basis of family background and status. People compete at giving gifts to rivals and arranging more costly feasts.

There is great rivalry and hostility between the younger sons and the eldest who is privileged. Marriage is also a contest for prestige. In marketing too there is a great deal of boasting and competition. Religious life too reflects their great drive for prestige and their stress on rank.

Child training is very strict and fits into their rank system. Children are often dipped into cold water to toughen them. Names are given to a child every year and gifts are distributed to members of the tribe till he achieves adulthood. Rivalry and competition at interpersonal level is high. Property is a symbol of great prestige and though shame is a great mechanism of social control competition pushes a child into adulthood and the struggle for rank pushes an aged person into a backwater. There is little stress on co-operation or group striving and even ceremonies are held against a background of struggle for rank and prestige. Religion involves a belief in the graded ranks of spirits which man tries to control. Zunis of the pacific south-west on the contrary play down competitiveness and stress co-operation instead. In Zuni culture it is not regarded as proper to set oneself off against the group. One does not work for oneself but for the family, the class, the association or the village. There is little emphasis on the private accumulation of property. All the men in a matrilineal household work together in the fields, and the food is stored in a common storehouse.

Some other primitive tribes are as follows:

The Ojibwa of Canada:* Fear of being shamed is very strong in Ojibwa, and accordingly much of violence that exists is by way of repudiation of insults. Outright murder is not common, but slashing seems to be more frequent. The most common form of expression for interpersonal hostility is through shamanism, by invoking bad medicine omens, starvation and attacks of paralysis. Murder is most commonly committed for trespass upon trapping grounds. It is avenged by a close relative of the deceased. Suicide is institutionalized and is most often committed to wipe out shame or disgrace. Hence the personality of Ojibwa is said to be hostile and aggressive.

*Tanala and Betsileo Culture**:* The Betsileo of Madagascar people are an ethnic cognate of the Tanala, whose culture they resemble in many ways. The subsistence economy of the Tanala, which consists of dry rice cultivation, is such as to provide relatively easy exploitation of the environment and so guarantee a fairly stable subsistence. There is, accordingly, no anxiety concerning food, each person is confident that he can master the food situation adequately. The Betsileo, on the other hand are full of apprehension regarding their subsistence economy. They give more importance to wet rice cultivation. In Tanala culture, value of property is much pronounced and is the sole mean of enhancing the self and the land is cultivated in common. Whereas, among the Betsileo, it has become a private property. Hence, this increased the competitive attitudes of people and made for numerous conflicts. Family ties have now easily broken and because of this increased hostility among individuals, crime has increased considerably. Hence personality is characterized as being aggressive and hostile.

The Maori: The Maori of New Zealand provide more opportunity for individual initiative, though it is a co-operative society***. The ideal of Maori behaviour is to work for the welfare of

---

* In describing the Ojibwa we rely on the following source: Ruth Landes, "The Ojibwa of Canada", in M. Mead, op. cit., Chap. iii.

** Tanala Betsileo Culture upon which the psychological analyses are based have been furnished by Ralph Linton. See R. Linton, "the Tanala of Madaagascar," in A. Kardiner, The Individual and His Society, Chap. vii.

*** B. Mishkin, "The Maori of New Zealand", in M. Mead, op. cit., p. 431.

other, but there is always a high degree of personal remark in this co-operation. Social recognition is achieved in generosity, toward others. Individual achievement is psychologically shared by all, so that excellence in any particular skill is acclaimed by the entire group. Rivalry is stimulated when it involves the welfare of the group. Finally, Maori society provide for an affective latitude of permissive behaviour. When conformity becomes too boring, or too oppressive, the individual can exercise his right to be unconventional. Notoriety is not condemned. Young people might show off by violating some taboos, though violation carries severe punishment.

The Ifugao: are brown-skinned Malaysian people who inhabit the interior of mother Luzon, in the Philippine islands. The culture places a high premium on individualism, which characterizes each family as a unit. The family pursues its individualistic ends of accumulating large stores of rice even at the cost of impoverishing other sections of the community* Limited co-operation exists beyond the family only in the case of severe drought. They are described as capitalistic society. Economic relations are competitive, family being pitted against family in almost every department of social behaviour.

The absence of competitiveness and the practice of co-operation exist only in relation to near kin. The Ifugao individual, therefore, is characterized by a duality of attitudes and habits.

Personality in Some Modern Cultures

Due to rapid means of communication and transport, and because of widespread desire to know and understand other types of people, there is a great commingling of people and cultures today. But even then slight shifts of cultural patterns bring in their wake differences in personality structures as we shall see hereinafter. But one caution is necessary. Literature and newspapers invest people from other lands' with characteristics which have no scientific basis and which are just prejudices. Not seldom national and political ties bind us to reality and friendly nations are favourably described. Again such descriptions are often based on impressions of travellers, journalists and the like.

---

* I. Goldman, "The Ifugao of the Philippine Islands, in M. Mead, op. cit., p. 158.

Another very popular concept used to describe basic personality characteristics found in any nation or similar group is 'national character'. But the term character is used in so many ways that discriminating writers use the term 'national characteristics' in its place. Again due to large-scale international mixing an Indian educated in England or America may resemble people of those countries more than he does an Indian farmer for example. But these facts do not negate the truth that a nation does have certain characteristics whatever may be the level of her development. Let us take a few illustrations.

The Japanese believe that their emperor is descended from the sun goddess and worship him with great reverence, loyalty, devotion, and obedience. They have a very high sense of duty and discipline supported by an equally strong feeling of shame. In order to save their face they would make any sacrifice. They have strong national and anti-foreign attitudes, and these spring largely from their great loyalty and devotion to their emperor. They are very patriotic, are devoted to their family, and have great pride and sense of honour, initiative, industry, and a sense of mission. They are quiet and cool. Though they are very indulgent to their children they bring them up very strictly teaching them cleanliness, manners and respect for authority very early in life. Boys are dominant and aggressive, girls are taught to be affectionate and submissive.

After the last Great War in which the Japanese were defeated they accepted the consequences of defeat partly because of their great regard for the emperor and partly to avoid shame and humiliation. But under American occupation their culture and personality underwent radical changes. The American influence tempered their rigid approach and made them more democratic and pacificistic.

That Americans have certain characteristics peculiar to them may appear doubtful in view of the large size of the country, the large variety of people inhabiting it and the numerous sub-cultures contributing to its general culture pattern. But there is no denying the fact that it is a dynamic country, that its people have within a short range of time transformed a land of undeveloped resources into a most prosperous and advanced country through sheer diligence, initiative, perseverance and foresight, that they attach the greatest importance to success and achievement, and that they are more concerned with the future than with the past. Their approach is practical and dominant, they enjoy competing and working hard, they have sympathy for the underdog, and are generous and charitable. They love their land, they love themselves and they love life. Democracy, individual freedom, race pride, faith in technology are basic to their personality structure. Their reading material is full of 'success stories'.

A number of sociologists and anthropologists like M. Mead, G. Gorer, R. Williams and others have dwelt at length on the major dimensions of American character. Others with a psychiatric approach have found in American way of life a basis for neurotic trends.

Before we conclude this discussion it may be pointed out that certain personality characteristics are normal in one culture and abnormal in another. Too much thinking is considered normal in India but it may be considered abnormal in America. Withdrawal, meditation and mystical experiences are normal in India but abnormal in the West. But of course there are certain personality traits which would be thought abnormal everywhere.

Deviance

An essential feature of social life is that it is possessed of a set of norms which regulate the behaviour of individual members. These standards of behaviour, as we have seen earlier, are called norms. But no society completely succeeds in getting all its members to behave in accordance with the social norms. Some of them fail to conform to these norms. Failures to conform to the customary norms of society is deviant behaviour or deviance. Thus, deviant behaviour is any behaviour that fails to conform to some specified standard.

Parsons defines deviance in two ways. *Firstly,* he defines it as a "motivated tendency for an actor to behave in contravention of one or more institutionalized normative patterns". *Secondly,* he defined it as "the tendency on the part of one or more of the component actors to behave in such a way as to disturb the equilibrium of interactive process. Deviant behaviour disturbs the social equilibrium. It is contravention of the social norms. It is a departure from the usual modes of behaviour. It consists of disapproved activities cheating, unfairness, malingering, delinquency, immorality, dishonesty, betrayal, corruption, wickedness and sin are examples of deviant behaviour.

Deviation is relative not absolute. Deviation is relative to the prescription and anticipation that govern particular patterns of behaviour at specified times and places. Societies are undergoing continual change. What is considered as intolerable at one time, becomes norm at another time.

Social deviation is non-conformity to the norms of the group

The juveniles and the criminals are social deviants because they do not conform to the norms of the group. The group expects its members to engage in interaction which is responsible and predictable and the group also expects its members to conform to certain ethical and legal practices, and the criminals are those who violates these practices. Normal individuals also transgress from time to time and may behave in irrational ways on particular occasions. Society distinguishes between those whose deviation is temporary and those whose deviation is of longer duration. The temporal point is, therefore, important in the conception of social deviants, who represent various social types, that is, more or less persistent constellations of personality traits. A criminal under the law is one who is found guilty of one or more crimes and a person who commits only one crime in his life time and is adjudged guilty is a criminal under the law. But when we speak of a criminal type, we usually have in mind someone for whom criminal behaviour is characteristic.

Two strategies have been developed to decide who is deviant. According to the first strategy developed by Robert K. Merton and Talcott Parsons deviant behaviour is conduct that objectively appears to violate a norm*. According to the second strategy developed by Edwin M. Lemert and Howard S. Becker, deviant behaviour is conduct that is perceived by others as contrary to the norms. In the later conception, less attention is paid to the actual social definitions of conduct by members of social groups. A conduct is regarded as deviant because it is harmful and dysfunctional.

---

* This strategy is the focal point of the work of Robert K. Merton and Talcott Parsons, for example, and through their influence in the work of quite a few others.

It may also be noted that deviant behaviour is usually related to specific situations. A person may be deviant in certain ways but may be conformist in others. A sex deviant may be fairly conventional in dress, food habits and many other activities. He may be honest and industrious. Similarly a non-conformist who is regarded a fool at one time may be regarded a genius at another time. The geniuses of all ages have suffered from the hostile attitude of the members of their communities. It has been said that people are not completely conformist or completely deviant. A completely deviant person would find it difficult to stay alive in society. And nearly all normal people are occasionally deviant. Most people have been guilty of deviant behaviour at one time or the other in one or the other respect. Nearly everyone in one society is deviant to some degree. Whether one is labelled as deviant depends upon the specific circumstances, attitudes, interests and tolerance limits of a specific society. It may also be noted that while deviation is condemned, in some cases it is praised. The genius, the hero, the leader and the saint are among the culturally approved deviants. However, the values of a culture will determine whether a particular deviant is praised or condemned. Each culture encourages some deviation and discourages others.

Deviant Sub-cultures

When an individual deviates from the norms of his sub-culture he is an individual deviant, but in a complex society there may be a number of deviant sub-cultures. By deviant sub-culture we mean the norms of deviant persons. It refers to a set of shared understanding, values and ways of doing things that are at odds with conventional society, and yet are accepted in common by members of a particular community. In such a sub-culture the participating members gain some of the gratifications and rewards, though it may be at the cost of rejection by the conventional world. Such a sub-culture usually develops whenever a relatively large number of individuals share a common problem of adjustment to conventional society and find difficulty in solving that problem within the conventional framework. Thus, in an area we may find a delinquent sub-culture in which many of the youths participate. In such areas delinquent behaviour is as normal as law abiding behviour. It is the group not the individual that is deviant from the conventional norms of society. A criminal gang has a deviant sub-culture. The members of such a gang are conformative within the deviant sub-group but at the same time they are alienated form the main institutional structure.

The deviant persons usually tend to join with similar other persons into deviant groups or they force others to their line. The bad boys in the college tend to form a clique. Individual hippies, drug addicts or homosexuals tend to drift together into groups of deviants. These groups reinforce and sanction the deviation and give the members emotional protection against critics. These groups of deviants develop a set of rigid behavioural norms of their own. These norms are called deviant sub-culture. The hippie culture may be called a deviant sub-culture.

Causes of Deviant Behaviour

Deviant behaviour may be caused due to inability or failure to conform. The inability to conform may be the result of mental or physical defect. On account of mental defect the individual has limited capacity to learn. On account of mental illness a person is unable to perceive and respond to realities in an orderly and rational manner. Hence he becomes a social deviant. The causes of mental illness may be both physical and social. The stresses and strains of modern social life produce mental illness. Cultural conflicts are also responsible for mental illness.

But some people fail to conform even though they are physically and mentally capable of learning conventional behaviour. Following theories have been put forward to explain such cases of deviation:

(1) Physical Type Theories (Lombroso, 1876 and Sheldon, 1949): These theories seek to relate deviant behaviour with body type. Lombroso was of the view that certain body types are more given to deviant behaviour than others. Deviants were classified into physical types to explain their behaviour. Lombroso (1876) compared the physical characteristics of Italian criminals with non-criminals taken from military personnel. He claimed to have found that criminals had more primitive facial features, large jaws, high cheekbones, large ears and so on, as well as being less sensitive to pain. They also tended to have extra nipples toes and fingers. A similar approach involving physical characteristics and criminal behaviour was

proposed by Sheldon (1949) who after examining the body shape and personality of over 400 male students concluded that there were three basic body builds: Endomorph, ectomorph and mesomorph. Endomorphs tend to be rather fat and who are sociable and relaxed. Ectomorphs are thin and fragile people who are introverted and restrained. Mesomorphs are muscular and hard, they tend to be aggressive and adventurous and more prone to delinquency. Sheldon tested his theory on delinquent boys and "normal" college students over an eight years period and found a strong connection between the mesomorph and crime. However, the physical types theories are no longer accepted.

(2) Psychoanalytic Theories: These theories attribute deviant behaviour to the conflicts in human personality. Freud was a leading psychologist who gave the concepts of id, ego and superego. Deviant behaviour according to him is the result of conflicts between the id and the ego or between the id and the super ego. Sometimes culture frustrates biological drives and impulses leading thereby to deviant behaviour. Thus, our culture makes no approved provision for the satisfaction of sexual drives of the unmarried, widowed or separated. If one gratifies such impulses in contravention of taboo, he is engaging in deviant behaviour.

(3) Failure in Socialization: Both the above types of theories fail to explain deviant behaviour adequately. Everyone affected with physical or mental illness does not become a deviant. Likewise, every member of a society is frustrated by the clash of his biological drives.

With the taboos of his culture, but not everyone becomes a deviant. The social scientists are of the opinion that some persons are deviant because the socialization process has failed in some way to integrate the cultural norms into the individual's personality. Where the socialization process is successful, the individual internalizes the social norms and he behaves in the expected manner. His lapses are rare. Family as we have studied earlier, is the most important agent of socialization. Behaviour norms are mainly learnt in the family. Although it is difficult to prove direct relationship between deviant behaviour and family atmosphere, yet a variety of behaviour difficulties have been traced to some disturbance in the parent child relationship.

(4) Cultural Conflicts: The society is an extremely heterogeneous society. There are many sets of norms and values which compete with one another. The family norm may come into conflict with the norms of trade union. One religion teaches one thing, another teaches a different thing. The school teaches respect and obedience, the party teaches resistance and revolt. The family teaches God worship, the state teaches secularism. The religious system teaches that one should be generous and self-sacrificing, but economic system rewards those who are ruthless and selfish. Our formal mores demand chastity until marriage, but our films present too much sex. The young people are exposed to obscene literature. Thus, culture conflicts are a unique feature of the modern complex and changing society. They are found virtually in all societies. And whenever they exist, culture conflicts encourages deviant behaviour. It may be said that a high rate of deviation is the price we pay for a complex, rapidly changing society.

(5) Anomie: Anomie is a condition of normlessness. By normlessness we do not mean that modern societies have no norms; instead it means that they have many sets of norms with none of them clearly binding upon everybody. As we have seen in the modern society with its elaborate division of major and complex institutional patterns, the difficulty of coordinating all the parts and of socializing all the humans to mesh their behaviours smoothly is formidable. The individual does not know which norm to follow, whether to follow the norms of the family or of the school. Anomie thus arises from the confusion and conflict of norms. People, in modern society move about too rapidly to be bound to the norms of any particular group. In traditional societies people were guided by a coherent set of traditions which they followed with little deviation. But the modern society lacks coherent traditions, different groupings having different norms. The society provides him no guide. Consequently his behaviour lacks consistency and conforms to no dependable norm. According to Durkheim, "when there is a sudden change, the normative structure of the regulating norms of society is slackened, hence man does not know what is wrong or what is right, his impulses are exclusive, to satisfy them, he seeks anomie." In the words of Merton, "Anomie may be conceived as breakdown in the culture structure occurring particularly when there is an acute distinction between cultural norms

and goals and the socially structured capacities of members of the group to act in accord with them."

(6) Personal Factors: Sometimes personal factors may also be involved in the genesis of deviation. As a result of their particular experiences, many of the people acquire deviant attitudes and habits. An ugly face may deprive some people of the opportunity to participate in the affairs of the community. Some persons are so seriously affected by an experience that they isolate themselves from certain groups of situations. Thus, some people may refuse to ride trains or automobiles because of some accident in which they were involved. The sight of a dead man led Lord Buddha to renounce the crown. A mouse eating the food offered to the idol made Swami Dayanand a critic of idol-worship. In some cases a deviant behaviour is supported by myths and legend.

(7) Social Location: The location of people in the social structure also causes deviant behaviour. The position a person occupies in the stratification system, his position in the age and sex structure of the society and his position in the special arrangements of the society make a difference in how he behaves. The life chances of people depend on the particular position they occupy in the society. The people who live in slums and are at the bottom of social hierarchy are more induced to certain forms of deviation than the people who form the upper strata of society.

Norms Differ from Society to Society

Norms differ from society to society. What is considered deviant behaviour in one society may be considered the approved behaviour in another society. The Hindu society regards polygamy as deviant behaviour, but the mohammedan society permits it. The West permits free-mixing of sexes but the East does not approve it. The scope of behaviour regulated by norms varies considerably in different groups. The norms of some groups relate chiefly to ethical matters, while the norms of other groups may cover wider area of life. Thus, non-conformity to norms is always relative to the society for example different groups have different ideas of permissible behaviour. The range of acts that would be approved by college students differs from that which would be approved by college authorities. In somewhat comparable manner, certain groups of delinquents share values that help to explain their delinquency. Middle class and working class children tend to grow up in social worlds, but in the schools and elsewhere, the working class children are judged by middle class standards, which many are ill equipped to reject. These frustrated children flock together in little gangs, where a sub-culture emphasizing malice (desire to harm others) and negativism is developed and in which delinquent behaviour is rewarded because it represents an attack on the values of the respectable middle class. These delinquents behave in accordance with the norms of a delinquent sub-culture of the gang (Glencoe, Illinois: The free Press, 1955). When speaking of norms, therefore, it is helpful to indicate whose norms are being referred to, especially in a modern society which is complex and rapidly changing.

Social Deviants Represent Failure in Socialization

Socialization is the process by which the individual learns to conform to the norms of the group. When he does not more or less systematically conform, he is a social deviant. Socialization may be viewed as the training of a performance, one who can play the roles required by the cultural plot (Ernest Becker, 1962).

Such training calls for mastery of a conventional code of rules of interaction, by which to keep one's own face and to protect the face of others. Details of this code have set forthwith insight by Erving Goffman, (1956) around the two central concepts of deference and demeanour and The Presentation of Self in Everyday Life. Society protects the integrity of the individual and yet includes him in social interaction by means of deferential rules of avoidance and deferential rules of presentation. The former relate to the principle that the self is in part personal and is entitled to privacy and protection; the latter concern the principle that the self is partly social and that everyone has the right to engage in interaction with others if the rules are followed. Effective interaction requires acceptable egos. Hence, the need for demeanour which is self-regard is reflected in proper dress, bearing and deportment. The mentally ill according to Gooffman's view are those individuals who are not able to project a sustainable self.

Factors Associated with Deviant Behaviour, Criminal Behaviour and Violence

(1) Urbanization

Almost everywhere, the spread of urbanization—in the United States, Europe, Latin America, Africa and Asia—has been accompanied by a marked increase in various forms of deviant behaviour. While city living has characterized some areas for centuries, urbanization has increased at such an accelerated rate over past century that today it encompasses hundreds of millions of people throughout the entire world. Urban life has produced what some people have called the mass society. It has greatly increased social differentiation, the clash between norms and social rules, and the break down of interpersonal relations (Gilbert, Geis, 1979).

Following the civil war, the United States changed from a society of rural communities to one of the most urbanized in the world. Urbanization leads to deviant behaviour. Since Greek and Roman times, writers have contrasted the morality of rural areas. On the whole, modern cities as compared with rural areas, do appear to have higher rates of crime, illegal drug usage, heavy drinking and alcoholism, homosexual behaviour and mental disorder (Clinard, Marshall, B., 1965). Over 50 years ago, the French sociologist Emile Durkhheim maintained that crime increases directly with the volume and density of the population. Urban life tends to foster increased individual freedom of normative choice. Norm and role conflict, or diversities of norms and behavioural standards, create situations in which no single standard is likely to upheld and in which deviation from it is not met with penalizing sanctions. The end result of urbanism is the creation and the strengthening of a variety of sub-cultures, and the norms of these sub-cultures are often conducive to deviance. The large city populations provide what is termed the "critical mass" of deviants as well as the opportunity to commit deviant acts.

(2) Rapid Cultural Change

Rapid social and cultural change and disregard for the importance of stability through the generations also characterize urban life.

Consequently, elements that are traditional, or "sacred", dwindle in importance. Sometimes the practical exigencies of urban life produce these changes; at other times, they seem to be an outgrowth of the failure of informal controls to uphold and to maintain the older values and ideologies. Urban living has brought such great changes in the modern family, as has been pointed out, that it is often referred to as the "urban family." The modern family is both a characteristic and a result of urban life. The reduced size of modern people are more often known for their gadgets than for themselves. People increasingly come to judge others by how well they display their wealth a display Veblen termed "conspicuous consumption". Parsons emphasize the importance of status symbols in urban society, and it is on the basis of such readily visible criteria that status is assigned. Because of the status which money and material goods provide, criminality, both in the lower and upper classes, becomes higher in urban areas.

(3) Mobility

Urban societies generally tend to regard mobility favourably, but frequent moves may have unsatisfactory effects. They tend to weaken attachments to the local community, particularly among primary or face to face contacts, to make persons less interested in maintaining certain communities, standards, and to increase contact with secondary groups of diverse patterns, thus weakening bonds which help to provide the basis for social control among members of local groups. As persons become more mobile they come in contact with many other different norms, and they begin to understand that other codes of behaviour differ from their own. Mobility often means the loss of such personal relationships and kinship and neighbourhood ties and fewer close friendships. As a result of these factors, social controls and also legal controls are weakened.

(4) Materialism

External appearances and material possessions have become a primary importance in modern urban society, where people are more often known for the gadgets than for themselves. People increasingly come to judge others by how well they display their wealth, a display Veblen termed "consumption". Under urban conditions, the types of clothes a person wears or the automobile he drives, the costliness of his home and its furnishings, the exclusiveness of the club or association to which he belongs, and the knowledge of his salary or the amount of his financial assets are the sole means others have to judging him or his success in life. Parsons emphasize the importance of status symbols in urban society (Erving Goffman, 1959), and it is on the basis of such readily "visible" criteria that status is assigned. Because of the status money and material goods provide, criminality, both in the lower and upper classes, becomes higher in urban areas.

(5) Individualism

Urban persons tend to regard their over interests and self-expression as paramount in their social relations. The "I" feelings come to replace much of the feeling of co-operation characteristic of rural life. People increasingly feel that they must look after their own interests and increase their status through their own efforts. The urban person's strong belief is hedonism or personal happiness as the ultimate goal of life is increasingly seen. Individualism leads to competition. The extreme individualism and the competition of urban areas account, in part for their higher rates of crime, alcoholism, suicide and mental disorder.

As urbanism increases and conformity to social norms becomes less affected by informal group controls, greater opportunities and inducements develop for behaviour which deviates from that of others or the norms of others. As impersonality increases and intimate communication declines in the city, normative violations produce less and less informed censure of the kind seen in the rural areas. The conflicting normative experience in an urban setting tend to weaken parental authority and other traditional controls over youth and also over all individuals. As a result, responsibility for controlling behaviour in cities is shifting more and more to the police, the courts, and other agencies of government that tend to enforce the norms of certain power groups.

Society with a Higher Crime Rate

Criminality involves the learning of norms and attitudes conducive to law violation whether it is matter of burglary, an income-tax violation, or false advertising. Some of these norms and attitudes are derived from society, and they may lead to criminality itself. Barron lists six values that are related to the high crime rate in the United States (Barron, Milton, L., 1974).

***(1) Success*:** Success is undoubtedly one of the prime values in the culture. When people come to the realization that they cannot attain success by conventional hard work and thrift, many are apt to turn to delinquency and crime.

***(2) Status and Power Ascendance*:** Americans have traditionally been status conscious, and the struggle for higher status marks the history of most of the immigrant groups coming into this country. When status and power desires are thwarted, they may be obtained through illegal means.

***(3) Pecuniary and Material Wealth*:** Money and the desire for success and status are closely interrelated, but money as much as any single symbol has come to denote "worthiness". "It is often not what a person is that matters, but rather what he has." Most of the crimes that are eventually punished through the courts are theft related.

***(4) Resistance to Authority*:** The "rugged individualism" and the "pioneer spirit" are still valued in U.S. society many years after their function in settling the country has waned. Americans tend to resist rules, and they prefer to be free from too many controls. In fact, complete conformity to rule is often ridiculed in our society because it indicates a person's failure to show independent spirit.

***(5) Toughness*:** This value is particularly associated with males, but females also demonstrate this in psychological ways. Males are often defined in terms of toughness and on specific occasions, they show others how tough they are.

***(6) Dupery*:** The best example of dupery relates to consumer fraud. The ability to manipulate people is an important value, it is prevalent for e.g., in the sometimes indistinguishable line between whiter collar crime and good hard business. Perhaps the best e.g. of dupery relate to consumer fraud. One study of a number of occupations showed that false repairs were made on merchandise actually in working order. This study reported that watch repairmen were the most honest of those surveyed, though they too were dishonest to some extent. For the watch repairmen, "the test. ... was made by loosening the little screw that fasten the winding wheel in the watch. Of the 462 watch repairmen investigated throughout the nation only

49 per cent lied, overcharged, gave false diagnoses, or suggested expensive and unnecessary repairs. A bare majority of 51 per cent were honest, only 8 of them charging nothing at all (Barron Milton, L., 1974).

A Low-Crime-Rate Society

Generally, high rates of conventional crime accompany a high degree of urbanization, industrialization, and affluence, as in U.S. society. Switzerland, however, represents an exception to this general rule. In terms of per capita wealth, it is the richest industrial country in the world, yet its crime rate is far less serious than it is in the next most affluent western countries (Sweden, the United States, and the Federal Republic of Germany). The crime rate in Switzerland is much lower than the aforesaid affluent countries due to the unique government and the political structure as well as to its historical development. The process of urbanization has been slow and the cities have never become too large (the largest Swiss city has a population of about 425,000 as compared with, for example Stockholm with nearly a million). The Swiss citizen's widespread sense of responsibility and active participation in community affairs affects each individual's behaviour and that of other, including compliance not only with the generally accepted social norms but also with the law. It is commonly said, that in Switzerland "everyone is his own policeman". The people are conscious of the judgement that others make of behaviour that violates laws and regulations and thus risks public censure. The possibility of public censure restrains many from getting into trouble; infact, the desire to avoid public censure is more conducive to conformity than fear of police reprimand. Here the family ties are very strong, even in urban areas which maintains the contacts between age groups and more conformity in the family due to which the crime rate is less, although it is developing due to urbanization process in industrialized societies in Switzerland (Clinard, Marshall, B., 1978).

Enforcement of Norms

Norms are enforced by means of sanctions. This term refers to the actions of other or of an actor himself that have the effect of rewarding conformity and punishing non-conformity to norms by facilitating or interfering with the need gratification of the individual. Positive sanctions involve the usage of reward or other forms of satisfaction such as approval or praise. Negative sanctions involve the use of punishment or deprivation of satisfactions. Further, where the source of reward or punishment is the behaviour of others, the term external sanction is employed. Where the source is with in the actor, internal sanction is used. Examples of external sanctions are giving an employee a raise in pay or docking an employee who is late for work. Examples of internal sanctions are a feeling of pride for having conformed to a norm in the face of strong temptation to violate it or a feeling of guilt for having failed to conform.

Social norms include not only an overt behaviour but also verbal behaviour associated with in individual's perceptions, thoughts or feelings. Thus, norm is defined as an expectation shared by group members which specifies behaviour that is considered appropriate for a given situation. Two features of expectations which are especially important for understanding the concept of social norms are their anticipatory nature and their normative quality.

***(a) Anticipatory Nature of Expectation*:** An individual regularly expects that he will-behave in a certain manner, and he actually has definite expectations concerning the behaviour of persons with whom he interacts. This anticipatory quality of interaction is important because it guides the behaviour of an individual. One anticipates how the other persons might react to his various actions and shapes his behaviour accordingly. Often these anticipations take the form of rehearsing one's social interactions before they transpire.

***(b) Normative Quality of Expectations*:** Stems from the fact that only when one is able to anticipate consistently the behaviour of others can one maximize one's reward—cost costumes. The extent to which expectations are normative varies in proportion to the importance of reward and costs involved.

Social norms come to govern individual behaviour through the process known as socialization. Social norms provide one of the most important mechanisms of social control of the behaviour of individuals within the society. By means of normative social control, the behaviour of individuals within an organized social system is regulated within acceptable limits that maximize the likelihood of survival of the system. It is through the process of socialization that cultural social values and norms come to govern individual behaviour. Without the process of socialization, societies would not endure in any consistent form.

Now a days social psychology is equally interested in the problems of norm formation and change. There is nothing final or absolute about social custom, tradition and values. Social norms grow slowly as a result of social interaction. Social norms do change, though very slowly at times. As a social psychological problem, the problem of social norms is atleast as important as the problem of conformity-deviation to existing standards. Social norms develop due to society and social influence in the form of its various agencies.

Conformity and Social Norms

Social influence refers to the change in an individual that occurs because of contact with other people in the process of producing this change, people are affected by the presence, opinion or behaviour of others. Social influence is exercised in six fundamentally different ways i.e. information, record, coercion, expertise, reference identification, legitimacy.

This is often asked as why do people change their views when they come in contact with other people. The answer to this widely asked question is social influence which leads to conformity. Conformity acts a source of social influence for adherence to social norms.

Social conformity facilitates social interactions. Conformity occurs when individuals change their behaviour in order to adhere to existing social norms—widely accepted rules indicating how people should behave in certain situations or under specific circumstances (Moscovics, 1985). Thus, it represents a crucial means through which groups or even entire societies mould the actions of their members. A clear example of conformity is provided by the fact that most persons speak in a whisper when in libraries or hospitals, even if they usually prefer to converse in louder tones. They do so because both formal and informal rules indicate that this is the correct way to behave. Pressure towards conformity exist in many ways/settings and often exert profound effects upon social behaviour. Krechetal (1962) assesses that the essence of conformity is the yielding to social pressure. According to Allen (1965) conformity is a change in the behaviour of a person due to group influence resulting in the increased congruence between the individual and the group.

Social influence is subject to external and internal factors. The various external or internal factors are cohesiveness, group size, social support, sex, social status and organismic factor of personality.

***(1) Cohesiveness*:** Is the degree of attraction to the influencing group. It is defined as the total field forces acting on members to remain in the group. Stemming from cohesiveness is the property called the "internal power of the group", which is defined as the magnitude of change, the group can produce in its members. The degree of internal power will be equal to the magnitude of the force on the number to remain in the group. Cohesiveness may be defined as the tendency to stick together and be in accord. The amount of cohesiveness not only varies from group to group but also within the group from time to time. The group cohesiveness refers to the degree to which the members of a group desire to remain in the group. Thus, the members of a highly cohesive group in contrast to one with a low level of cohesiveness, are concerned with their membership and are therefore, more strongly motivated to contribute to the group welfare. It implies co-operation among members, affiliation and loyalty to the group. Thus, attraction toward a particular group to which we belong, or towards its individual members, is usually described by the term cohesiveness and there is little doubt about the impact of this factor upon conformity. The more cohesiveness of the group, the more will be conformity or adherence to the social norms. Cohesion is developed through social interaction. There are fewer deviates from highly cohesive groups than from less cohesive groups (e.g. Forsyth, 1983).

In experiments, too, group members who feel attracted to the group are more responsive to its influence (Berkovitz, 1954, Lott and Lott, 1961; Sakurai, 1975). Fearing rejection by people they like, they allow them a certain power. In his Essay Concerning Human Understanding, the seventeenth century philospher John Locke recognized the cohesiveness factor: "Nor is there one in ten thousand who is stiff and insensible enough to bear up under the constant dislike and condemnation of his own club".

Thus, the more attractive a group is to its individual members, the greater the probability of their conforming to group goals and expectations and the more likely prospective members are to be willing to adjust their attitude and behaviour patterns in order to obtain membership. The highly attractive group can demand more than other groups can because the individual member will get more in return, such as higher satisfaction and status. College fraternities and sororities are a good e.g. of these processes.

The more cohesive the group, the more likely it is able to impose negative sanctions on non-conforming group members. Sanctions imposed by less cohesive groups to which members are less committed are likely to lack the effectiveness that coincide with high cohesiveness and commitment.

However, cohesive groups are not only characterized by higher levels of conformity, but they also face the very real danger of non-conformity. Thus, the more amiability and esprit de corps amount the members of an in group of policy-makers, the greater is the danger that independent critical thinking will be replaced by group think which is likely to result in irrational and dehumanizing actions directed at outgroups according to Janis. A high degree of group cohesiveness is conducive to a high frequency of symptoms of group think, which is then are conducive to a high frequency of defects in decision-making. Cohesiveness, then, is an important factor affecting conformity, but its consequence can be functional as well as dysfunctional.

(2) Group Size: Second factor that exerts important effects upon our tendency to conform is the size of the influencing group. One might guess or think that the greater the number of persons around us who act in the same manner or who state some opinion, the greater our tendency to do the same i.e. to conform. But, this is not true. In fact, the relationship between the size of the group and conformity is complex. Conformity pressures rise quickly upon 3-4 members but, beyond this level, it has less additional effects as individuals exposed to social pressure may begin to suspect collusion (e.g. Gerard, Wilhelmy and Conolley, 1968). They may conclude that members are not expressing individual views of behaving in accordance with individual preference. They are working together to exert influence.

(3) Social Support: Does having an ally help! In Asch's research and in many later studies of conformity, subjects were exposed to social pressure from the unanimous group. Although the other persons present seemed to hold views different from their own. Under such condition, it is hardly surprising that many individuals yielded to social pressure. What would happen, if persons facing such pressure discovered that they had an ally—someone who shared their views, or at least failed to endorse the same position as the majority. Under such conditions, perhaps conformity might be reduced (e.g. Allen and Levin, 1971 and Morris and Miller, 1975). In these investigations subject provided with an ally or partner showed much less conformity than subjects not supplied with social support. Isolation from other people is one of the severest forms of punishment. Removal of social support is the means of inducing the psychological breakdown known as "brainwashing" (See Figure 22).

Figure 22: Isolation from other people is one of the severest forms of punishment. Removal of social supports is the means of inducing the psychological breakdown known as "brainwashing".

(4) Sex: In our culture, and in many others, there would appear to be a pronounced difference in the definition of sex roles in regard to the matter of conformity. The typical feminine role tends to be defined as involving promulgation of the conventional values of the culture, dependence upon the group, submissiveness to the male, avoidance of disagreement with others in the interests of group harmony. The typical masculine role tends to lay more stress on the ideals of self-sufficiency, self-assertion, independence of thought, standing on one's two feet and casting a shadow.

It goes without saying that women are slightly more influenceable because they are more concerned with interpersonal relations and attribution the difference to personality. Eagly and Wendy Wood (1985) believe that gender differences in conformity may instead be a product of men's and women's typical social roles. Male-female differences are not just a gender difference but also (or instead) status differences. In every day life, men tend to occupy positions of greater status and power, so we often see men exerting and women accepting influence. This explains why people perceive a much greater gender difference in everyday conformity than has been found in experiments that assign men and women identical roles. What causes them (females) to conform are the traditional expectations society holds for women, which suggest that women should be concerned more than men in getting along well with others.

Thus, the socially dictated meaning of the group pressure situation might be expected to differ in significant aspects for males and for females, and females might be predicted to conform more readily in it. In Crutchfield's (1955) study, females consistently earned higher conformity score than did males. High conforming females tended to be generally characterized by easier acceptance of the conventional feminine role. On the contrary, many of the females who independently resisted the group pressure tended to be characterized by marked signs of conflict in their feelings about the conventional feminine role, by rejection of a dependent relationship with parents and with others and by hostile attitude towards family. On a personality scale intended to measure "socialization" (Gough, 1960), the independent females scored significantly lower than did the conforming females. Among males, it is interesting to note that there was little difference in socialization scores between the independents and conformers.

Many early experiments on conformity yielded a result that females seemed to be much more yielding to social pressure i.e. more conforming than males (e.g. Crutchfield, 1955). According to Baron and Byrne, (1988), females in general seem to be much more conforming than males. This is so because men are tough and women are more yielding, and females are easier to push around than males because males are believed to be more influential than females. These findings were consistent with the then prevailing views about the supposed characteristics of the two sexes (e.g. men are "tough" and women are "yielding"). Thus, this result was quickly accepted as true by many social psychologists. Indeed for more than two decades, the view that females are more susceptible to social influence than males went largely unchallenged. Beginning in the early 1970s, however it was subjected to renewed examination. The results of this "second wave" of research were directly contrary to those of the first. No large or consistent difference between the sexes with respect to the tendency to conform were uncovered.

Thus, on the whole it is concluded that in number of researches, women have been found to be more easily influenced. But Eagly, (1987) after carefully reviewing these studies conclude that these sex differences arise because females are more concerned with social rational aspects of a group situations than males are, and they are especially concerned with maintaining social harmony and ensuring smooth interpersonal relations.

***(5) Social Status*:** Has an important impact on social influence. It is believed that people who are low in status are easier to influence than higher status people. (Driskell and Mullen 1990) Many also believe that, on average, females have lower status than males both in society and in a range of most settings. Together these beliefs lead to the assumption that low status persons come round easily than higher status people. People who are low in social status develop low self esteem due to which they lack confidence and are thus highly susceptible to punishment. So due to fear of success, they yield to social influence/social pressure to gain others' friendship in order to avoid the rejection by the group and to maintain the friendly support and status-quo within the group. Thus, on the whole it is concluded that lower status people are easily influenced by others in the group than the high status people.

Culture and Conformity

Does cultural background help predict how conforming people will be? Indeed it does. James Whittaker and Robert Meale (1967) repeated Asch's experiments in several countries and found similar conformity rates in most 31 per cent in Lebanon, 32 per cent in Hong Kong, 34 per cent in Brazil but 51 per cent among the Bantu of Zimbabwe, a tribe with strong sanctions for non-conformity. When Milgram (1961) used a different conformity procedure to compare Norwegian and French students, he consistently found the Norwegian students to be the more conforming. However, cultures may change. Replications of Asch's experiment with university students in Britain, Canada and the United States sometimes trigger less conformity than Asch observed two or three decades earlier (Lalancette and Standing, 1990; Larsen, 1974, 1990; Nicholson and Others, 1985; Perrin and Spencer, 1981).

When researchers in Germany, Italy, South Africa, Australia, Austria, Spain and Jordan repeated the obedience experiments, how do you think the results compared to those with American subjects? The obedience rates were similar or even higher—85 per cent in Munich (Mantell, 1991, Meeus and Raaijmakers, 1986 and Milgram, 1974).

In a study of "administrative obedience" in the Netherlands, Win Meeus and Ouinten Raijmakers (1986) ordered Dutch adults who had volunteered for an experiment to distrupt a job applicant who was taking an employment test, causing the applicant to fail the test and supposedly remain unemployed. In the guise of an experiment on the effects of stress, the subjects had to trigger 15 derogatory computer messages that caused the applicant to become progressively more upset. As the applicant's tension turned to irritation and finally to despair, the subjects found the procedure and their task disagreeable. Yet by shifting responsibility to the experimenter, 90 per cent fully complied.

So, conformity and obedience are universal phenomena, yet they vary by culture (Bond, 1988; Triandis and Others, 1988). Euro-American cultures teach individualism: you are responsible for yourself. Follow your own conscience be true to yourself. Define your unique gifts. Meet your own needs. Respect one another's privacy. Asian and non-western cultures are more likely to teach collectivism. Your family or clan is responsible for its individual members, whose actions therefore reflect shame or honour upon it. So bring honour to your group. Be true to your traditions. Show respect for elders and superiors. Cultivate harmony, and do not criticize another publicly. Be loyal to family, company, nation. Live communally, without assuming that you have a private self-separate life from your social context. An analysis by Red Bond and Peter Smith (in press) of 133 studies in 17 countries confirms that these cultural values have an impact on conformity. Compared to people in individualistic countries, those in collectivist countries are more responsive to other's influence. In sum, it may be inferred that even in most individualized societies the obedience to authority shall always be at moderately higher rate because of the fear of breaking down or lest chaos may prevail.

Internal Factors Affecting Conformity

There are individual differences in conformity proneness. Common observation over the ages seems to make obvious the point that individuals vary widely in their tendencies to conform. Some individuals give way to group pressure and others do not may only mean that their situations are different. One man yields because he fears reprisals of the group against his family, another man resists the same group because he has no family that can be threatened through him.

Personality and Conformity

There are numerous basic personality factors associated with tendency to conform or with tendency to remain independent under group pressures.

(a) Cognitive Functioning: The conformists are prone to be significantly less intelligent than the independent persons. For e.g. the correlation of conformity with scores on the Concept Mastery Test (Terman, 1956), a high level test of intelligence, is .50 or higher. Conformists show greater tendencies toward rigidity of cognitive processes and poverty of ideas, as contrasted with the greater capacity for cognitive restructuring and for novel ideas found in the independent subjects.

***(b) Motivational and Emotional Functioning*:** The conformists are lower in ego strength and in ability to cope under stress. For example, a measure based on the readiness of soldiers to fire their guns effectively under battle conditions in the Korean conflict is found to correlate .38 with conformity score in a sample of military officers. The conformists tend to exhibit emotional constriction, lack of spontaneity, repression of impulse, and indirect expression of hostility to a greater degree than do the independents. They also tend to be more anxious. (Score on the Manifest Anxiety Scale, Taylor, 1953) correlate in the range from .30 to .40 with conformity scores.

***(c) Self-conception*:** Conformists are inclined toward pronounced feelings of personal inferiority and inadequacy. They lack self-confidence. They tend to be less insightfully and realistic in their self-perceptions than are the independent subjects. For example, their self-descriptions on an adjective check list (Gough,1960) tend to differ much more from the composite adjective descriptions of them given by an expert assessment staff than do those of the independent subjects.

***(d) Interpersonal Realities*:** The conformists exhibit intense preoccupation with other people, as contrasted with the more self-contained, autonomous attitudes of the independent persons. The interpersonal behaviour of the conformists tend to show far more passivity, suggestibility, and dependence upon others, while at the same time there is considerable evidence of basically disturbed and distrustful attitudes toward other people. More over the conformists prove to be poorer than others, the independent person in his ability to judge other people's trait accurately.

***(e) Personal Attitude and Values*:** The conformists express attitudes and values of a far more conventional and moralistic nature than do the independent subject. This is often coupled with a "low tolerance for ambiguity" and a rigid dogmatic, authoritarian outlook. Thus, Nadler (1959) reports that F-scale scores correlate .48 with conformity scores as measured in the Asch technique. Conforming subjects tend to have occupational interest pattern as measured by strong Vocational Interest Inventory (Blank) which are similar to those professions generally regarded as placing more stress on conventional social values.

Reasons of Adherence to the Norms

We have seen that society, as represented by our associates, exerts a steady pressure upon us to adhere to the norms and that in the case of some norms—the laws—these pressures are institutionalized and applied by agencies. It is easy to see that we do not enjoy the disapproval and displeasure of our fellows, that we can hardly sustain the pain of ostracism from our own groups. It is easy to see in addition that we do enjoy the approval and approbation of our fellows and that in most cases this is a large reward and one that we endeavour to earn by our conformity. But hope of reward and fear of punishment are not the only reasons we conform to the norms of one society. There are other basis for adherence which are as follows:

(1) Indoctrination: The first reason we adhere to these norms is that we have been indoctrined to do so. From our earliest childhood we are taught to observe the norms of one society. Like other aspects of culture they are ready for us when we arrive upon the human scene and we accept them, as we accept the ideas and the material, without conscious thought or reflection. We are taught, for example to take our meals at certain times of the day, to use certain kinds of utensils at the table, to address our elders with respect, to omit certain vulgarities from our speech and so on. The "Socialization" of the child, in effect, is the process of learning the norms of his own society. After a while, these norms seem to give him the right and proper way of doing things, and sometimes, indeed, the only way. In many cases, therefore, we adhere to the norms because we know no alternative—for the same reason, in short, that we use English instead of Hindustani. This is the process of indoctrination, a process that is continuous and constant from the beginning of our lives.

(2) Habituation: Is the second reason of adherence to the norms. What is customary in many cases becomes habitual. We are indoctrinated in the use of knife, fork and spoon, and after a while their use is a matter of habit. Repetition has thus made a habit, and a folkway comes to be rooted in a sense, in the organism. When one has become habituated to a practice, he observes it automatically, without reflection or effort. Thus, habituation reinforces the norms and guarantees the regularity of conformity.

(3) Utility: The third reason why we conform to the norms of one society is that frequently we can appreciate their utility. As reflective individuals we can see that norms are useful, that they enable us to interact with others in a way conducive to the best interests of all, that they contribute to the ease of social intercourse. It is apparent to us, for example, that the fair way of distributing tickets to a play for which only a limited number of seats are available is to sell them first to those who come first to purchase them. We see that rationality in the expression "first come, first served". We recognize that an orderly line/queue is a superior device, socially speaking, to a disorderly rush, in which someone, perhaps ourselves, might be trampled.

We recognize further that the flow of traffic at busy intersections is smoother and less dangerous when lights are installed. Thus, we stop at a red light and go on a green one, not only because we are indoctrinated and habituated to the practice, but because we recognize that this kind of regulation is useful to everyone, ourselves included.

***(4) Group Identification*:** Is the fourth reason of why we adhere to the norms of our own social group norms, for example, rather than to those groups to which we do not belong, not because we regard our men as superior, and not because we are particularly indoctrinated or habituated to them, but because in conforming to them we express our identification with these groups.

Thus, a norm may not specify what kind of behaviour is expected by the group or society but it usually also specifies the degree of conformity to the norm that is expected by the group as reasonable adherence to the norm. They are generally conservative mechanisms. They serve as a rule to maintain the status-quo with in the group which the child respond to and regards in a rather absolute fashion. Although he lapses from them under the grip of momentary desire or in the flux of fantasy, they tend to be regarded as final and inflexible, resting on the authority of father or mother. However, as a child matures and as he interacts with other children, he grasps the notion of reciprocity with others. Interaction in reciprocal relationships makes possible co-operative activities and co-ordination of individual efforts.

In the process of reciprocal interaction, the child comes to see rules or norms as based on mutual agreements. He finds that they can be changed and that new rules can be made. When he begins to take part in the process of changing and making rules himself, they truly become his own rules by which he abides through inner autonomy.

Thus, the crucial condition for willing, autonomous and even enthusiastic internalization of social norms is the participation in reciprocal interactions with other people.

Formation of Social Norms

The problem of the formation of social norms may be studied from two angles: how norms arise in a group and how children come to acquire social norms.

It must be clearly recognized that social norms are shared norms. They are the standards or values of the group and arise in connection with matters of importance to the group. The conduct, strivings and aspirations of members of the group are regulated by these norms. These norms cannot be known or inferred from the behaviour of single individuals. They emerge from group or social interaction and can be known from group or social situations. Readers must have realized by now that the behaviour of individuals in group interaction is different from individual behaviour and cannot be explained in terms of the latter, and therefore, we must draw a line between individual psychology and social psychology.

Now what are the characteristics of social situations in which norms arise? Sherif (1935) distinguishes between 'structured' and 'unstructured' situations, the former being compelling, strong and clear, and the latter, weak, ambiguous, and vague. It is the latter type of 'unstructured' situations that social norms arise because they offer alternatives for experience and behaviour. In structured situations the objective factors are strong and compelling and mostly determine experience and behaviour. Amidst tools, buildings, timetables, things of definite magnitudes, proportions and limits the responses of an individual are more or less accurately determined. He has definite scales and standards to measure size, speed, and the like. But it is in unstructured situations like birth, death, marriage, illness, quarrel, and the like that customs and traditions arise. What we eat and how we eat, how we dress, what ceremonies or rites should regulate marriages in any group, how we treat strangers and intimate friends, how patients should be nursed, and the like are vague indefinite situations which leave room for a number of alternatives for experience and behaviour, and that is why customs, traditions, standards and values have full scope to develop with regard to these matters. The various alternatives are compared and the desirable ones are stabilized or confirmed through processes of social interaction, through past experience, and through established social relations and goals. When social norms arise those situations become structured and definite. The type of experience and behaviour possible at the time of birth or death in an orthodox Hindu home is very precisely determined because of the decisive role of accepted social norms. For poor people in Indian villages there are no social norms with regard to taking tea in the afternoon, but richer people who have separate tea or drawing rooms with crockery, tea trolleys, and a host of other things, have social norms which make almost a ritual of tea-taking.

The second question with regard to the formation of social norms is how children develop and acquire them. Murphy, Murphy and Newcomb* maintain that moral judgements are clearly not simply assimilated readymade from the preceding generation, but are reworked in terms of the child's needs and degrees of identification with and respect for other individuals. Many moral judgements of children are in violent conflict with those of their parents and of the social world in which they live, if a type of behaviour related to their need is involved. Many children protest with tears when dogs or domestic animals are cruelly beaten by their parents or other adults, and are moved to pity when they read in fairy stories about the cruel treatment given to wolves or giants. The needs of children are not only biological but also products of social experience.

Many psychologists and educationists have studied the growth and development of moral ideas among children, and they show that to begin with, the child is very self-centred and it is only gradually that he comes to acquire altruistic moral ideas. In the early thirties the Swiss psychologist J. Piaget published his studies of the development of ideas of right and wrong among children of the lower class in Geneva. He showed that the moral judgements of the child pass through four stages or levels. In the first stage they just do what people around them do. They played marbles as older boys did and enjoyed doing it without any consideration of right and wrong. This stage is amoral and if they were asked who won the game they replied that everybody won. The second stage was marked by 'moral realism'.

**Experimental Social Psychology* (New York: Harper and Brothers).

The rules of the game must be strictly enforced; what is right is right and what is wrong is wrong. If any person does wrong he must be punished regardless of his motives. If they are told that other boys have different rules, they do not understand it and do not care. Children of the age group 4-5 are of this type. A little later at the age of 7-8 years they enter the third stage and begin to realize that rules are not objective and absolute but are made by people and reflect group values. Through social interaction they recognize that such rules are a matter of mutual arrangement and can be changed and replaced by other rules. In fact they do devise new games and make new rules. Geneva children which Piaget was studying remain at this stage till the age of 9-10. Then around adolescence they reach the fourth stage when they realize that mutual arrangement is not the only criterion of rule making. Rules should be altered by considerations of justice and equity. If the rule applies to all it is satisfactory, but there may be cases where rigid universal application of the rules may be unfair, for example, a lame or handicapped boy may be given a start in a race, or a sick or new boy may be allowed to have two turns. Piaget's conclusions have been supported by other investigators in the field, but his explanation that early conception of moral rules as rigid and absolute is due to the strict authoritarian discipline of the parents seems to be too naive. It may be due to lack of proper understanding of the implications of moral rules and tacit acceptance from adult members of the group.

The fact of conformity behaviour as well as the factors that enhance its occurrence have been demonstrated by laboratory and field studies. Muzafer Sherif, (1935) conducted his classical study on the development of social norms. He developed the notion that norms emerge in response to ambiguity. He employed what is called the autokinetic effect in studying the process of norm formation. This is the phenomena that occurs when a pinpoint of light is viewed in an otherwise totally dark room: a totally stationary light will appear to move. In one of his experiments, Sherif brought a group of subjects into a dark room to observe a pinpoint of light and then asked them to estimate how far the light moved. Sherif created a totally ambiguous situation, in that there were no criteria for the subjects to use in estimating the movement of light. After a series of trials, Sherif observed a most interesting social-psychological phenomenon: the range of estimates by his respondents began to converge toward the mean. After the first trial, the range of estimated movements varied from two or three inches to 15 inches. After additional trials, the more extreme estimates tended to become less extreme and therefore move toward the mean. Eventually, the group came to establish a norm—in this case, a generally agreed-upon estimate of light movement. Respondents who helped to develop this group norm then tended to continue to use it in later trials when they were by themselves. In other words, a social norm developed to provide meaning to an ambiguous situation. In this experiment the patch of light remains stationary, but the pupil of eye does not remain stationary. The movement of the pupil is directly related to the physical movement in terms of inches. So the patch of light will appear to move.

The power of group pressure to induce conformity of judgement in the individual is dramatically revealed in the widely known experiments of Asch (1951, 1952, 1956). In the experiments, subjects thought they were participating in a test of perceptual skills with a group of six other subjects. The subjects were shown one card with three lines of varying length and a second card which had a fourth line that matched one of the first three.

The task was seemingly straight forward. The subjects had to announce Aloud which of the first three lines was identical in length to a "standard" line. Because there was always an obvious answer, the task seemed easy to the participants.

Indeed, since the subjects all agreed on the first few trials, the procedure was quite a simple one. But then something odd began to happen. From the perspective of the subject in the group who got to answer last, all of the first six subject's answers seemed to be wrong—in fact, unanimously wrong. And this continued. Over and over again, the first six subjects provided answers that contradicted what the last subject felt was the correct one. The dilemma that this situation posed for the last subject was whether to follow the group and repeat the answer that everyone else was giving.

As one might guess, the situation in the experiment was more contrived that it first appeared. The first six subjects were actually confederates of the experimenter and had been instructed to give unanimously erroneous answers in many of the trails. And the study has nothing to do with perceptual skills. Instead, the issue under investigation was that of conformity through indirect social influence/ pressure.

What Asch found was that in about one-third of the trials, subjects conformed to the unanimous, but erroneous group answer, with about 75 per cent of all subjects conforming at least once. However, there were strong individual differences. Some subjects conformed nearly all the time, whereas, other never did so.

Since Asch's pioneering work literally hundreds of studies have examined the factors affecting conformity, and we now know a great deal of phenomenon (Moscovics, 1985; Tanford and Penrod, 1984). Among the most important variables producing conformity are the following:

***(a) The nature of the group*:** The more attractive the group, the greater its ability to produce conformity. The lower the status—the social rank held within the group—of a person and the greater the similarity of the individual to the group, the greater is the power of the group over the individual's behaviour.

***(b) The nature of the individual's response*:** Conformity is considerably higher when people must make a response publicly than when they can respond privately, as our founding fathers noted when they authorized secret ballots in voting.

***(c) The kind of task*:** People working on tasks or questions that are ambiguous (having no clear answer) are more susceptible to social pressure. Giving an opinion, such as on what type of clothing is fashionable, is more likely to produce conformity than answering a question of fact.

***(d) Unanimity of the group*:** Conformity pressures are most pronounced in groups that are unanimous in their support of a position. But what of the case in which people with dissenting views have ally in the group who agrees with them. Having just one person present who shares the unpopular point of view is sufficient to reduce conformity pressures (Allen, 1975).

Another experiment that produced even more dramatic results on conformity was on obedience to authority. This experiment was done by Stanley Milgram (1963, 1965, 1974), in a laboratory of Yale. Milgram selected eighty men of various ages and occupational backgrounds and asked them to take part in what he said was an important experiment in learning. Each subject was assigned to a group of four people—the other three of whom unknown to the subject were Milgram's assistants. One of the assistants was the "learner" in the make believer experiment. The other two assistants and the subject were the "teachers", and their job was to instruct the "learner" by punishing him with an electric shock when he made an error. The subject was put at the controls that regulated the amount of shock. Actually, no electricity was hooked up to the controls and no learning took place. The "learner" deliberately made errors and only pretended to feel pain when punished. Of the so (eight) subjects, half were placed in a control group. These subjects were not subjected to any pressure to raise the shock level and did not raise them very high. Thirty four of these forty control subjects stopped at shock levels listed as "slight" or "moderate". Only six went above 120 volts. But it was a far different story with the other forty subjects. These forty were strongly urged by their fellow "teacher" to raise the amount of electricity higher and higher and they did. Only six of them refused to go above 120 volts. The other thirty four went right on, even though the "learner" at first shouted that the shocks were becoming painful and later began to groan and finally scream in pain. Seven of the subjects went up to what they thought was maximum they could deliver—a "highly dangerous shock of 450 volts. Many of the experimental subjects showed signs of doubt and stress about engaging in such a sadistic act, yet they conformed anyway to the pressures of their group (see Figure 23).

Figure 23: These photos show the apparatus and basic set up used in the Milgram experiment—the shock generator, the "learner" with electrodes attached to his wrist, and the subject receiving a sample shock from the generator.

Social Norms are Changing Rapidly

Social norms are changing rapidly (see Figure 24) due to various reasons. The three major themes—power, social problems and conflict are enormously complicated by the swift pace of change in social norms in modern societies. The following are the causes of these changes in norms:

Figure 24: Social norms are changing rapidly. The photograph shows the deviation of sexual norms i.e. from bedroom to drawing room and from drawing room to open.

(1) The Technology Explosion

Much of what we see every day—telephones, televisions, cards, electric lights, stereos, refrigerators—have been invented since 1900. In fact, if we took a count of all the inventions in mankind's history, more of them would have been invented in the last two generations than in all the generations of mankind before (Ogburn, 1955) (see Figure 25).

Imagine that we took the last 10,000 years of man's existence and compressed them into one hour. The startling conclusion, illustrated in Figure 26, is that most of the technological inventions have been made in the last minute.

25 (a): Picking cotton by hand.

25 (b): Mechanical cotton pickers.

Figure 25 (a & b): Technological innovations change man's occupations and his organizations.

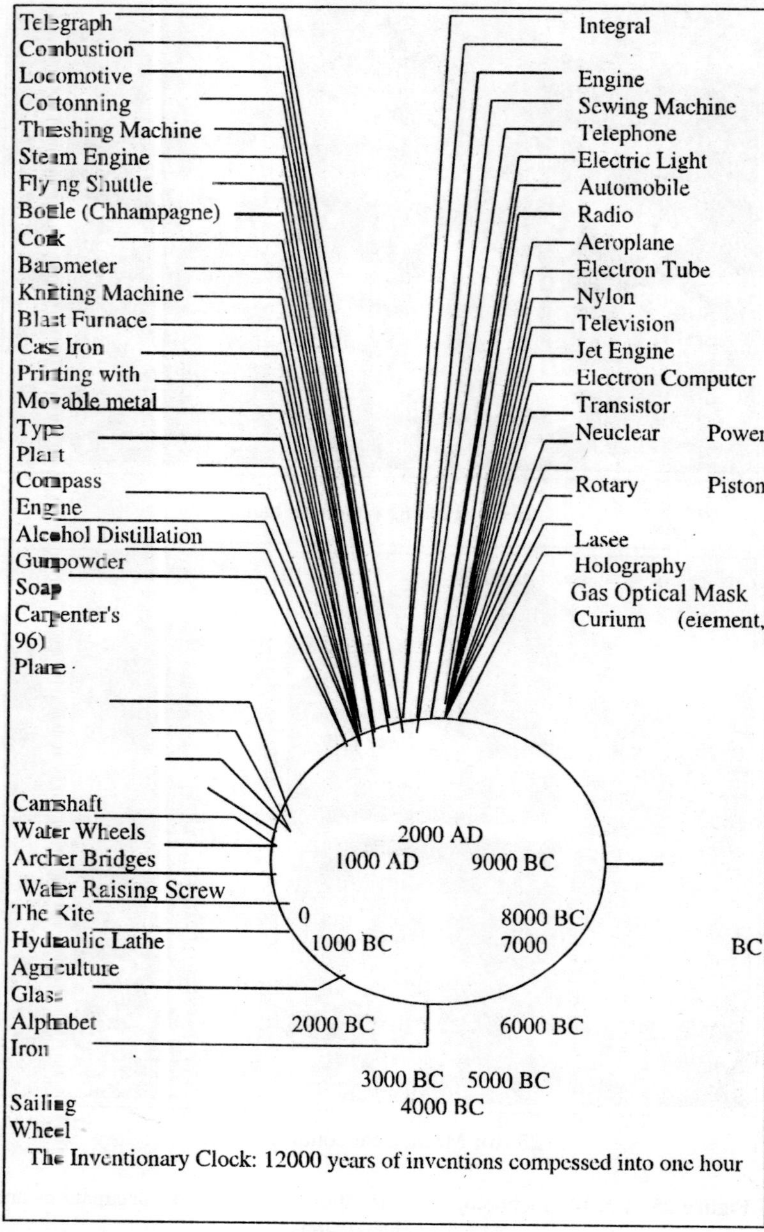

The Inventionary Clock: 12000 years of inventions compessed into one hour

Figure 26: The Technology Explosion.

The same rate of technological innovation may be seen in the rapid increase in patents for inventions used in the United States in 1790, there were three inventions patented; in 1835 there were 752; in 1900 there were 24,644; by 1973 the figure was over 65,000. Thus, technology is reshaping over whole social life by its fantastic growth. Thus, change is caused by improvements in technology and shifts in the economic structures. This theory is often called "technological determinism," since it argues that changes in the social system are produced by developments in technology.

(2) The Population Explosion and Demographic Changes

There are more people alive at this very second than there have been in all time before 1900, combined. Everything about modern social life is influenced by the sheer numbers of people—over 3.5 billion—who are living now and who are reproducing at a staggering rate. The quality of government, the possibility of war, the fear of mass starvation, the hope of modernizing underdeveloped nations, the dream of world cooperation—all of those precious dreams and nightmarish fears hinge precarious on the tick-tock of the population bomb (see Figure 27).

Figure 27:
Almost 200 years ago Malthus predicted that the human race would inevitably grow beyond the limits of its food supply. Today rapid population growth has brought the world to the brink of the Malthusian nightmare of misery and mass starvation.

The world population increased very slowly throughout the last 500,000 years, but all of a sudden, in the last few years, the population leaped upward at a staggering pace. Major social upheaval caused by shifts in the amount of population or in its physical distribution with in society such as urbanization. Thus, population explosion gives rise to change in the social structure which ultimately gives rise to change in social norms.

(3) The Knowledge Explosion

In addition to the technology explosion and the population explosion, the contemporary world is experiencing a knowledge explosion. Take few examples:

Ninety per cent of all the scientists who ever lived are alive right now. There are presently more books written in the world each day than were written in most centuries up until 1600; there are probably more students in colleges and universities at this moment than there have been in all history up to 1950; The United States now spends about 7½ per cent of its Gross National Product (value all goods and services) on education, a staggering $75 to $80 billion a year; Government, Industry and Universities now spend huge sums of money on "Research and Development", on deliberately planning future change. Once change came accidentally at its own pace; now the society plans for it.

This knowledge explosion feeds the technology explosion, which in turn promotes social change and then to change in norms. Francis Bacon once said "Knowledge is power"; Alvin Toffler speaks more to our age: "Knowledge is change".

(4) The Urban Explosion

Three out of four Americans now live in a urban area. Before 1850 no society had a majority of its population living in urban areas, and by 1900, only Great Britain was an urban society. Today, however, almost all industrialized nations are highly urbanized. While non industrial societies are still predominately rural, even they are rapidly becoming urban. Cities are growing quickly, but the sub-urban areas around the city are mushrooming even faster. All over the world the growth of cities is much faster than the growth of the general world population. It is estimated that more than 20 per cent of the world's people now live in cities of 100,000 people or more and the trend is toward increasing urbanization as more countries industrialize (see Figure 28).

Figure 28: The aerial view of Tokyo exemplifies the worldwide urban explosion caused by population growth and industrial development.

Urban society is considerably different from the rural society man has known so long. In addition to the obvious physical differences (large concentration of people, high-rise buildings, tangled highway networks), there are important social consequences of urban living. Some of these consequences are negative: poverty, racial serration, pollution and ecological destruction, crowding and intense social conflict. Other results of urbanization improve the human situation better economic efficiency, a concentration of manpower and brainpower, expanded opportunities for many people in health care, occupation, recreation and art. Thus, it can be concluded from the aforesaid studies that urbanization is one of the major causes of social change and change in social norms. Urbanization leads to modernization which is a complex process involving many transformations shown in (Figure 29).

Figure 29: Traditional and Modern Societies: Dimensions of Difference.

	Characteristics of Traditional Societies	*Characteristics of Modern Societies*
	Scale of Life	
	Small scale; population typically small and widely dispersed in rural villages and small towns	Large scale; population typically large and concentrated in cities
	Cultural Patterns	
Values	Homogeneous; scared character; few sub-cultures and counter-cultures	Heterogeneous; secular character; many sub-cultures and counter-cultures
Norms	High moral significance; little tolerance of diversity	Variable moral significance; high tolerance of diversity
Orientation	Present linked to past	Present linked to future
Technology	Pre-industrial; human and animal energy	Industrial; advanced energy sources
	Social Structure	
Status and Role	Few statuses, most ascribed; few specialized roles	Many statuses, some ascribed and some achieved; many specialized roles
Relationships	Typically primary; little anonymity and privacy	Typically secondary; considerable anonymity and privacy
Communication	Face-to-face	Face-to-face communication supplemented by mass media

(Contd.)

(Contd.)

Characteristics of Traditional Societies		*Characteristics of Modern Societies*
Social Control	Informal gossip	Formal police and legal system
Social Stratification	Rigid patterns of social inequality; little mobility	Fluid patterns of social inequality; considerable mobility
Gender Patterns	Pronounced patriarchy; women's lives centered on the home	Declining patriarchy; increasing number of women in the paid labour force
Family	Extended family as the primary means of socialization and economic production	Nuclear family retains some socialization function but is more a unit of consumption than of production
Religion	Religion guides world view; little religious pluralism	Religion weakens with the rise of science; extensive religious pluralism
Education	Formal schooling limited to elites	Basic schooling becomes universal, with growing proportion receiving advanced education
State	Small-scale government; little state intervention into society	Large-scale government; considerable state intervention into society
Economy	Based on agriculture; some manufacturing within the home; little white-collar work	Based on industrial mass production; factories become centers of production; increasing white-collar work
Health	High birth and death rates; brief life expectancy because of low standard of living and simple medical technology	Low birth and death rates; longer life expectancy because of higher standard of living and complex medical technology
	Social Change	
	Slow; change evident over many generations	Rapid; change evident within a single generation

(5) Strained Social Institutions

What difference does all this change make for social life—the real point of concern for social psychologists? For one thing, our social systems are becoming outmoded, inefficient, and unresponsive. The government is a prime example. At the local level most municipalities, town, and counties were established years ago, when transportation was slow, communication difficult, the population small, and problems essentially local. Now that network is falling apart, totally unable to cope with massive regional problems of pollution, population shifts, organized crime, and a withering tax base. At the national level, the monster bureaucracies seem unresponsive to the needs of the people, isolated, and hopelessly slow to act. The watergate scandal of the early 1970s shook the public confidence in the basic integrity of the nation's leaders. At the international level, the prospect is even gloomier. Although the existence of atomic weapons necessitates increased cooperation among nations, there is little evidence of major countries working together to settle their differences.

The family is another social institution that feels the brunt of change. Children rebel against their parents; parents find that there mate choices are not satisfactory under changing situations, and the divorce rate shoots out of sight; aged grandfathers are shuffled out of "senior citizen's homes", instead of receiving the honour and dignity of their position. Young people live together instead of marrying, middle-aged people get married but feel a vacuum of meaningless partnerships, and old people watch their painfully built beams shattered by social change.

Educational institutions are also changing as the society demands more from them than ever before. Not only must the schools do their traditional job of teaching the three R's—reading, riting, and rithmetic—but they must also train a labour force for the technological society, instil values and increase the world's knowledge through research.

Value Changes

Social change happen when major shifts occur in the values, beliefs, ideologies and religions that support the culture of a society. Social change is caused when active sub-groups form social movements and try to overthrow the established order. Revolutions, political upheavals, and social reforms have nearly always depended on the deliberate efforts of social movements (Yinger, 1977).

Thus, as the society changes many of the traditional values and processes of economic institutions are challenged (see Figure 30).

The twentieth-century feminist movement has found most of its supporters among white, middle-class, college-educated women. This social base has recently expanded to include larger numbers of working-class and black women.

Figure 30: Feminist movement: An outgrowth of change of values.

Conclusion

Thus, to conclude, much of what we engage in as individuals is idiosyncratic. Since every personality is unique, many actions and types of behaviour displayed by different people are also unique. Indeed existence would be dull if the social world were not invested with a high level of human diversity. However, in order for social organization to remain intact and for the humans as a species to survive, we still must will to adhere to norms. Norms provide an important source of stability to society. Norms are of great importance to society. It is impossible to imagine a normless society because without norm, behaviour would be impredictable. The standards of behaviour contained in the norms give order to social life (relations).

Interactions go smoothly if the individuals follow the group norms (March, 1954). The normative order makes the factual order to human society possible. Man needs a normative order to live in society because human organism is not sufficiently comprehensive or integrated to give automatic responses that are functionally adequate for society. One can hardly think of a society apart from norms. A society without norms would be to use the words of Hobbes, "solitary, poor, nasty, brutish and short." The normative system gives to society a cohesion without which social life is not possible. They influence individual's attitude and his motive. They impinge directly upon a person's self conception. They are specific demands to act made by this society.

B. GENDER AND SOCIAL NORMS

Ever since his birth, man has been classified into male and female. This obvious distinction is based on the basic physiological difference between the two sexes. The fact that women were physically weaker than men seemed to suggest an all-round weakness, which included mental traits too for centuries many people have believed that women are distinctly different than men in their general intellectual abilities, with some people believing that women had no intelligence. In the days before suffragette movement and women's lib, it used to be taken for granted that men were superior to women with respect to intellect (Eysenck and Wilson, 1976). Aside from those with such radical opinions, other believed women to have different sets of skills than men, women were to excel in perception, memory and language development, and were thought to be deficient in logical functioning and inability to think analytically and critically. Males were considered to be more adept than females at problem solving, and research in this area support this belief (Bedell, 1934; Billings, 1934; Sweeney, 1953; Terman and Tyler, 1954; Maier and Casselman, 1970; Roll, 1970; Constantinople, 1974; Raheim and Kaufman, 1974; Felen, 1975; Maxwell, 1975; Singer, 1975; Mcways, 1976; Hayes, 1978; Johnson, 1984; Kumar and Kapila, 1987 and Hasija et. al., 1989). These researches suggest that the biological gender is not the only determiner of problem solving ability. Present day psychology favours the idea that sex differences are mainly determined by upbringing that is from complex process of socialization (Martin and Parker, 1995). The survey of cross-cultural data strongly suggest that "The sex-roles depend upon cultural definition and conditioning. Without the influence of society, people's sex-role would not define their identities or determine their personality styles" (Mead, 1935). Mischell (1976) indicated that there are three theoretical positions that explain how sex differences may develop. First of these is biological theory, which states that the boys and girls simply inherit the physiological characteristics that lead to these differences. The second theory is that of sociological one that explain these differences on the basis of socialization processes in which observational learning plays an important part. The third position is that of psychological theory which states that children first achieve an understanding of the permanence of their own sexual identities and then construct for themselves patterns of sex-appropriate behaviour.

It would be worthwhile to study the genetic and cultural variables responsible for these differences to understand the psychodynamic factors responsible for their greater socialization.

Sex-role Orientation

The distinction between male and female serves as a basic organizing principle for every human culture. Although societies differ in the specific tasks they assign to the two sexes, all societies allocate adult roles on the basis of sex and anticipate this allocation in the socialization of their children. Not only are boys and girls expected to acquire sex specific skills, they are also expected to acquire sex-specific self concepts and personality attributes, to be masculine or feminine as defined by that particular culture (Barry, Bacon and Child, 1957). These psychological characteristics and behavioural pattern characteristics of each sex are refered to as "sex-roles". Sex-roles are conceptualized in terms of masculinity and femininity and sex-role orientation is the differences among individuals as how confident they feel about their sex-identity (Bem, 1974, 1975, 1977).

In a process of learning his/her sex-role, a person first learns to discriminate between the patterns of behaviour for the two sexes, then to generalise from specific events to new situations and last to perform appropriate sex-typed behaviours. Garnets and Pleck (1979) defined sex-role salience as "the extent to which individuals do or do not experience and organise personality characteristics as parts of larger constructs of masculinity and femininity". These roles are different in different places and times (Mead, 1935), but there are certain biological limits within which these roles can vary.

Friedan (1964) has focused on the way women were socialized to accept subsidiary roles as partners, housekeeper and overpossessive mother, at the same time their over individuality and potentialities were over-ridden. The human personality according to Millett (1970), is formed along sex lines. Thus, aggression, intelligence and efficacy characterize the male, docility, passivity and ignorance the female. The second factor sex-role elaborates the code of conduct and attitudes appropriate for each sex. The third factor, the status bestowed on each sex group, reinforces their temperament and role thus, women are accorded lower status than men.

Sex-role consists of behaviours socially defined as appropriate to one's status as male or female. It represents the abstracted concept of ideal male or female as defined by the culture. English and English (1974) defines "masculinity as a state or condition of an organism that manifests the characteristic appearance and behaviour of a male and femininity as a state or condition of an organism that manifests the characteristic appearance and behaviour of a female". Similarly, Baken (1966) associates masculinity with the agentic orientation, a concern for relationship between one's own self and others and femininity as a concern for the self but in relation to others (communal). Erikson (1964) anatomical distinction between 'inner (female) and outer (male) space represents an analogue to a quite similar psychological distinction between a masculine fondness for building or destroying and a more ethical feminine commitment to resourcefulness in peace keeping and devotion in healing.

Parsons and Bales (1955) associate masculinity with instrumental orientation, cognitive focus on getting the job done and femininity with expressive, supportive and effective orientation. Studies of certain other researches have shown that traits associated with masculine personality are independence, assertiveness, aggression, power, smartness, rationality, stability and intelligence, while femininity is associated with traits like elegance, attractiveness, sociability, warmth, submissiveness and peacefulness (Sharma, 1979).

According to Sandra Bem (1974, 1981, 1984, 1987, 1993) sex-roles are the set of expectations defined by a particular society that indicate what is appropriate for men and women with certain sex specific personality attributes called masculine and feminine where masculinity is associated with instrumental (task) orientation and femininity with interpersonal orientation and they tend to behave in this likely manner in their daily life activities (Williams, 1982).

Starting from the moment of birth, with blue blankets for boys and pink ones for girls, most parents and other adults provide environments that differ in important respects according to gender. For example, the kinds of toys that are given to boys and girls vary, and father play more roughly with their infant sons than with their daughters. Even our nursery rhymes reflect these differences such as: "Sugars and spice and all things nice, that's what little girls are made of; Snips and snails and puppy dogs tails, that's what little boys are made of". Adults frequently treat children differently on the basis of their gender (Power, 1981; Eccles, Jacobs and Harold, 1990; Jacklin and Reynolds, 1993). Such differences in behaviour and there are many more, produce different socialization experiences for men and women. Socialization is the process by which an individual learns the rules and norms of appropriate behaviour i.e. boys and girls are taught and rewarded for performing behaviours that are perceived by society as being appropriate for men and for women respectively. According to Sandra Bem (1987, 1993) socialization produces a gender schema, a cognitive frame work that organizes and guides a person's understanding of information relevant to gender. On the basis of what their schemas are regarding what is or is not appropriate behaviour for a male or a female, children begin to behave in ways that reflect society's gender roles (Sears *et al.,* 1965).

It is not just parents, of course, who provide socialization experiences for children but, society as a whole communicates clear messages to children as they are growing up for example, children's reading books have traditionally potrayed girls in stereotypically nurturant roles, while the boys were most physical and action-oriented

(McDonald, 1989; Crabb and Pristash, 1992). Television too, acts as a particularly influential source of socialization. The potency of television as an agent of socialization is underscored by data indicating that the more television children watch, the more sexist they become (Morgan, 1982; Liebert and Sprafkin, 1988 and Carter, 1991).

Our conclusions about what is or is not an appropriate behaviour for others and ourselves are based on gender roles which are societal expectations about appropriate behaviour for women and men already stated above.

If men's and women's gender roles were equivalent they would have only minor impact upon our lives. However, expectations about men and women differ significantly, which in turn may result in favouritism toward members of one of the sexes. Gender roles may also produce stereotyping, judgements about individual members of a group based on their membership in that group.

People in every society hold particularly well-defined stereotypes about men and women and these prevail regardless of age, economic status and social and educational background. Men are more apt to be viewed as having traits involving competence, such as independence, objectivity and competitiveness. In contrast, women tend to be seen as having traits involving warmth and expressiveness, such as gentleness and awareness of other's feelings.

What's more, cross-cultural research finds remarkable similarity in the content of gender stereotypes in different societies. For example a twenty-five nation study identified a core set of descriptors that were consistently used to describe men and women (Williams and Best, 1990). Women were seen as sentimental, submissive and superstitious while men were seen as adventurous, forceful and independent (See Table 3a).

Descriptive Adjectives for men and women: The following items represent adjectives that were found to apply most to men or to women, respectively in atleast twenty of the twenty-five countries studied in the Williams and Best (1990) study.

Table 3(a): Descriptive Adjectives for men and women.

Items Associated with Males		*Items Associated with females*
Active	Lazy	Affected
Adventurous	Logical	Affectionate
Aggressive	Loud	Attractive
Ambitious	Masculine	Charming
Arrogant	Opportunistic	Curious
Assertive	Progressive	Dependent
Autocratic	Rational	Dreamy
Clear thinking	Realistic	Emotional
Coarse	Reckless	Fearful
Courageous	Robust	Feminine
Cruel	Rude	Gentle
Daring	Self-confident	Mild
Determined	Serious	Sensitive
Disorderly	Severe	Sentimental
Dominant	Stern	Sexy
Egotistical	Stolid	
Energetic	Strong	
Enterprising	Unemotional	
Forceful	Wise	
Hardheaded		
Hardhearted		
Independent		
Initiative		
Inventive		

Source: Adapted from Table 3.5, page 77, in Williams, J.E. and Best, D.L. (1990). Measuring sex stereotypes: A multidimensional Study. Newbury Park, C.A. Sage.

According to Bem Sex Role Inventory, (see Table 3b) following are the characteristics of the male and female stereotypes.

These stereotypes about men and women have proved to be remarkably enduring. Though the feminist movements' influence has been far reaching, gender stereotypes have shown little change (Martin, 1987; Bergin and Williams, 1991 and Alper, 1993).

Table 3(b): Characteristics of male and female stereotypes

Characteristics of male stereotype	*Characteristics of female stereotype*
Act as leader	Affectionate
Aggressive	Cheerful
Ambitious	Child like
Analytical	Compassionate
Assertive	Does not use harsh language
Athletic	Eager to soothe hurt feeling
Competitive	Feminine
Defends own beliefs	Flatterable
Dominant	Gentle
Forceful	Gullible
Has leadership abilities	Loves children
Independent	Loyal
Individualistic	Sensitive to the needs of others
Makes decision easily	Shy
Masculine	Soft spoken
Self reliant	Sympathetic
Self sufficient	Tender
Strong personality	Understanding
Willing to take a stand	Warm
Willing to take risks	Yielding

Source: Based on information in Bem, 1974.

Traditional Notions of Gender Identity

Traditionally, all societies generally hold unfavourable attitude towards the female members. It does not hold them in equally high regard and not evaluate them as favourably and positively as men. According to traditional nations of gender identity following traits are associated with males and females which are give in Table 4.

Gender roles (sex roles) are attitudes and activities that a culture links to each sex.

Sex is a biological distinction that develops prior to birth. Gender is the meaning that a society attaches to being male or female.

Further, Williams' (1982) analysis reveals that the male personality reflect high needs in autonomy, aggression and exhibition but low needs for deference and nurturance. By contrast female needs have been found to be strong in succorance (helpful) and abasement but weak in dominance. Bennet and Cohen (1959) summarized the nature of the differences under five general principles.

(1) Masculine thinking is a modification downward in intensity of feminine thinking.
(2) Masculine thinking is oriented more in terms of the self while feminine thinking is oriented more in terms of the environment.
(3) Masculine thinking anticipates reward and punishments determined more as a result of the adequacy or inadequacy of the self while feminine thinking anticipates rewards and punishments determined more as a result of the friendship or hostility of the environment.
(4) Masculine thinking is associated with the desire for social love and friendship.
(5) Masculine thinking finds value more in malevolent and hostile actions against a competitive society while feminine thinking finds value more in freedom from restraint in a friendly and unpleasant manner.

Table 4: Traditional Notions of Gender Identity.

Feminine Traits	*Masculine Traits*
Submissive	Dominant
Dependent	Independent
Unintelligent and Incapable	Intelligent and Competent
Emotional	Rational
Receptive	Assertive
Intuitive	Analytical
Weak	Strong
Timid	Brave
Content	Ambitious
Passive	Active
Cooperative	Competitive
Sensitive	Insensitive
Sex object	Sexually Aggressive
Attractive because of physical appearance	Attractive because of achievement

Source: Based on information in John J. Macionis, 1987.

It is commonly acknowledged that the male's role carries greater advantages. The female is infact punished for being a girl through being accorded a lower status and denied equal autonomy. Man's role carries with it greater opportunity. The consequence of the masculine role brings much ego satisfaction. The traditional male role in our culture is that of a wage earner and head of the family and traditional female adult sex-role in our culture is that of a mother and wife. She is supposed to be affectionate, sympathetic, understanding, compassionate, soft spoken, warm, tender etc. It is said that their role has certain advantages for instance, the girl is said to be secure from life's strain because she is sheltered as a child and upon marriage simply transfers her dependency from parent to husband. In actuality, females because of socialization learn dependence. And this leads to fear of success.

Fear of success is a psychological dimension which is a subsidiary product of cultural norms of sex-role appropriate conduct and is a natural consequence of the endemic condition of female life rooted in the contradictions of social structure and the pervasive ideology of female inferiority. It is a stable latent disposition acquired early in life as a part of sex-role socialization. Fear of success is also known as "success anxiety" i.e. the motive to avoid success (M-S) where the females lower their performance as a fear of deviance from sex-role standards and thus conform to socially accepted values absorbed in their minds in early years (Horner, 1968). Horner (1968) suggested that most women have disposition to become anxious about achieving success because they expect negative consequences such as social rejection and/or feeling of being unfeminine as a result of succeeding. Horner (1972, 1974) suggested that while men become unsexed by failure, women become unsexed by success. Condry and Dyer (1974) and Shapiro (1979) also suggested that fear of success may be conceptualized as a fear of deviance from sex-role standards. Sehgal (1990) and Kapila (1992) also found that female's achievement on variety of problem solving tasks get hampered due to fear of success that might threaten her femininity and results in social rejection as compared to their masculine counterparts. Mead (1949), observed that a female had too choices either she proclaimed herself as a woman and therefore, less on achieving individuality, or an achieving individual and therefore, less a woman. Miller (1976) says that female underlies her accomplishment so that she may not inflame the male's ego. Thus, females do poorly in most of the competitive tasks may it be education, job or any organization (Sharma and Malhotra, 2003). The effect of this is two fold that is feminine women and those coupled with women having success anxiety conform more. And alongwith androgynous women in particular consider the value of norms, also conform to the existing norms and impart them too.

Traditionally men were found to prefer instrumental values such as job security, risk taking, and high financial rewards, whereas women preferred the expressive and socially oriented values of true friendship and altruism (Buchholz, 1978; Herzog and Bachman, 1982; Maguire, Romaniuck and MacRury, 1982; Feather, 1984 and Maxwell and Cumming, 1988). In contrast, men, more than women, valued behaviour that was extrinsically motivated and resulted in material rewards (Deci and Ryan, 1985).

In the area of achievement motivation, theorists have suggested that since young women are largely preoccupied with their potentiality as child bearers and don't expect the same reward for their accomplishments as men, women might be expected to be less motivated to achieve than men.

The sex-roles are taught by the culture to the children at a very early age. Successful reassignment can be accomplished only if it occurs before the age of three or four (Hampson, 1965) and by nursery school age, normal children start behaving according to their assigned sex-roles, boys are aggressive both physically and mentally and restrict themselves to verbal and presocial forms of aggressions (Sears, 1965). Boys prefer blocks transportation, climbing where as girls prefer playing house, painting, dolls, clay and stories (Fagot and Patterson, 1969). Young children know that their parents want their sons and daughters to act differently. As children grow older, sex differences become even more pervasive. Males are more motivated toward achievement and power, females are more and more motivated toward affiliations and dependency. Men are more competitive, women are more cooperative (Oetzel, 1966). Whether a particular behaviour remains stable from childhood into adulthood actually depends on whether or not it is congruent with society's sex-role standards. Becoming "psychological" male or female is thus one of the major accomplishments of childhood. Gender stereotyping in self-concept leads persons to choose activities which are consistent with the self and to avoid activities which are inconsistent with it. By and large, however, stereotypes about females are more negative in content than those about males. For example, in many cultures, males are assumed to possess such desirable traits as decisiveness, forcefulness, confidence, ambition and rationality. In contrast the corresponding assumptions about females include less desirable traits such as passivity, submissiveness, indecisiveness, emotionality and dependence (Deaux, 1993; Unger, 1994). Alongwith race, gender has been over the past 30 years, and remain today, one of the most contested concepts. Gender is what one culture symbolizes and means by maleness and femaleness. These terms are further defined through the prescribed roles of men and women, boys and girls, husbands and wives. The physical characteristics of male and female bodies combined with their sexual and reproductive functions, carry strong symbolic meanings. Natural differences between males and females are perceived by many as an indisputable basis for assigning different gender roles.

Natural differences translate into inequitable power and opportunity for men and women, as seen in social, economic and political arenas. In other words, natural differences translate into differences in rank, power and prestige at home, at work, in churches, mosques or synagogues in school, and at play.

No doubt, meanings surrounding gender involve historical processes. Gender meanings are also the product of dominant structures reinforced by traditions, customs, and our dominant notions of common sense. A thorough understanding of gender is hindered without consideration of these factors. However, gender meanings are currently influx in our society.

At community High, for example, aggressive behaviour by boys toward girls has generated a provocate response from girls. Girls have regendered some of their social practices by adopting the aggressive language and posturing of boys as a defense against the boys (Cousins and Mabrey, 1998). Many of Tina's female peers have abandoned ascribed characteristics such as passivity, weakness and inactivity (lack of agency), which are part and parcel of the traditional meanings assigned to female gender roles (Ortner, 1996). One consequence, in school and beyond, is that those girls have been defined as unladylike and loud (Fordham, 1993). By contrast, the aggressiveness and loudness of boy have been defined as "boys being boys" being who they naturally are and doing what they naturally do as males. In the domain of sexual activity, strong traditions and entrenched frames of reference among school staff and some students still render the girls as the polluted or promiscuous participants in sexual liaisons. Underlying these gender relations are traditions and customs that have shaped how girls' and boys' bodies and activities are defined. Girls redefining themselves in response to environmental forces, however is a good example of praxis (Practice).

Signorrella and Janison (1986) tested the mediating effect of sex-role stereotypes on the relationship between gender and cognitive performance. They found that individuals of both sexes who viewed themselves in stereotypically masculine terms performed better on masculine tasks of mathematics and spatial perception than those who viewed themselves as feminine individuals (irrespective of the sex).

According to Kagan (1964) and Kohlberg (1966) the highly sex typed individual is motivated to keep his behaviour consistent with an internalized sex-role standard, a goal that might be presumably accomplished by suppressing any behaviour that might be considered undesirable or inappropriate for his sex. Thus, whereas a narrowly masculine self-concept might allow an individual to freely engage in both masculine and feminine behaviours. Even though males and females may be typed as masculine and feminine, it has recently been suggested that masculinity and femininity do not represent the bipolar ends of a single continuum, but instead are independent, uncorrelated dimensions (Constantinople, 1973; Bem, 1974; Berzins, 1975 and Spence et al., 1975). Thus, it is possible for persons of either gender to simultaneously endorse both masculine and feminine characteristics about themselves, i.e. psychological androgyny.

Bem (1974, 1975, 1976) conceives of androgynous person as adaptive, flexible and effective in particular interpersonal contexts. Accordingly, the androgynous person can be both instrumental (assertive, competent, forceful, independent) and expressive (nurturant, warm, supportive, compassionate), depending on the demands of the situation. Review of literature suggests that high level of sex-role development does not necessarily facilitate general psychological or social adjustment. Rather, it is now the androgynous person capable of incorporating both masculinity and femininity into his/her personality who is emerging as more appropriate sex-role ideal for contemporary society.

According to Maccoby (1966) greater intellectual development seems to be associated with cross-sex typing, i.e., with masculinity in girls and femininity in boys by showing a curvilinear relation between masculinity/femininity and intelligence. Sex typing can also produce defensive trait like consistency, whereas androgynous self-concept may enable a person to modify his behaviour to be effective in particular situation without worrying about his sex-role appropriateness (Bem, 1976). A more androgynous view has recently been found to be accompanied by greater maturity in one's moral judgement (Block, 1973) and by a higher level of self esteem (Spence et al., 1975). Androgynous individuals not only perform cross-sex behaviour with little reluctance or discomfort (Bem and Lenney, 1976), but furthermore, they display high levels of both 'masculine' independence and feminine nurturance when the situation seems to call for it (Bem, 1975).

For all androgyny advocates, the ideal man and ideal woman would display the best qualities of both sexes, that is, both greater instrumentality (dominance and agency) and greater expressivity (warmth and communion). The concept of androgynous individual is in accordance with changing society. Now a days both masculine and feminine activities are being made available to both sexes. Some people are androgynous because they are not subjected to strong stereotyped pressures.

Bem (1974, 1975) in an important series of articles challenged the literature that persons who adopt a conventional masculine or feminine role are somehow healthier. Bem argued that internalising culturally imposed, appropriate sex-role may inhibit the development of full and satisfying behavioural repertoire. By contrast, the androgynous individual who identifies with both desirable masculine and desirable feminine characteristics is free from such sex-role limitations and is able to move comfortably and effectively engage themselves in both masculine and feminine behaviour across variety of social situations.

Bem et al., (1976) and Bem (1977) concluded that feminine women have a narrow range of behavioural options than androgynous females who have a much broader range of behavioural options in terms of their attitudes and life choices.

Three important conclusions may be drawn from the foregoing discussion, (1) Since the level of expectation from both the sexes are different from a very early age hence the women do not strive for higher achievement because that does not seem to be in conformity with the assigned sex role, (2) Whosesoever, women have shown more independence i.e. higher traits of masculinity (Milton, 1957; 1959) they have been able to achieve at par with men, (3) The concept of psychological androgyny as put forth by Bem (1976) has clearly demonstrated that high traits of both masculinity and femininity that is sex-role that encompass traits thought typical of both sexes seems to be more efficacious in dealing with a situation than mere sex-typing in consonance with the sex-role of either masculinity or femininity.

According to the traditional model of sex-role orientation deviations from culturally sanctioned sex-role behaviour were considered maladaptive and undesirable (Kagan, 1964; Kohlberg, 1966 and Mussen, 1969). In the present society, the concept of androgynous individual is emerging as a sex-role ideal because now a days both masculine and feminine activities are being made available to both the sexes. According to Mead (1959) "men are behaving a little more like women and women are behaving little more like men, in short, both are behaving more like people." In short both have started incorporating each other's role. But androgynous individual who identified with both desirable masculine and desirable feminine characteristics is capable to engage more comfortably in both masculine and feminine behaviours across a variety of social situations. In number of studies (Bem, 1975; Bem and Lenney, 1976; Bem, Martyna and Watson 1976 and Sahoo, Rout and Rout, 1985) it was found that androgynous individuals were behviourally and emotionally more adaptable than rigidly sex-typed individuals because of their greater behavioural flexibility. Not only this, women classified as more androgynous showed overall adjustment and higher self-esteem than those classified as less androgynous. In general androgynous subjects show more adjustment than feminine subjects (Orlofsky and Windles, 1978).

The possibility that a single individual can embody a both masculinity and femininity has, of course, been expressed by Jung (1923), Gray (1957) and Baken (1966) also.

In nutshell, androgynous is good for e.g. compared to gender typed individual, androgynous men and women are found to be better liked, better adjusted and more adaptable to situational demands, more flexible in coping with stress, more comfortable with their sexuality, more satisfied interpersonally and in an elderly sample both are satisfied with their lives. Whereas, strong adherence to traditional gender role is often found to be associated with gender schemes and negative consequence for example men who identify the extreme masculine role behave more aggressively and not only this they often defy/thwart the norms set by the society than men who perceive themselves as having some feminine characteristics. Similarly females who are high on masculinity, i.e. who have more of masculine features and less of feminine characteristic behave like tomboys and thus violate the norms very often. Hence, it is the females and androgynous males who adhere to the norms. It is the females, the primary agents of socialization in the family who have strong faith in these values and norms and internalize the same. They do all religious work and hence pass all this to the next generation especially the females and it is due to these females that the society is functioning smoothly.

Thus, it can be inferred from the above discussion that females are socialized in such a way that they abide by the norms of the society whereas, males have casual disposition towards social norms.

C. CONCEPT OF PERSONALITY

The socialization practices are uniformally imparted in a blanket manner to the children by all the agencies in their respective cultures that also help them to grow as males and females.

But, besides the socialization agencies which are responsible for gender roles and learning of norms by the respective cultures – One significant factor which Eysenck emphasized is the personality disposition in terms of E/I differences. The E/I is genetically oriented and determined at birth.

The term personality is derived from the Latin word "persona" which means the mask worn by Roman actors. In this sense personality means the individual as seen by others.

There is the other sense of the term personality which includes the whole individual, his physique, temperament, skills, interest, hopes, feelings, habits, intelligence and achievement. It includes what he is today and what he hopes to be in the future. It includes the way in which he relates himself to other people. In a broadway, it may be said that personality is affected by three major factors (i) hereditary potential and primary characteristics of reactivity, (ii) the environmental situation in which a person has been brought up and in which he finds himself, and (iii) the subjective meanings and interpretations he gives to his experiences and the way in which he wants to shape them, in short, his aspirations.

Thus, personality is not a static concept but a dynamic concept which is changing constantly. It is the most distinctive feature of an individual. This is the overall integration of his structures, modes of behaviour, interests, attitudes, aptitudes and many other distinguishable characteristics. Thus, the personality refers to the whole individual. It is an important variable in most behavioural responses, and study of human behaviour is incomplete without the variable of personality. Personality of each one is unique; each individual has a unique personality. Though the children are brought up by the same parents in one house, there is variation in heredity, in experience and in ideals; not even the identical twins have the same personality.

Personality has dozens of meanings: popular, legal, grammatical, ethical, religious, economic and psychological (Allport, 1937). At the core of all these different meanings however, common feeling is: a person is both unique and important. Thus, the word gives direction and energy to the vague human desire for individuality. In psychology, the field of personality is concerned not only with the total individual but also with individual differences.

In the common man's language the term personality is used in many ways. For example, consider such statements as 'Raju has a good personality, Ashish has a poor personality' and 'Pankaj has no personality' may refer to attractiveness or handsomeness of appearance. The phrase a 'poor personality' may indicate that the person has certain characteristics which are not considered to be good. The term 'no personality' may indicate that the person does not make an impact on others. But these statements are based on superficial observations and evaluation of people and do not represent a scientific interpretation of the term personality. The term personality refers to physical, mental, social and emotional characteristics of a person and their integration into a behavioural pattern which is characteristic of the individual. Personality, thus, has many components or dimensions and is affected by heredity, learning, motivation, emotion, intelligence, perception, thinking, creativity and many other factors that make an individual what he is at any particular moment. There are various definitions of personality given by various psychologists which may be grouped according to whether they lay emphasis on superficial outer observable objective appearance or whether they stress on the inner subjective essentials.

Kempf (1919) has defined personality as "the habitual mode of adjustment which the organism reflects between its own egocentric drives, and the exigencies of the environment. As phrased, this would include practically all of human behaviour since the vast majority of our responses do consist of such habitual ways of thinking.

Prince (1924) defined personality as the sum total of all the biological innate dispositions, impulses, tendencies, appetites and instincts of the individual, and the acquire disposition and tendencies. This definition emphasizes subjective aspect of personality.

Warren and Heist (1966) defined personality as "the entire mental organization of a human being at any stage of his development." In this definition, an attempt has been made to treat the physical structure and psychological traits as two separate units.

J.F. Dashiell (1939) has defined personality as "His (man's) system of reaction possibilities as viewed by fellow members of the society. It is the sum total of the behaviour traits manifested in his social adjustments." This definition shows that personality is the way of the reactions and the behaviour. It does not treat the personality as important and composite but in this definition, the factors of the environment that do not form part of the personality have also been included. According to Kimball Young (1930), "personality is the more or less integrated body of habits, traits, attitudes and ideas of an individual as these are organized externally into specific and general roles and as they relate internally to earned self consciousness and the concept of the self and earned the ideas, values and purposes, which are related to roles, motives and status.

Allport (1937) states that "personality traits may be considered as so many important dimensions in which people may be found to differ." This seems too inconclusive, for example: it includes physical dimensions, which are only indirectly of importance for personality. Watson (1924) has called attention to the fact that character is a part of personality. He says "personality includes not only these (character-conventional) reactions, but also the more individual personal adjustments and capacities as well as their life history." In 1925 Watson decreed that personality is but the outcome of our habits.

Symonds (1928) has defined personality as "the portrait or landscape of the organism working together in all its phase" and May (1929) speaks of "the social stimulus values of the individual." Later Allport defined (1937) personality as "the dynamic organization with in the individual of those psychophysical systems that determine his unique adjustments to his environment. The term dynamic in the definition of personality indicates that the different characteristics of a person interact with and modify one another. It also points out that changes can occur in the way a person behaves in a situation. The word 'organization' implies that personality is made up of a number of different traits, each one of them closely related to the other. The relationships between traits often undergo changes, with certain traits becoming more dominant than others because of changes in the individual and in his environment. The term psychophysical implies that personality has both mental and physical elements. The psychophysical system include the habits, attitudes, values, emotional states, and motives of a person which are psychological in nature but have a physical basis in the neural glandular and general bodily states of an individual. Guthrie (1944) has defined personality as "those habits and habit systems of social importance that are stable and resistant to change." According to Cattell, (1950), personality is that which permit a prediction of what a person will do in a given situation.

Personality is the most adequate conceptualization of a persons behaviour in all its detail (McClelland, 1951). Guilford (1959) defined personality as a person's unique pattern of traits. According to Eysenck (1960) personality is more or less enduring organization of a person's character, temperament, intellect, physique which determine his unique adjustment to the environment. According to Allport (1961), personality is the dynamic organization within the individual of those psychophysical systems that determine his characteristic behaviour and thought. Personality is used to mean the configuration of individual characteristics and ways of behaving which determines individuals unique adjustment to his environment. Hence, personality includes any characteristics, that is important in the maintenance of self respect (Hilgard, 1962). Eysenck (1965) states that there is some agreement that personality refers to some enduring disposition in the constitution of individuals and that it is the basic reality underlying individual differences in behaviour. Eysenck's dimensional approach has ushered a new era in the psychological arena of experimental research in personality. According to Mischell (1976), Personality usually refers to the distinctive patterns of behaviour (including thoughts and emotions) that characterize each individuals adaptation to the situations of his or her life. According to Klienmuntz (1967), Personality refers to unique organization of traits characterizing an individual and influencing his interaction with his environment, social and non-social.

According to Brody (1972), the study of personality rests ultimately on the fact of individual differences. The true search for the understanding of individual differences, temperamental peculiarities and other deviations from the strictly average behaviour i.e. personality can in the real sense said to have a beginning with Hippocrates and Galen. They identified four major temperamental types on the basis of humors: melancholic, choleric, sanguine and phlegmatic. These four types are supposed to be responsible for difference in behaviour. Their physiological theory is now regarded somewhat quaint, but the descriptive system is still used which has given birth to modern personality theory. However, most agree that personality includes the behaviour patterns a person shows across situations or the psychological characteristics of the person that lead to those behaviour patterns.

Personality has been defined and studied in a number of different ways. Some have developed broad theories to explain the origins and makeup of personality. Others have focused only on one or two issues, such as the influence of heredity on personality.

The first approach i.e. theory construction, was popular for many years. As a result, we have many broad personality theories. Most of these broad theories can be grouped into four categories.

(i) Type and Trait Approaches: Which focus on people's characteristics—stubbornness, shyness and so forth—and how these characteristics are organized into systems. They emphasize the dimensions and organization of personality.

***(ii) Dynamic Approaches*:** Which emphasizes ongoing interactions among motives, impulses and psychological processes. They emphasize motivational factors and the lively interplay of various components of personality.

***(iii) Learning and Behavioural Approach*:** Which emphasize the ways the habits are acquired through basic conditioning or learning processes.

***(iv) Humanistic Approaches*:** Which emphasize the self and the importance of the individual's subjective view of the world. These various viewpoints are that of Watson, Allport, Cattell, McClelland, Murray, Maslow, Spence, Taylor and Guilford. They have tried to provide different frameworks of personality in order to explain behaviour which has led to a lot of disagreement regarding the structure of human personality.

Until the 1950s, new born babies were considered to be a psychological 'blank slate'. Today personality is seen to be atleast partly biologically determined. The biological approach claims that individual inherit psychological characteristics in much the same way that inherent physical characteristics. One of the leading proponents of this view was Hans Eysenck.

However, an Eysenck's personality model in terms of extraversion/introversion has been used to see the development of norms and the performance differences among different personality groups i.e. introverts and extraverts vis-à-vis Sherif's autokinesis, Asch's visual line drawing test, serial learning and anagrams of problem-solving tasks. It would be in the fitness of things to give a conceptual framework and review of studies.

Hans Eysenck (1916-1997) proposed a hierarchical structure of personality. Unlike earlier trait theorists, Eysenck claimed that there are just three and not five 'super traits'.

***(1) Extraversion*:** According to Eysenck, the extravert is typically sociable, enjoys parties, has many friends, needs to have people to talk to, does not like reading or being alone. This clearly parallels the 'big five' definition of Extraversion (Eysenck, 1957).

***(2) Neuroticism*:** Neurotics are typically seen as excitable, aggressive, depressive and emotionally sensitive/over-responsive.

(3) Psychoticism: Psychotics are typically egocentric, aggressive, impersonal, cold, impulsive and lacking in empathy and/ or concern for other people.

Eysenck's Hierarchical Structure of Personality

Eysenck proposed a hierarchical model to explain his three-factor model. This comprised four levels of behaviour trait relationship which differed according to specificity and/or regularity (Eysenck, 1992) (See Figure 31).

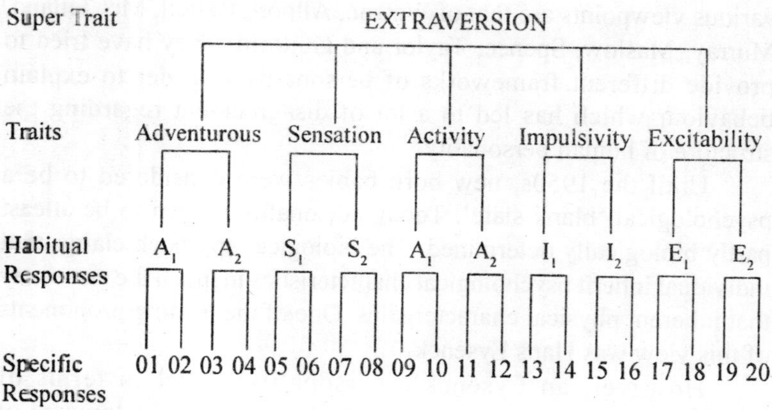

Figure 31: Eysenck's Hierarchical Structure of Personality

(1) Specific Responses: Lowest level relates numerous pieces of behaviour that are specific to a given time and setting e.g. man goes on adventure weekend in wales, or reading in a bus.

(2) Habitual Response: Next level relates to habitual responses which are typical ways of behaving or behaviour that is repeated over time in different places e.g. man goes on several adventure weekends.

(3) Trait: At the third level lie the traits that explain the habitual responses for example 'sociability' includes the habitual responses of 'going to parties' and taking part in team games. Behaviour that is repeated over different settings e.g. man enjoys not only adventure weekends but also dangerous sports such as sky diving, mountaineering, deep sea, diving and murder mystery weekends. These behaviours suggest a high score on the trait 'adventurousness'.

(4) Super Trait: At the top of the hierarchy is the type level/ super trait that tend to be highly inter correlated e.g. adventurousness correlates positively with sensation seeking, activity, impulsivity and excitability. These correlations suggest a high score on the super-trait 'extroversion'.

A Review of Eysenck's Personality Theory

The personality theory as forwarded by Eysenck (1947) and as it stands now (Eysenck, 1952, 1957, 1960a and b, 1963a and b, 1966a and b, 1971, 1981, 1985) has undergone a lot of modification to reach its present status. To begin with Sigal *et al.* (1958a and b) Hamilton (1959), Foulds (1961) and Bannister (1977) created much doubt regarding—Eysenck's theory of personality in general, and the way it has been validated especially the criterion analysis in particular. But the theory has passed through the ordeal of time and criticism through great experimental evidence which has accumulated with the passage of time and has strongly supported and approved his concept of personality. Eysenck has given a dimensional approach to personality with descriptions at two levels. The major dimension being Extraversion-Introversion (E/I), Stability-Neuroticism (S/N), Psychoticsm and Intelligence. These four dimensions were the resultant of hypothetico-deductive techniques and elaborate factor analyses (Eysenck, 1956a and b, Eysenck and Eysenck, 1963a and b). Apart from Intelligence, Extraversion/Introversion and Neutroticism have been found to relate mostly to learning and performance. These two dimensions are independent of each other (Eysenck, 1947, 1952, 1957; Madan, 1967; Child, 1964; Bull and Strongman, 1971; Mohan and Kumar, 1973).

Similar to Eysenck's Extraversion and Neuroticism, Cattell (1956) and Guilford (1934, 1959), extracted factors which closely resemble them. On the other side, Taylor's (1953) Manifest Anxiety has been found to correlate highly with Neuroticism (Bending, 1957 and Eysenck 1963). The mutual independence of Neuroticism and Extraversion has been reviewed and supported by Carrigan (1960). Eysenck contends that these two factors contribute to the description of personality more than any other set of factors in the non-cognitive field. As regards the study of Extraversion/Introversion and Neuroticism, Eysenck (1964) believes that it can be analyzed at the two levels i.e. causative and descriptive.

Extraversion/Introversion

Although the term Introversion and Extraversion are today often associated with the name of the Swiss Psychiatrist C.G. Jung, they may be found in the earliest English dictionaries. Dr. Johnson's dictionary, published in 1755 used the term in a physical sense, but by the late 19th century they were defined in ways very similar to current usage. Extraversion was described as a "turning outward of mind" on to people and objects in the external world; introversion as "inner directedness", a preference for abstract ideas rather than concrete objects. Today, the scope of these terms is rather broader; Extraversion also refers to impulsive, sociable tendencies, and introversion implies controlled and responsible behaviour.

The following Figure (Fig. 32) shows how these two major dimensions of personality relate to the Greek typology. The advantage of the dimensional system over the categorical system is that an individual can be described more flexible by assigning him a point anywhere within the space formed by the two factors. Most people congregate in the middle range on these dimensions with fewer number falling toward the extremes.

Eysenck describes the dimensions of Extraversion as measured by the Eysenck Personality Inventory as follows:

High E Scores are indicative of Extraversion on the descriptive side. High scoring individuals tend to be outgoing, impulsive, and uninhibited having many social contacts and frequently taking part in group activities. Eysenck (1957, 1967) deduced the concept of E/I from nosologicial categories based on Jung's (1923) views and supported by Hilderbrand's study (1958). According to Eysenck and Eysenck (1968), 'the typical extravert is sociable, likes parties, has many friends, needs to have people to talk to, and does not like reading or studying by himself. He craves excitement, takes chances, often sticks his neck out, acts on the spur of the moment and is generally an impulsive individual. He is fond of practical jokes, always has a ready

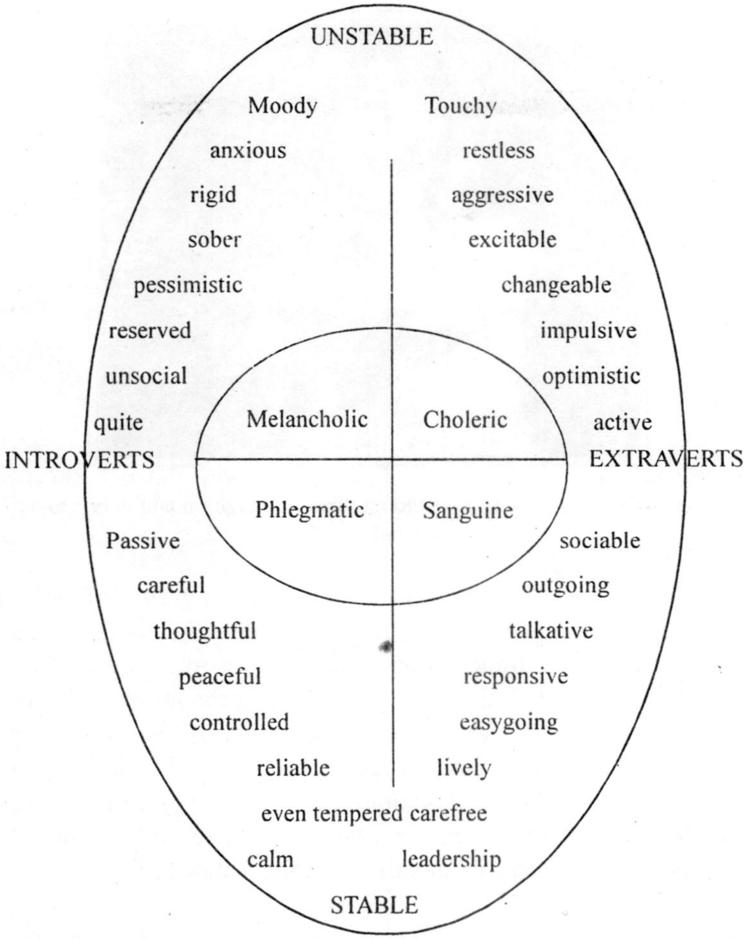

Figure 32: Two major dimensions of personality revealed by Factor Analysis compared with the 4 Greek categories (from Eysenck, 1967).

answer and generally likes change. He is carefree, easygoing, optimistic, and likes to "laugh and be merry" (see Figure 33). He prefers to keep moving and doing things, tends to be aggressive and to lose his temper quickly. His feelings are not kept under tight control and he is not always a reliable person.

Figure 33: An extravert is outgoing, likes stimulation and likes to be around people.

The typical introvert is a quiet, retiring sort of person, introspective, fond of books rather than people; he is reserved and distant except to intimate friends. He tends to plan ahead, "looks before he leaps", and distrusts the impulse of the moment. He does not like excitement, takes matters of everyday life with proper seriousness and likes a well-ordered mode of life. He keeps his feelings under close control, seldom behaves in an aggressive manner, and does not lose his temper easily. He is reliable, somewhat pessimistic, and places great value on ethical standards.

The Excitation Inhibition Theory of Introversion and Extraversion

On the causative side, Eysenck has attempted to relate individual differences in Introversion-Extraversion to hypothetical inherited differences in the functioning of the nervous system. For this purpose, Eysenck refers to the Pavlovian concepts of excitation and inhibition (Pavlov, 1927) balance of Central Nervous System (CNS), Hull's concept of reactive inhibition (Ir) and Gray's (1965) level of arousal. In his review of personality, Eysenck (1963a and b) gave evidence that difference in individuals on E/I were deeply embedded in the constitution of the individuals, especially in the ascending reticular formation of the central nervous system. Eysenck initially traced this differentiation in individuals to Pavlov's experiment with dogs, who found that not all dogs condition alike. There were some dogs in whom the excitation was quicker, built up of inhibition slower and as such they could be conditioned better.

Eysenck (1955a and b) extended Pavlovian views to be the Jungian typology of Extraversion/Introversion. For doing this he took the help of Hullian concept of reactive inhibition based on Hull's (1943) first submolar principle "all responses leave in the physical structure a state which acts directly to inhibit the evocation of activity—this inhibitory substance manifest itself through reactive potentials. This negative action is called Reactive Inhibition (Ir) an increment of which is assumed to be generated by every repetition of the response whether reinforced or not and these increments are assumed to accumulate except as they spontaneously disintegrate with passage of time."

Eysenck (1957) has tried to derive most of the known differences between introverts and extraverts by the excitation inhibition theory. He states his fundamental assumptions as follows:

Individuals in whom excitatory potentials is generated slowly and in whom excitatory potentials so generated are relatively weak, are thereby predisposed to develop extraverted patterns of behaviour and to develop hysterical-psychopathic disorders in the case of neurotic breakdown; individuals in whom excitatory potential is generated quickly and in whom excitatory potentials so generated are strong, are thereby predisposed to develop introverted patterns of behaviour and to develop dysthymic disorders in case of nervous breakdown. Eysenck postulates the existence of a ratio of inhibition to excitation (I/E). The value of this ratio is relatively low for introverts and relatively high for extraverts. Excitation is relatively a straight forward concept. It refers to the neural processes upon which the development of learned associations between stimulus and responses depend. Thus, all other things being equal, individuals with strong excitation potentials would be more able to form learned connections between stimuli and responses than individuals in whom excitatory potentials are weak. Inhibition is rather a more complicated concept. The term reactive inhibition comes from Hull (1943). Eysenck's conception of inhibition involves a modification of views held by Hull and Paolov. Reactive inhibition may be conceived of as fatigue like neural state which occurs as a inevitable consequence of any excitatory process.

There is another important feature of Eysenck's physiological theory. Eysenck (1967) relates his conception of the physiological differences between introverts and extraverts to a distinction used by Russian Researchers especially Sokolov (1963) and Teplov (1963) of the organisms with "weak" nervous system (Gray, 1965). Soviet work on the dimensions of personality known as the "strength of the nervous system" and "equilibrium in dynamism" is compared with the Western work of Introversion-Extraversion, in the light of suggestions that each of these dimension is related to level of arousal (Gray, 1967). Organisms with "weak" nervous system are assumed to respond at lower levels of stimulation and are assumed to respond with greater intensity to stimuli than organisms with 'strong' nervous system. However, the weak nervous system as a result of its extreme reactivity is more subject to protective or transmarginal inhibition than the strong nervous system. The concept of protective or transmarginal inhibition implied that when the levels of excitation are reached which are above some optimal value, inhibition occurs, which serves to decrease such excitation. Eysenck (1967) believes that introverts are more subject to transmarginal inhibition than extraverts. Eysenck's theory thus assumes some upper level of arousal which is reached at lower level of stimulus intensity by introverts than by extraverts. Once this level is reached, new inhibitory processes occur which reduce excitation. As a result of the operation of this form of inhibition it is possible that at high levels of stimulus intensity, cortical arousal should be lower for introverts than for extraverts.

Eysenck (1970) also believed Ascending Reticular Activating System (ARAS) to be responsible for producing arousal under identical stimulating conditions which is higher for introverts than in extraverts, hence behavioural and experimental predictions are forwarded on the basis of differences in degree of arousal rather than in degree of reactive inhibition.

Eysenck's (1967) Base-Rate Arousal Model/Theory of Introversion and Extraversion (The Physiological Basis of Personality)

The most highly developed theory of Extraversion is that of Eysenck (1967). Eysenck developed his three-factor model by suggesting that each 'super trait' has a biological basis. Specifically, individual differences in each factor reflected individual differences in ***base-rate levels of cerebral cortex arousal*** (See Fig. 34).

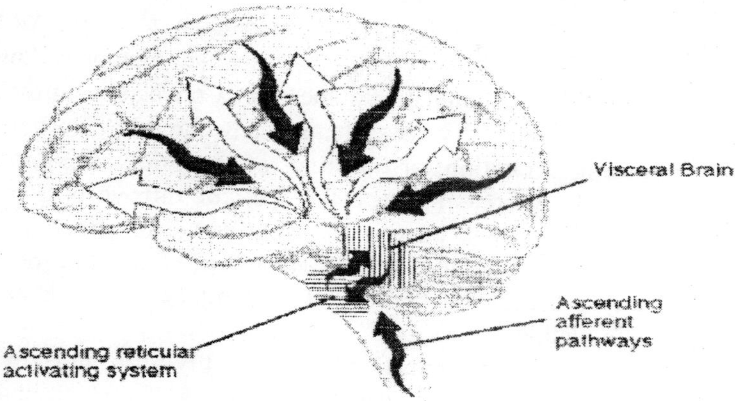

Figure 34: Showing the ARAS.

(1) Extraversion: Extraverts have low base rate level of arousal and so need external stimulation to boost levels i.e. to maintain an optimum cerebral activity level (Fordham, 1991 and Hayes, 1994). Introverts in contrast, have high base rate of cortex arousal and so avoid further external stimulation as would lead to over stimulation. Cortical arousal is controlled/mediated by activity in a particular part of the brain—the ascending reticular activating system (ARAS) which is easily activated in introverts, but responds more slowly in extraverts as illustrated in Figure 34.

The figure shows that the incoming (ascending) afferent pathways take messages to the receptor areas in the brain, but collaterals also go to the ARAS, which in turn sends out messages to the neo-cortex to keep it in a state of arousal, ready to deal with the incoming messages. There is also a reciprocal flow of information from the neocortex to the ARAS, informing it that the messages, say are repetitive, and do not require a high state of arousal, thus shutting down the ARAS. Also included in the diagram is the visceral brain or limbic system, which governs the expression of emotions, and is causally related to neuroticism. The two systems are relatively independent, but as indicated by the arrows, in a high state of limbic system activation, the ARAS is also affected; clearly it would be impossible to have strong feelings of fear or anger and also a low state of cortical arousal. Extraverts have 'strong' nervous system—the ARAS is biased to inhibit neural impulses which 'dampens down' the effects of stimulation of the brain. Conversely, introverts have 'weak' nervous systems where the ARAS provides strong excitation, or boosting, of incoming stimulation, thereby increasing its effect i.e. for introverts a little stimulation will have a relatively powerful effect, while extraverts may need a large amount of stimulation before any effect is felt hence—their tendency to seek extra stimulation.

(2) **Neuroticism:** Neurotics have a highly arousable, over-reactive autonomous nervous system (ANS) which makes them highly responsive to stress. The sympathetic division of the ANS is active when emotion is felt and it controls bodily changes associated with strong emotional reactions (e.g., increased pulse and heart rate, sweating, churning stomach). In neurotics, the ANS reacts more quickly and strongly to stimulation causing them more readily to experience anxiety than their stable counterparts.

Psychoticism: There is no place for psychoticism within the base-rate arousal model (Eysenck, 1967) but psychotics are typically egocentric, aggressive, impersonal, cold, impulsive and lacking in empathy or concern for other people.

He believes that differences between extraverts and introverts are due to individual differences in the functioning of the reticular activating system. This structure in the brain stem is thought by neurophysiologists to be responsible for producing non-specific arousal in the cerebral cortex in response to external stimulation, and Eysenck hypothesizes that introverts are more highly aroused than extraverts given the same conditions of stimulation. Paradoxically, this results in the introverts showing more restrained or "inhibited" behaviour because the cortex is exercising control over the more primitive, impulsive, lower brain centers. The arousal concept is thought to explain most of the differences between extraverts and introverts, that have been observed in the laboratory and real life for example, introverts are supposed to acquire conditioned responses more readily than extraverts because their higher arousal facilitates the formation of connections. The difference in conditionability in turn accounts for the different types of abnormal behaviours to which introverts and extraverts are prone. The most direct way of testing the notion that introverts are higher in arousal than extraverts would seem to be to examine EEG's (brain waves) of the two personality groups. The EEG consists of moment to moment fluctuations in voltage across two points on the scalp—1000 amplitude and high frequency is believed to reflect high arousal.

Gray (1970a and b), has tried to elaborate Eysenck's stand (1957, 1967) on the theory of personality with the more localized function. This theory is concerned both with physiological and psychological nature of Extraversion, although the evidence supporting his contention comes from animal physiology. Gray 1971 offers a more elaborate system "consisting of ARAS together with orbital frontal cortex, medial septal area and hippocampal system which determines the degree of introversion. This system is able to carry out the essential psychological function believed by Eysenck to underlie introversion/extraversion. The more sensitive or active this system is, the more introverted will the individual be."

While outlining the role played by the septal area and the hippocampus, Gray (1971) has stressed that hippocampus displays a theta rythm at times as a result of neural input from the medial septal area. But there is good evidence that (Stumpf, 1965) the pacemaker cells in the medial septal area act to produce a theta rythm as a result of neural input received from the midbrain reticular formation. As a voltage of the stimulating current applied to the midbrain reticular formation is gradually increased, a theta rythm first appears in the hippocampus and then increases in frequency, until the same limiting stimulus voltage, the theta rythm is replaced by a fast, low voltage, desynchronized hippocampal. EEG (Stumpf, 1965). As well as with this reticular septal-hippocampal circuit, there is a hippocampal-reticular formation connection, which is evidently of an inhibitory nature. As shown by Adey, Segundo and Livingston (1957) stimulus of the hippocampus causes an upstream conduction from the midbrain reticular formation to be thalamic portion of the ARAS; and this inhibition is disrupted by small doses of barbiturates, indicating the likelihood that it is normally exercised at times when the hippocampus displays a theta rythm. Thus, there is every reason to suppose that the ARAS and the septo hippocampal system whose operation is indicated by a theta rythm are coupled together to form a negative feedback loop. That is to say an increased activity in the ARAS results in an increase in hippocampal activity and one result of this increased hippocampal activity is to inhibit any further increase in the activity of the ARAS. In this way for a given sensory input and under given conditions, a temporary equilibrium between reticular activation and hippocampal is reached.

Gray (1971, 1972) has overemphasized inhibition while almost neglecting excitation and arousal, whereas, Eysenck has put forward the view that on the basis of experimental evidence and EEG studies extraverts are characterized by low, and introverts by higher states of cortical arousal. These differences might be caused in turn by differential threshold levels in the reticular formation whose main function is control of arousal and inhibition level in the cortex. He also makes the assumption that individual differences on the threshold level of arousal of visceral brain were responsible for phenotypic differences in E/I. The dual nature of interaction in the cortex also gains support from neuroanatomical studies (Rhine and Magoun, 1946, 1947; Sprague, 1953; Sprague and Chambers, 1954; Grossman, 1967) which reveal excitation as not separate entities, but go hand in hand to determine differences in human behaviour. Gray's hypothesis regarding the physiological explanation of E/I emanates from electrophysiological studies. The set of interactions between the ARAS and he frontal cortex-septohippocampal system described by Gray is remarkably similar to the psychological relationship which Eysenck (1957) has already postulated as lying at the root of the dimension of Extraversion/Introversion (E/I).

Eysenck (1955, 1957) has emphasized time and again that learning and performance are related to each other because of individual difference in consolidation of the learned responses. Eysenck (1966a) proposed a consolidation theory according to which performance sets up cortical events which in order to become available to organisms, require rest for consolidation. He also postulated that consolidation interferes with performance, along the lines of Walker's theory (1958). Walker (1958) has suggested that cortical arousal is related to strong consolidation and Eysenck has argued that introverts are characterized by higher level of arousability than extraverts (Eysenck, 1962a, b, 1963a, b, 1964, 1966a, b and c, 1967, 1971). For the poor consolidation of extraverts, it can be argued that the cortical arousal might be playing an important role. To substantiate this, EEG studies have provided evidence that there is a lower level of cortical arousal in extraverts (Gale, Coles and Blaydon, 1969 and Shagaas and Canter, 1971). On the basis of EEG studies, Eysenck concluded that introverts typically have low alpha amplitude and high alpha frequency while extraverts typically have high alpha amplitude and low alpha frequency. These are the EEG characteristics respectively of high and low arousal groups (Eysenck, 1970).

The relationship of Extraversion in relation to performance with conditioning, reminiscence, acquisition of efficiency and KR, academic attainment and intelligence like problem solving tasks has often been explored. The relationship of Extraversion to that of socialization and criminal behaviour and antisocial behaviour has also been explored. But Extraversion and development of Social norms should be empirically tested because no such studies have been conducted in this area. So it would be relevant to observe the relationship of said factors in Extraversion within the Eysenckian framework of inhibition excitation balance and level of arousability.

Franks (1954) conducted an experiment on eyeblink conditioning with matched groups of hysterics, dysthymics and normals and found that dysthemics condition better and more quickly than hysterics. This finding by no means left the other exponent of Hullian theory quiet who emphasized the role of Drive in conditioning. Spence and his colleagues (Spence, 1956, 1958, 1964; Spence and Beecroft, 1954; Spence and Taylor, 1951, 1953; and Taylor, 1951) working within the Hullian framework emphasized that response strength (R) in conditioning is a function of Drive and this total Drive is a part of level of internal anxiety of the subject. Franks (1956) conducted another experiment with PGR and eyeblink conditioning and found conditionability to be related to Introversion/Extraversion and not to Neuroticism. Franks (1956) explained the results of Iowa group on the ground that in a mixed group of neurotics the predominance of dysthymics can easily distort the results. Eysenck (1956b) has pointed out that the studies which compared the effects of Introversion/ Extraversion and Neuroticism, used sometimes a UCS which was strong enough to evoke anxiety and as such distorted the results in favour of anxiety hypothesis. Madan (1967) has at length explained this apparent diversity of results in the following manner:

"The crucial experiments conducted by Field and Branglemann (1961) with eyeblink conditioning, Vogel (1961) with measures of CSR conditioning, Quay and Hunt (1965) with conditioning were related to Introversion/Extraversion and not to Neuroticism. Bending (1957), Eysenck (1963a) and Child (1964) found that Anxiety is not only related to Neuroticism positively but also significantly negatively with Extraversion. This implies that individuals with high score on Extraversion will have less of anxiety, whereas, those low on Extraversion will have high anxiety. Eysenck (1963b) too maintains that anxiety is a conditioned fear and since introverts are more conditionable, they would show more of anxiety. Thus, more introverted subjects who condition better would at the same time be scoring high on Anxiety who according to Spence-Taylor hypothesis should also condition better.

Coming down to the relationship of Introversion/Extraversion to conditioning some studies have reported that extraverts condition better than introverts. According to Brody (1972) "Levey found that introverts showed more rapid conditioning than extraverts under partial reinforcement conditions. Extraverts showed more rapid conditioning than introverts under total (100%) reinforcement conditions. Levey reported that under both short CS-UCS interval and low UCS intensity, introverts condition more rapidly, whereas, under both long CS-UCS interval and high UCS intensity, extraverts condition more rapidly. Eysenck (1966b, 1967) argues that these findings are predicted by his theory and are in no way contradictory to his theory, Eysenck (1965)." Thus, Eysenck (1970) explains the differences between introverts and extraverts in conditioning in terms of the differential build up of reactive inhibition, though he mentions the possibility that the differences might also be due to differences in excitatory potential. Reactive inhibition is conceptualized as a kind of "neural or cortical fatigue" which acts as a—negative drive and subtracts from the positive drive under which the organism is working.

The relationship of Extraversion with reminiscence has been an established one. Eysenck (1967) proposes that extraverts should have higher reminiscence score on pursuit rotor learning tasks and was supported by Staats (1957), Claridge (1960), Lynn (1960a and b), and Meier (1961), Feldman (1964a and b), whereas, Ray (1959), Rechtscaffen (1958) and Becker (1960) provide contrary evidence derived from experiments done with faulty designs" (Kumar, 1974). But later it was found that many other facts were difficult to reconcile with an inhibition theory of reminiscence for pursuit rotor learning (Eysenck, 1965). According to the consolidation theory of Eysenck (1966a) argues that organisms require rest for consolidation and during the state of rest the extraverts dissipate the accumulated Ir.

In learning situations the effect of Introversion/Extraversion on the acquisition of efficiency with Knowledge of Results has been invested in many studies. Mohan and Deol (1970) using time estimation, Mohan and Gupta using weight estimation found that Introverts were performing insignificantly better than extraverts. Mohan and Kumar (1973) studied the effect of Introversion/ Extraversion on performance of 'Backward Alphabet Writing' when 100 per cent Knowledge of Results was administered. The results of the study showed that introverts were superior to extraverts from the beginning to end, but on time taken only in the beginning extraverts were superior but later on introverts were significantly superior. The result of the study can be attributed to Madan (1967) who in the review of Eysenckian personality theory had experimentally substantiated that the introverts opt for accuracy over speed.

Relation of Extraversion/Introversion to Intelligence, Educational Attainment and Problem Solving.

Sufficient evidence has shown that academic attainment, problem solving and intelligence are related positively to Introversion.

Two individuals may possess the same native ability, yet one may set up very high standard of expectations out of himself and another may set up very low one. This setting of goals has been called the level of aspiration (Lewin, Dembo, Festinger and Sears, 1944). A parallel phenomena is the achievement oriented behaviour called achievement motivation or need for achievement (Atkinson and

Feather 1966). Both act as a motivating force to put in more effort in performing a task. Eysenck (1957, 1960a and b) and Lynn, (1962) have deduced that introverts condition better due to which they would show a greater degree of socialization as they learn the social norms and expectations faster. An expectation may follow that since the introverts are more socially aware, they would be having a higher level of aspiration (Eysenck, 1947) and be high on achievement motivation (Eysenck, 1962). This was earlier borne out by Eysenck and Himmelweit (1946) when they found that the dysthymic subjects had definitely a much higher level of aspiration giving rise to a much greater goal discrepancy score (GDS) than the hysteric subjects. Broadbent (1958) reported that level of aspiration was positively related to Introversion.

Lowell (1952) found that individuals high on achievement motivation showed a higher level of performance on both arithmetic and verbal task than persons low on achievement motivation. Atkinson and Litwin (1960) also found similar results. Hence the deduction may be permitted that introverts being high on achievement motivation and on level of aspiration, will show better performance in educational tasks than the extraverts. This setting of higher goal for a prolonged period of time is essential in any long-term programme of academic achievement.

Sufficient evidence has shown that academic attainment is positively related to introversion. Himmelweit (1946) found that hysterics (Extraverts) have a bad vocabulary in relation to their intelligence. Broadbent (1958) and Furneaux (1956) observed that students who do well in the University examination have a lower score in Extraversion. Lynn (1960b) and Lynn and Gordon (1961) found that university students were more introverted and there was positive relationship between Introversion, persistence and vocabulary. Child (1964, 1966) too detected that promoted children were more introverted than demoted ones significantly. Madan (1967) has demonstrated that introverts perform better on both vocabulary and educational attainment in the age group of 20 to 25 years.

Overall, extraverts and introverts do not differ in intelligence. However, recent work has shown that performance on cognitive tasks such as those found in IQ tests may be broken down into at least three independent components: speed, accuracy, and persistence. When this is done, extraverts are found to be faster but less accurate and less persistent than introverts (e.g. Brierley, 1961). The extraverts are also inclined to start well but slip back progressively relative to introverts. An illustrative study is that of Mohan and Kumar (1976) who conducted a detailed analysis of the performance of introverts and extraverts on the Standard Progressive Matrices IQ test. The performance of 100 students, balanced for sex was examined in terms of items done correctly, wrongly, abandoned and not attempted. These four outcomes were related to the difficulty level of the problems and time spent on the test. As expected, the extraverts began with an edge over the introverts but showed a greater deterioration in performance, thus allowing the introverts to draw ahead by the end of the test (See Fig. 35).

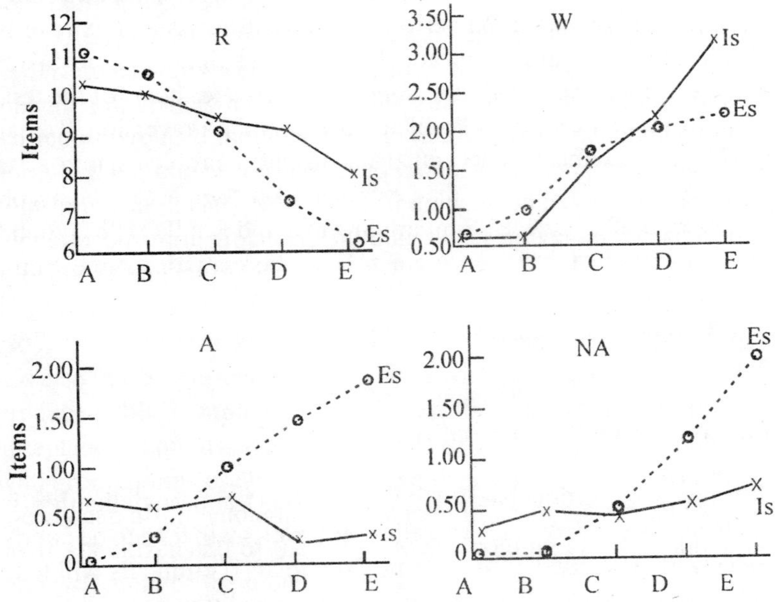

Figure 35 : Performance of Introverts and Extraverts on SPM.

The relationship of Introversion/Extraversion with problem solving has also been the subject of investigation in many studies. Eysenck (1959) conducted a study on problem solving by administering Morrisby Compound Series Test to 28 introverts and 19 extraverts. The results indicated that extraverts show greater work decrement by taking longer to obtain correct solution towards the end of the test as compared with introverts and giving up more easily towards the end. At the beginning of the work, extraverts were significantly faster than introverts. The introverts would also perform better on intelligence test because their cortical arousal is quicker, accumulation of Ir (reactive inhibition) slower and its dissipation faster, this standpoint was reaffirmed by Eysenck (1967) when he said that the introverts had a higher arousal and more efficient consolidation and hence performed better than extraverts who had lower arousal and less efficient consolidation. Farley (1966) reports that on stressed version of Nufferno intelligence test extraverts were significantly faster than introverts and ambiverts. Subjects with medium N performed significantly better than low on N and high on N subjects. Prior to Farley (1966), Furneaux (1956) conducted a study in which he compared the performance of introverts and extraverts Nufferno intelligence test and he observed that on time taken extraverts took proportionately longer time on later items of the test.

In a specific study of Problem Solving and Extraversion, Kumar (1974) reported that on conceptual and insightful problems, introverts were significantly superior than extraverts, on complex problems on a sample of 320 subjects. Similarly, Kumar and Kapila (1987) found that on four insightful problem solving tasks with a time limit, introverts were significantly better than extraverts. On the problems of set, Kumar and Kumari (1988) reported that introverts outperformed the extraverts.

Extraversion and Criminality

Extraverts condition badly (Eysenck, 1964) and socialization is mediated by conditioning. Therefore, extraverts will tend to be poorly socialized. Two predictions follow from this: (i) criminals will tend to be extraverted, (ii) criminals will tend to condition badly. There is evidence that extraverts take more risks than introverts. Figuratively and literally they are greater gamblers. This is in line with Eysenck's description of the extraverts as impulsive, and Gray's view of extraverts as reward seekers who are inclined to disregard the possible unpleasant consequences of their behaviour, Both writers see introverts as more controlled, responsible and fearful. Similar considerations would lead us to expect a greater amount of anti-social behaviour from extraverts than introverts. From Eysenck's theory such an association is predicted because extraverts are supposed to be less susceptible to the kinds of conditioning that constitute the socialization process, and Gray's theory would predict that extraverts would be more prone to crime and anti-social behaviour because they are impulsive reward seekers. Whatever the reason, this has been found to be the case: a part from their violations on the road, extraverts break institutional rules of all kinds and find their way to prison more often than introverts (Eysenck, 1971). Extraverts are also more likely to become recidivists than Introverts (Eysenck and Eysenck, 1974). Extraversion, however, is not the only temperamental predictor of delinquent behaviour and anti-social behaviour. The above relationships are usually stronger when high levels of Neuroticism are also involved, and the psychoticism factor is a better predictor than either Extraversion or Neuroticism.

Eysenck (1961) found that extraverts tend to be "tough-minded" in their attitudes and introverts relatively "tender-minded". And as such tough-minded people (E) tend to favour euthanasia, easy divorce, compulsory sterilization, and capital punishment as against the religious and humanitarian values expressed by tender-minded people. They enjoy social and aggressive humor (preferably fairly explicit). Whereas, introverts prefer more cognitive styles of humor, such as puns and incongruity-jokes. As regards sexual behaviour, extraverts have intercourse more frequently, in more different ways, and with more partners than introverts (Eysenck and Wilson, 1976).

Eysenck (1964) proposed that because of poorer condition ability and thus poorer socialization of extraverts, the incidence of crime would be higher in that group. Further combination of high E and N would produce a strong drive resulting in tendency towards anti-social behaviour. Eysenck's 'typical' criminal, therefore, would be a neurotic extravert. Later, criminality was linked also to high levels of Psychoticism (Eysenck and Eysenck, 1970). Evidence being equivocal. Professor Eysenck believed that the criminal is an extravert by basing his theory on various studies that look at the speed to which extraverts and introverts will condition (Little, 1963). He argued that the extravert is slow and therefore difficult to condition, whereas, the introvert is quicker and easier to condition. The theory suggests that it is therefore the criminal, and in particular the recidivist, that does not learn by his/her oven mistakes, and does not adjust to what society expects from each individual and therefore becomes delinquent. Earlier study has also found support for this view (Bartholomew 1959). Eysenck also suggested that other factors interact with temperament, including general intelligence (g) and environmental factors (Eysenck and Gudjonsson, 1989) to produce personality and behvioural styles. For example, Eysenck indicated that above average intelligence (g) provides anti-social behaviour. In general it was predicted that criminals and sociopaths would have high scores on P, E and N (Psychoticism, Extraversion and Neuroticism) (Eysenck, 1977 and Eysenck and Gudjonsson, 1989).

Eysenck (1994) further suggested that anti-social behaviour is egocentric and demands immediate gratification. He argued that because the introvert conditions better, they are more likely to adapt to socially acceptable behaviour. He then postulates that individual differences in the speed of conditioning will lead to a relationship between personality and criminality.

To conclude, all criminals are good extraverts but all extraverts are not criminals. They may not conform to the norms/the expected standards of society because of individualistic nature, the offshoot of which is criminality.

Eysenck also argued that extraverts are people who have a (Nervous system) NS that require more stimulation than most people, and also that they are more difficult to condition. Slower conditioning leads to poorer socialization which in turn leads to anti-social behaviour. Similarly, neurotics, who are very emotional people are also difficult to condition and this coupled with their emotionality makes them more likely to exhibit anti-social behaviour. Psychotics often have a poor grasp of reality and may even experience delusions. This by itself could lead to criminal behaviour, but coupled with a personality that is cold, lacking any empathy and is tough minded and impulsive, this is almost a perfect recipe for the aggressive or violent offender–hence the dimension of Psychoticism make sense and compliments Extraverts and Neurotics in committing some undesirable activities.

Extraversion/Introversion and Social Influence

Studies in the areas of suggestibility, conformity and compliance have produced complex findings with respect to the differences between extraverts and introverts.

In some circumstances, extraverts appear to be more open to social influence than introverts. They are more inclined to change their judgements under the influence of prestige suggestions (Sinha and Ojha, 1963) and to change their evaluation of paintings after discovering the name of the artists (Mohan and Kumar, 1973). They are more field dependent as measured by the Rod and Frame Test (Fine and Danforth, 1975; Malhotra and Makkar, 1999), and extraverted children are more responsive to peer influences regarding antisocial behaviour (Rim and Seidenross, 1971).

On the other hand, introverts are more susceptible to the autokinetic effect, that is seeing a stationary light in the dark as moving when there is some social pressure to do so (Panek, 1962). Also, their judgements of taste intensity are more likely to change in parallel with manipulations in the intensity of ambient light (Wilson and Gregson, 1967). Organ (1975) gave bonus points to business school students for performance on random quizzes which tested daily preparation. The introverts received (obtained) more bonus points throughout the program and maintained a steadier performance record over a period of time. Extreme extraverts actually showed a significant downward trend over time, which suggests that they were progressively loosing interest.

When an introvert encounters an extravert with different views on a controversial topic, the Introvert is more likely to be persuaded to modify his position (Carment, Miles and Cerwin, 1965). It is not clear whether this is because extraverts are more stubborn, more assertive, more plausible, or simply more talkative. In a study of religious conversion, Roberts (1965) found virtually no difference between extraverts and introverts except for a slight tendency for the introverts to show more gradual change in religious conviction.

Results in the area of hypnotic susceptiblility have been particularly complex and contradictory. Lang and Lazovik (1962) found that extraverts were easier to hypnotize than introverts and Hilgard and Bentler (1963) found that subjects in the neurotic-extravert (hysteric) quadrant were most readily hypnotizable. However, in the series of studies by H.B. Gibson and his associates (Gibson and Corcoran, 1975; Gibson and Curran, 1974) there has emerged a consistent tendency for neurotic introverts and stable extraverts to be most suggestible. No adequate explanation of these inconsistencies has yet been suggested, though Gibson has put forward some interesting hypothesis for future research. One is that the type of hypnotic induction procedure might be critical; neurotic introverts might be more susceptible to an authoritarian procedure which emphasizes "taskmotivating instructions," while stable extraverts might respond to permissive procedures that maximize interpersonal reinforcement. A second suggestion is that an uncomplicated correlation between hypnotizability and Extraversion might emerge if the effect of neuroticism was minimized by administration of a tranquilizer. When these experiments have been done, we might be close to an understanding of the connection between personality and hypnotic susceptibility.

In summary, it seems that either extraverts or introverts may appear as more open or susceptible to social influence, depending upon the particular conditions of motivation. When social rewards and excitement are offered as incentives, the extraverts appear more likely to comply and cooperate. In conscience arousing situations, and those that are relatively impersonal, the introverts are often more motivated to comply. In nut shell, the organismic variables and most of other variables impinging upon the subject may be tenable while the suggestion is made.

Conditionability: One of the most significant psychological effects relates to the relative ease or difficulty with which individuals become conditioned (e.g. Franks, 1956, 1957) who found that introverts could be conditioned to produce eye-blinks in response to a buzzer more quickly than extraverts. The biological explanation suggests that since introverts produce a higher level of arousal than extraverts, their nervous systems are more likely to form the necessary associations. Shackleton and Fletcher (1984) suggest that the introvert, whose social conditioning has been more effective is likely to be more conformist and cautious than the extravert. Eysenck suggests that children learn to control anti-social behaviour through the formulation of a consience, this being a conditioned emotional response. Eysenck (1977) further believes that the speed at which a person will be conditioned, depends upon an individual's personality, and particularly in terms of Extraversion and Neuroticism. The theory predicts that high Extraversion and high Neuroticism combinations lead to poor conditioning and then such individuals will lack social control and will therefore be over represented in offender populations.

Conversely low Extraversion and low Neuroticism would lead to effective control and socialization and therefore not be represented in offender populations. In terms of conditioning, Eysenck further argued that extraverts may condition less well than introverts due to levels of Neuroticism or Emotionality. Neuroticism is suggested to be related to the workings of the Autonomic Nervous System (ANS). High Neuroticism individual may have an unstable ANS and may show mood swings and anxious behaviour, while low Neurotic individuals have a stable ANS and therefore display calm and even tempered behaviour. It is suggested that high Neuroticism affects conditioning because of the effects of anxiety.

In the present study, the dimension of Neuroticism has been controlled i.e. by taking only those subjects who scored between 8 to 12 on EPI. In the current investigation, it has been done so in order to see that the Neuroticism score may not have a spill over effect in terms of the results atleast viz-a-viz on the development of norms or indirect persuasion or to obedience to authority. When combining the scores of Extraversion and Neuroticism, it can be seen that those that score high on both Extraversion and Neuroticism will condition least well of all individuals, and these are the people who are likely to show criminal tendencies and those low on the scores of Extraversion and Neuroticism are likely to condition better and thus conform to the norms of the society. Hence, in Eysenck's view social behaviour (normal or anti-social/acceptable or unacceptable behaviour) is a product of socialization, which in his view meant conditioning, in a Pavlovian sense.

Role of Socialization in the Development of Introversion

Introverts are relatively highly susceptible to punishment (Gray, 1970). Chief among them is the fact that this hypothesis can help resolve an important difficulty in Eysenck's approach to the process of socialization. This process is of central importance in his general theory of introversion-extraversion.

It is easier to understand Eysenck's theory of Introversion if we first consider the problem to which this theory is an attempted solution. The starting point for this theory lies in the relation of the dimensions of Introversion and Neuroticism to each other as well as to a cluster of psychiatric disorders called by Eysenck (1957) "dysthymic" and to a second cluster of offences against society called "Psychopathic". These relations are set out in Fig. 36a. The problems they posed for the student of personality are these (1) what are the psychological and/or physiological variables which differentiate neurotic individual along the dimensions of Introversion-Extraversion (which is quite independent of Neuroticism) and which cause the introverted neurotic to be susceptible to the dysthymic disorder, but the introverted neurotic to display antisocial behaviour of a psychopathic kind? (2) what are the psychological and or physiological variables which result in the high susceptibility of individuals with high degree of Neuroticism both to dysthymic disorders and to the commission of psychopathic offences? Although there have been many changes, but Eysenck's solutions to these problems have remained fairly constant over the years; they are set out in a highly simplified manner in the following Figure 36a showing the basic structure of Eysenck's theory of Introversion-Extraversion (see p. 173).

(1) The first link in Eysenck's chain of explanation is to describe the dysthymic neuroses as disorder of over-socialization and psychopathic behaviour as a disorder of under-socialization (e.g. Eysenck and Rachman, 1965). In the introverted neurotic the establishment of the conscience treated by Eysenck as a cluster of classically conditioned fear reactions has proceeded so effectively that the individual concerned is disabled in adulthood by a variety of manifestations of his conditioned fears in the form of phobias, obsessions and compulsions, frank anxiety states, reactive depression, etc. In the extraverted neurotic, by contrast, there has been a relative failure of socialization, resulting in the lack of a sense of responsibility towards society and the various forms of antisocial behaviour: juvenile delinquency, sexual delinquency, lying, careless or drunken driving or more serious breaches of the law displayed by the psychopath.

(2) Introverts form the conditioned reflexes comprising the conscience with greater ease than extraverts because they are in general more highly conditionable.

(3) The greater condionability of the introverts is attributed by Eysenck (e.g. 1967) to a relatively high level of arousal at this pole of the Introversion-Extraversion dimension.

(4) The higher level of arousal in the introverts is due to a higher level of activity in the ARAS (ascending reticular activating system)..

	Level	
1.	Socio-Psychiatric	Introverts: Dysthymic disorder Extraverts: Psychopathic disorder
2.	Socialization	in Introverts: Good in Extraverts: Poor
3.	Conditioning of fear	in Introverts : Good in Extraverts : Poor
4.	Conditionability	in Introverts : Good in Extraverts : Poor
5.	Arousability	in Introverts : High in Extraverts : Low
6.	Physiological	in Introverts: High activity ARAS in Extraverts: Low activity

Figure 36a: Basic Structure of Eysenck's Theory of Introversion and Extraversion.

Gray (1970a) suggested that this theoretical structure must be modified at point (4), in so far as the evidence suggest that the physiological basis of introversion must consists of a more complex system comprising ARAS (arousal level) together with the inhibitory circuits present in the orbital frontal cortex, the medial septal area and the hippocampus (susceptibility to punishment) function as a single feed-back loop: the higher the activity in the ARAS the greater the arousal level, the stronger is the activity in the inhibitory part of this loop, i.e. the greater the inhibition of behaviour (susceptibility to punishment).

Gray (1970b) modified some of the details of Eysenck's 1957 theory on both psychological and physiological grounds the resulting theoretical edifice of which is presented in Figure 36b.

Level		
1.	Socio-Psychiatric	Introverts: Dysthymic disorder Extraverts: Psychopathic disorder
2.	Socialization	in Introverts: Good in Extraverts: Poor
3.	Conditioning of fear	in Introverts : Good in Extraverts : Poor
4.	Susceptibility to punishment	in Introverts : High in Extraverts : Low
5.	Arousability	in Introverts : High in Extraverts : Low
6.	Physiological	Feedback loop comprising ARAS, frontal cortex, septal area and hippocampus — Activity in introverts: high in extraverts: low

Figure 36b: Proposed Modification of Eysenck's 1957 Theory of Introversion and Extraversion.

As Gray (1970b) discussed, the evidence mainly derived from experiments in Eyeblink Conditioning (Eysenck, 1965, 1967; Spence, 1964; Levy, 1967; Ominsky and Kimble, 1966, Eysenck and Levy, 1972) gives support to the following conclusions:

(1) Introverts are better than extraverts at eyeblink conditioning under some conditions but not all.

(2) These conditions can be predicted on the hypothesis that introverts are relatively more highly aroused than extraverts.

(3) The superior conditioning of the introverts appears in experiments which involve at least some degree of threat. Introverts condition better than extraverts only under some conditions. It appears that these conditions are, in general, relatively under arousing ones (Eysenck, 1967, Gray, 1970a and b). But there is no reason to suppose that the parental conditioning technique presumably involved in the

> formation of the conscience are more often underarousing than overarousing, so that there is no longer any reason to predict the over socialization of the introverts which is critical to Eysenck's theoretical edifice. Therefore, it may be suggested that the introvert is more susceptible to punishment/fear.

Earlier, Eysenck (1947) had proposed on the basis of his observations that not only introverts are more socialized but also follow social norms and expectations faster due to their sensitivity of the situation and hence show outward agreement and inward disagreement in situation warranting compliance and make all possible adjustments in day to day activities in order to smoothen the process of routine affairs than extraverts who can easily flout the norms.

Thus, the present research is mainly focused on the empirical observation of the development of social norms in different personality and gender groups because so far no such studies have been conducted.

3

Aims and Hypotheses

The aim of the present investigation is to understand how social norms develop amongst different personality and gender groups. Social norms vary from culture to culture but two things predominantly are to be underlined: first the socialization process play a key role in adherence and second the personality. Eysenck in this regard, does the analysis in terms of causative and descriptive aspects of human personality. In the same culture also, some people conform to social norms more and some do not. This is mainly due to genetic make up and environmental influences. There are qualitative differences in the learning of norms. Eysenck (1947) traces the differences in learning of social norms to conditioning. Conditioning is the main factor which aids in learning of social norms. Socialization is mediated by conditioning. Thus, the ones who condition better are likely to adhere to norms and behave in accordance with the expected standards of behaviour than those who condition slowly. According to Eysenck (1947) introverts condition better and learn the norms and expectations faster as compared to extraverts who condition slowly and deviate from the norms. Similarly, gender differences are due to socialization practices. According to the process of social learning theory, males and females are taught and are rewarded for performing behaviours that are thought by society to be appropriate for men and women respectively. The gender differences lead to differences in learning of social norms. Females are expected to abide by the norms and males digress from the norms very often as it is considered as being their privilege. Thus, females due to the expected standards of behaviour follow social norms seriously and retain the same as compared to males (Eysenck, 1947). Thus, for gauging this effect, Sherif's autokinesis and Asch's perceptual tasks are employed.

Alongwith two tests i.e. anagrams and serial positioning effect are also administered to know their vocabulary and performance i.e. to know whether introverts or extraverts and males or females learn faster as based on observational contentions of Eysenck. A factorial design of 2 × 2 is to be employed in the present study consisting of two groups of personality viz. introverts and extraverts and two levels of sex: males and females. In all there will be four conditions or 4 cells, each comprising of 25 subjects who will be tested on perceptual behavioural norm tasks alongwith anagrams and serial positioning effect. Thus, 100 subjects will be taken for final individual experimentation.

There is a point to be proved in this study that learning of the higher order tasks and norms in terms of convergence and pressure would be studied in the investigation undertaken currently for the first time to the best of the investigator's knowledge.

Hypotheses

In the preceding chapter, development of social norms in different personality groups i.e. in extraverts and introverts and sexes i.e. in males and females have been studied in quite detail. Similarly, learning ability too has also been studied among different personality groups and both the sexes in detail. Presently, for the purpose of forming hypotheses, only salient researches regarding this area would be presented.

Social Influence and Personality

Hypothesis I

It has been already mentioned in the review of literature that extraverts would show more variation in terms of judgement of movement in autokinesis because of their excitement and seeking behaviour in comparison to introverts. To support the above contention, it can be argued in the form of some indirect evidence that Wundt in 19th century had suggested that extraverts are changeable and introverts are subject to lesser variation. On this basis, Eysenck (1947) labelled those who are changeable as extraverts and those who are not changeable as introverts. Attention of extraverts may wander and show more variation in movement than introverts. Moreover introverts are stimulus hungry and are geared to inspect, whereas extraverts are response hungry and are geared to respond (Brebner and Cooper, 1974 and Kumar, Malhotra and Jerath, 1986, 1989).

Qualitatively speaking introverts because of higher cortical arousal (Eysenck, 1957, 1967; Gale Coles and Blaydon, 1969; Shagaas and Canter, 1971; Kumar, 1974 and Kapila, 1992) and serious predisposition in general may show lesser movement in the autokinetic experiment. The introverts like to pay close attention to the task undertaken as compared to extraverts. Hence in the autokinetic experiment their movement of the pupil may be lesser than their counterparts. Because extraverts are geared to respond quickly and in the hurry may show wider variation in the judgement of the tiny light. Hence, because of their i.e. introverts' serious disposition they would retain the social norms better than the extraverts who may diverge and drift lesser from the convergence point as reached the preceding week. In the present study the subjects would be tested for retention after a week also apart from 4 readings in the initial stage of the experimentation.

Social Pressure and Personality

Hypothesis II

Ironically, introverts may yield to social pressure more because they believe that yielding is desirable to social pressure even if erroneous. Secondly, they i.e. introverts are more susceptible to punishment (Gray, 1972 and Kumar, 1974) hence, would find it difficult to withstand the pressure of the group as compared to extraverts.

Thus, with regard to social pressure, introverts would yield to social pressure more as compared to extraverts who breach the norms very often and do not come under pressure. Introverts may conform to group pressure more in visual perception task of Asch's line drawing cards than extraverts due to high susceptibility to punishment in the form of rejection by the group and conditioning in introverts is good and high as compared to extraverts (Gray, 1972, 1973).

Social Influence and Sex

Hypothesis III

On sex differences, it can be presumed that females would retain the norms significantly more and yield to social pressure/influence more than the males. The expectation is in line with the patterns of socialization and upbringing available to the two sexes. Females do not challenge the norms and adhere to them in order to win social approval. Females would show convergence more easily and would retain the norm longer than males. They yield to social pressure significantly more due to the fact that they consider influence as conforming to social norms. Not only this, expected behaviour from males and females are differently viewed i.e., when females digress from norms, they are looked down upon and when men break the norms, it is viewed as it being their prerogative (Kapila, Malhotra and Sharma, 2000).

Personality and Problem Solving (ANAGRAMS)

Hypothesis IV

A review of studies clearly substantiate that introverts are better problem solvers than extraverts in variety of problem solving tasks. Eysenck (1959) and Mohan and Kumar (1976) have clearly demonstrated the better performance of introverts over extraverts on problems taken out of various intelligence tests. Kumar (1974) found that on difficult insightful problem solving tasks, introverts consistently and significantly performed better than extraverts on both trials and time taken. These results were explained through the arousal and inhibition excitation hypothesis of Eysenck (1967) and Gray (1972). Kumar and Kapila (1987) and Kapila (1992) substantiated the superiority of introverts over extraverts on insightful problem solving.

Presently here anagrams of problem solving tasks are being employed for the experimentation and it is presumed that introverts (dysthemics) would perform better than extraverts because their vocabulary is better and hysterics have a bad vocabulary as empirically shown by Himmelweit (1946), Kumari (1987), Ohri and Malhotra (1989), Kapila (1992) and Makkar and Malhotra (2000).

Sex and problem solving i.e. Anagrams

Hypothesis V

By and large it is clearly observed that males are better than females to solve the different kinds of problem solving tasks right from school children to adults (Bedell, 1934; Billings, 1934; Sweeney, 1953; Terman and Tyler, 1954; McNemar, 1955; Staats, 1957; Maier and Burke, 1967; Priested and Hunsker, 1967; Eysenck and Cookson, 1969; Maier and Casselman, 1970; Roll, 1970; Constantinople, 1974; Raheim and Kaufman, 1974; Felen, 1975; Maxwell, 1975; Mcway, 1975; Singer, 1975; Hayes, 1978; Benbow and Stanley, 1980; Jacob and Dominowski, 1981; Johnson, 1984; Luchins and Luchins, 1984; Pesh, 1985 and Kumar and Kumari, 1988). A variety of reasons have been offered for the poorer problem solving of females (1) Attitude towards problem solving (Carey, 1958; Hoffman and Maier, 1961 and Kumar, 1983), (2) Masculinity/Femininity (Parsons and Bales, 1955 and Milton, 1957). (3) Fear of success (Horner, 1968, 1972 and 1974).

Since women's attitude toward problem solving is poor and they are high on femininity and low on masculinity and again high on fear of success, hence they perform poorly. In the present study it may be pointed out that only anagrams are taken which are vocabulary items in nature. This is contrary to the early researches as mentioned above which were qualitative in nature and the present task consists of vocabulary which is quantitative in nature. Females are better in vocabulary and have inherited better verbal ability. Not only this, females due to their articulation level take their tasks more seriously as compared to males. Thus, it is presumed that females would perform better than males.

Personality and serial learning

Hypothesis VI

Eysenck (1955 a, 1957) has emphasized time and again that learning and performance are related to extraversion because of individual differences in cortical excitation and inhibition. EEG studies have provided evidence that there is lower level of cortical arousal in extraverts (Gale, Coles and Blaydon, 1969). Eysenck (1967) attributes better performance of introverts to their higher arousal and poorer performance of extraverts to their poor arousal plus quicker cortical excitation and slower accumulation of reaction inhibition (Ir) and its faster dissipation in introverts.

Thus, due to differences in cortical arousal and physiological concomitants as proposed by Gray (1972), introverts are likely to learn the nonsense syllables in serial order in serial learning significantly in lesser number of trials than extraverts.

Sex and serial learning

Hypothesis VII

In the present study both the sexes have been included in equal number to observe the differences if any on serial learning tasks. To the best of investigator's knowledge no systematic attempt seems to have been made to study sex differences vis-à-vis serial learning tasks (Verbal learning tasks) so far. The reasons for including both the sexes in the present research are that since there is no available evidence concerning sex differences in verbal learning, in the present study sex has been included as a variable in order to avoid the biasness effect. If one sex is taken and no differences are looked for, then the actual behaviour of the other sex may be ignored. On the other hand, if such differences are assumed, resulting investigation may simply provide a rationalization of existing relations between the sexes (Berkovitz, 1975).

In the present research work, the performance of two sexes on serial learning task will itself prove or disprove the null hypothesis about the sex differences.

But still, it is presumed that females as they are better in vocabulary and due to their higher articulation will show superiority in serial learning task than males as it is also a verbal task and not a mathematical or abstract task.

4

Methodology

Design of the Study

A factorial design of 2 x 2 has been employed in the present study. There are two conditions of personality, i.e. introverts and extraverts and two conditions of sex, i.e. males and females. In all, there are four conditions or four cells each consisting 25 subjects who will be tested on perceptual and behavioural norm tasks alongwith serial positioning effect and anagrams. Thus, in all, there are 100 subjects in the four experiments.

	Males	*Females*
Extraverts	25	25
Introverts	25	25

2 × 2 factorial design

Selection of Sample

1. Initial Sample

A sample of 500 students (250 males and 250 females) of University level was drawn randomly from Himachal Pradesh University, Shimla for the present study.

The subjects were taken in a group of 10-15 each. First of all they were given Eysenck's Personality Inventory (Eysenck and Eysenck, 1968) to obtain their personality scores on Extraversion/ Introversion dimension.

Final Sample

The final sample of 100 subjects was selected on the basis of their scores on personality inventory. Students scoring between 8 to 12 on Neuroticism were considered as medium neurotics and at the same time students scoring either 12+ or –8 on the dimension of Extraversion were termed as extraverts and introverts respectively. The labelling of introverts and extraverts on the basis of their above mentioned scores are in accordance with the norms based on Indian samples e.g. (Mohan, 1974). Thus, the final sample of 50 males and 50 females was selected and the design turned out to be having the 100 Ss, the layout of which i.e. 2 × 2 factorial design is presented in Table 5.

Table 5: Design of the Present Study.

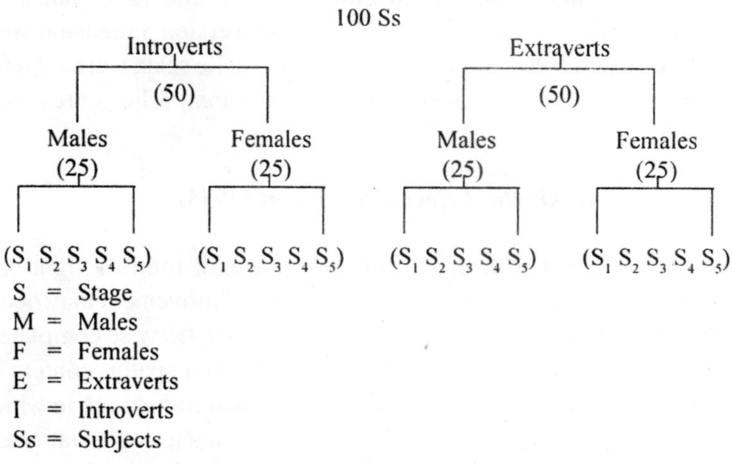

S = Stage
M = Males
F = Females
E = Extraverts
I = Introverts
Ss = Subjects
Stages are only for social influence under Sherif's study

Tools used

***1. Eysenck's Personality Inventory. (EPI)*:** (Eysenck and Eysenck, 1968).

Eysenck's Personality Inventory (EPI) has been used to select personality groups. It consists of 57 questions. Twenty-four items are for the dimension of extraversion/introversion. Twenty-four for Neuroticism and rest of the nine items constitute the lie scale.

Following instructions were given to the subjects and all the doubts were cleared before the proceedings started:

"Here are some questions regarding the way you behave, feel and act. After each question, you are supposed to encircle 'Yes' or 'No'. Try to decide whether 'Yes' or 'No'. It represents your usual way of acting or feeling, work quickly and do not spend too much time over any question. We want your first reactions, not a long drawn out thought process. The whole questionnaire should not take more than few minutes. Work quickly and remember to answer every question. There are no right or wrong answers and this is not a test of intelligence or ability but simply a measure of the way you behave." After that, forms were taken back and scoring was done with the help of scoring stencil which was placed along the anchoring points on the test booklet. Their scores on Extraversion and Neuroticism dimension were written on the top of the forms. Lie scores were also counted. Subjects who scored more than 12 and less than 8 on neuroticism dimension and –8 to 12+ on extraversion dimension were selected. Also Ss who scored 3 or less than 3 on lie scale were selected for the experiment i.e. subjects scoring more than 3 lie scores were rejected.

2. Sherif's Autokinetic Effect Experiment (1935)

Autokinetic effect is a visual illusion; in a dark room, a light will appear to move around. In this an experience of movement may occur when fixating on a stationary point of light in the otherwise completely darkened room (environment). In this condition a spatial context of background is lacking and there is no fixed visual framework to which the point of light may be referred. The result is that a single stationary point of light appears to drift or wander irregularly about a phenomena termed autokinetic movement. Typically, the point of light appears to make small excursion, but considerable movement is also noted. There are wide individual differences in the extent and the direction of the apparent movement which is shown to be significantly affected by social influence (Sherif, 1935). Autokinesis is an instrument which is placed in a darkened room (see Figure 37). The walls were not visible and there were no physical frames of reference for subjects.

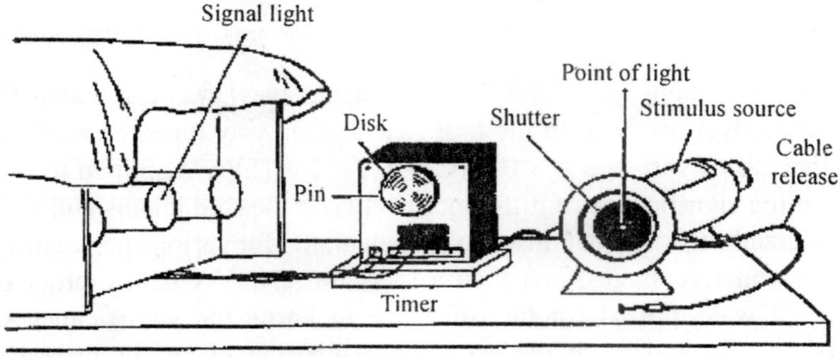

Figure 37: Drawing of apparatus used in autokinetic experiments in 1935-1936 (point of light, timer, signal system).

In this experiment, subjects were made to sit comfortably in a completely darkened room in a group of 4 consisting of 2 males and 2 females, 2 introverts and 2 extraverts. They were asked to give their precise judgements regarding the movement of the patch of light in terms of inches i.e. 3 inches, 4 inches, 5 inches and so on. There were 4 sessions spread over 2 days i.e. the first two sessions were taken the same day and next two session took place the following day with an interval of 15 minutes between sessions. In the first session, they gave the individual judgement because they did not know each other. After that session terminated, the same group of students were asked to make judgments concerning the movement after 15 minutes. In this session they made a judgement to each other and then to the experimenter. Similarly, 3rd and 4th readings were taken. The final i.e. the 5th reading was taken after the interval of one week to see the retention of group norms among different personality groups and two sexes formed at the 4th stage of convergence due to social interaction.

Before starting the experiment, the following instructions were given to the Ss. "This is a test of autokinetic effect. You will see a patch of light on a screen. Look at it. It will wave up and down and you have to tell how much the light moved as it followed its erratic course. First you will be tested individually and then in a group. In all there will be 5 sessions taken separately."

Scoring

The judgement for all the five readings (stages) was summated for the analysis of data. In the first case a three way repeated measure analysis of variance A × B × (C) i.e. 2 × 2 × (5) was applied to find out the significance of differences between the said means and their interaction. After that means were calculated for various personality, sex and five stages, and then a separate ANOVA of the order of 2 × 2 was applied for the 5th stage to know the significance of personality and sex. In the last, t-values were calculated for differeces between 4th and 5th stage to know how the two sexes and personality groups divulged from their respective convergence effects.

Asch's Visual Perception Test (1951)

This is a visual perception test of line drawing cards. This test of visual perception contains 4 cards. One of these cards contain the standard line and the other three cards contain the comparison lines. In Asch's visual perception test, 6 subjects were accomplices i.e. confederates of the experimenter and one was critical/naive subject. Thus, in all there were seven subjects who participated in this experiment. First, the subjects were made to sit comfortably around a table with 6 confederates of the experimenter. The confederates were instructed in advance to give wrong judgements of which the naive subject was unaware. In this experiment the subjects thought that they were participating in a test of perceptual skills with a group of six other subjects. They were first shown the standard line and then were asked to identify which of the three comparison lines best matched the standard line. They were asked to state publicly one after another their judgements. First, the confederates stated their judgements publicly one after another and then naive subject stated his/her judgement in the last. This procedure was repeated three times with different stimulus cards carrying comparison lines (see Figure 38 a and b). It was always the slightly longer line which the confederates stated as equal to the standard line. This experiment was done with all the 100 subjects. In order to determine the difference between sexes i.e. males and females and two personality groups viz. introverts and extraverts in yielding to group pressure.

Before starting the experiment, the following instructions were imparted to the subjects:

"There are 4 cards. One card contains the standard line and the other 3 cards contain the comparison lines. This is a test to measure your perceptual skill.

Your task is to announce about which of the three comparison lines was identical in length to a standard line. There are three trials and in each trial you have to repeat the same process. Is it clear to you? Now let us start doing the experiment."

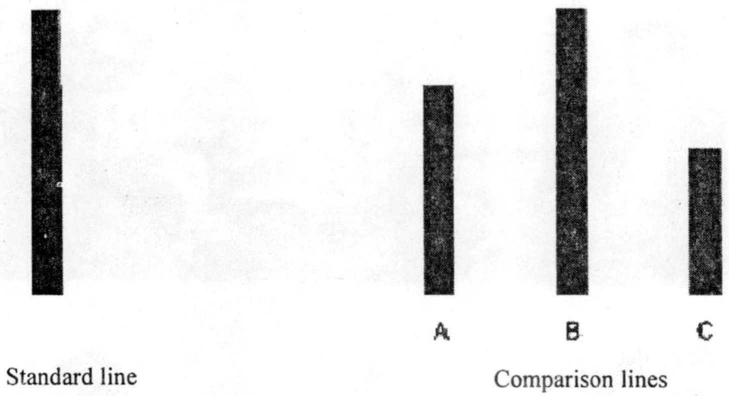

Figure 38 (a): Asch's Line drawing cards.

Scoring

Yielding responses were taken into consideration for each of the three trials, for example if the subject yielded 2 times out of three trials then score of 2 was to be given for the purpose of analysis of data. ANOVA of the order of 2 × 2 was applied for this test.

Figure 38 (b): These photos were taken during the Asch's experiment. The man in the middle is the subject; all the rest are confederates of Asch.

Anagrams (Adapted version of Dominowski, 1966 Adapted by Sehgal in 1990 and Kapila in 1992)

An anagram consists of several letters which are jumbled up and the subject must rearrange them to form a meaningful word. Anagram structure is the most commonly and frequently used task in research on problem solving. Several attempts have been made to account for the difficulty of anagrams in terms of their structural properties. Dominowski (1966), proposed the letter moves i.e. the No. of letters whose position movement might be related to solution difficulty. Thus, for the word camel, the anagram mceal can be solved with a minimum of two moves i.e. C to the first position and A to the second while mclea requires 3 moves. The fewer the moves, the better the performance. In this problem solving task, subjects had to rearrange the given 15 anagrams in the questionnaire with the time limit of ten minutes. After they sat comfortably, questionnaires were given to them and following instructions were imparted before they started their work which were printed on the problem sheet:

"Here are some jumbled up words given below. You have to remake the correct words of these in 10 minutes. Please write the correct words in the space given in front of each word. Work quickly and don't miss any word."

Scoring

Right responses were taken into consideration from the given answers for the analysis of data.

Serial Learning (Use of Nonsense Syllables)

Herman Ebbinghaus developed this method of studying learning and memory. Nonsense syllables are formed by putting a vowel between two consonants. He selected nonsense syllables because he believed that were essentially free of the influence of past experiences and the emotional factors associated with prose, poetry or common words. A list of 15 nonsense syllables was made. The syllables were arranged and written down in series and the subjects were asked to memorize the list in the same order as it appeared in the series. This type of learning is called the serial learning. In view of the limitations of three letter syllables, four letter syllables were used in which the initial or final consonant is double. This list was shown through the memory drum apparatus (see Figure 39). The paper strip containing the nonsense syllables is bound around a drum. When the drum is in place on its shaft, the peg on the small wheel engages the cogs of the drum and gives the drum each time a quick push which brings the next line into view. Reduction gear causes the driving wheel to rotate once in 3 secs, which is the interval between exposures when only one peg is inserted.

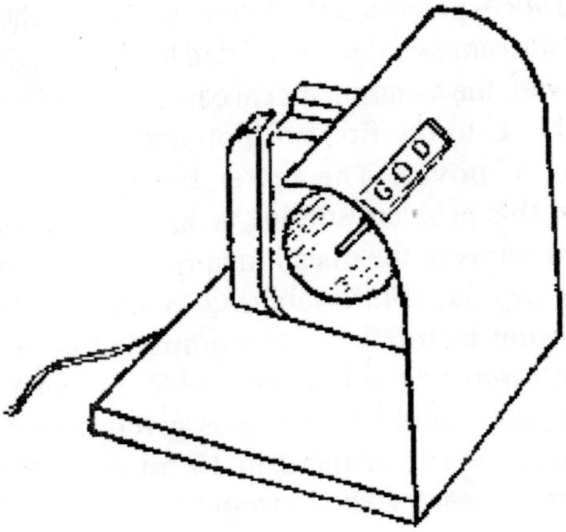

Figure 39: Memory Drum. The drum moves intermittently, providing a brief exposure to items of a list attached to the surface of the drum.

A more rapid rate can be secured by inserting two or three pegs. After the list was exposed to the subjects they were asked to recall the syllables in the same position i.e. in the same order as it appeared in the series. The trials were repeated until the subject was able to recall all the nonsense syllables correctly and in the same order. Following instructions were imparted to the subjects before starting the experiment:

"I, the 'experimenter' will show you the list containing 15 nonsense syllables through the memory drum apparatus. Your task is to go through the list in one exposure and then reproduce the same in the serial order as it appeared in series in the list. I will try to see how soon you can learn these nonsense syllables and how many trials will you take to reproduce the list. Is it all clear? If you have any doubt regarding the experiment kindly ask me and make yourself clear. When I say 'ready' kindly attend the exposure point on the memory drum."

Scoring

In this task, number of trials taken to recall the items in serial order were noted for the analysis of data.

5

Results

The present investigation was undertaken with certain aims in mind i.e., to know how social norms develop among different personality and gender groups and also who retain or adhere to these norms better and longer and which group shows compliance in the face of erroneous majority. The compliance was measured through Asch's line drawing test. The norms were studied through Sherif's autokinetic effect. Not only this, the present investigation was also designed to study the percentage yielding to social influence/pressure by the group in Asch's experiment of perceptual learning test among introverts and extraverts and males and females. As social norms vary from culture to culture, they are learnt differently due to their personality and genetic make-up irrespective of the cultural differences. Thus, the present investigation centered around the main theme that is, why do some people follow these norms more closely than others even when the imparting agencies are the same? The study was carried out keeping in view the analysis done by Eysenck, in this regard in terms of causative and descriptive aspects of human personality.

Alongwith this, the present investigation was also done to know the vocabulary performance and learning ability of the personality groups viz. introverts and extraverts and two sexes males and females through anagram solution of problem solving task and serial positioning effect.

Thus, in short, the present study aimed at: (i) analyzing differences if any between introverts and extraverts and males and females in retaining the social norms and yielding to social pressure/ influence of the group. Alongwith, vocabulary and verbal learning tasks were also studied to analyze differences if any among different personality and gender groups.

These effects were gauged through the following experiments:

(i) Sherif's autokinetic effect (1935)
(ii) Asch's visual perception test (1951)
(iii) Anagram solution (Dominowski, 1966)
(iv) Serial positioning effect (Gamble, 1909, 1927)

In Sherif's autokinetic effect experiment, a repeated measure of analysis of variance of the order of 2 × 2 × (5) was applied to study the significance of differences between the said means and their interactions. For rest of the experiments, ANOVA of the order of 2 × 2 was applied (Edwards, 1969). The details regarding each analysis are given as under. The details of the experiments have been presented in the preceding chapter of methodology.

Comparative Means' Analysis for all the four experiments

*In Sherif's autokinetic effect the means of movement (of the patch of light) in inches for all the five stages for introverts and extraverts are 2.48 vs. 4.81 regarding the patch of light and for males vs. females are 4.57 vs. 2.67. This indicates that introverts and females show lesser movement as compared to extraverts and females. (for details see Table 6 and Figure 40).

*In the second experiment of Asch's visual perception test, means of trials yielding to group pressre for introverts vs. extraverts are 2.46 and 1.82 (out of 3 trials) and for males vs. females are 1.88 vs. 2.40 thereby depicting that introverts and females yield to/come under group pressure more as compared to extraverts and males (For details see Table 6 and Figure 40).

Bars showing the comparative means for Sherif's autokinesis (mean of movement in inches); Asch's visual perception test (mean trials yielding to presssure out of 3 trials); Anagram problem solving task (means of correctly solved anagrams our of 15) and Serial positioning effect (mean trials of recalled nonsense syllables in serial order).

Table 6: Comparative means for all the four experiments
(i) Sherif's autokinetic effect (ii) Asch's visual perception task,
(iii) Anagram solution and (iv) serial positioning effect.

	Introverts	*Extraverts*	*Males*	*Females*
1. Sherif's autokinesis (Mean of movement in inches)	2.48	4.81	4.57	2.67
2. Asch's visual perception test (Mean trials yielding to group pressure out of 3 trials)	2.46	1.82	1.88	2.40
3. Anagram problem solving task (Mean of correctly solved anagrams out of 15)	12.48	6.14	9.08	9.54
4. Serial positioning effect (mean trials taken to recall the nonsense syllables in serial order)	6.68	10.08	8.44	8.32

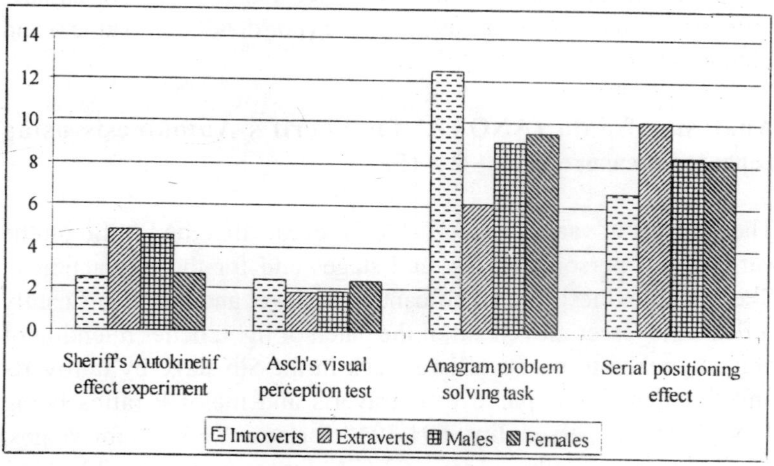

Figure 40: Comparative Means for Sherif's Autokinsis, Asch's Visual Perception Test, Anagram Solution and Serial Positioning Effect

Vertical line depicts

(1) means of movement in inches.
(2) mean trials yielding to pressure out of 3.
(3) means of correctly solved anagrams out of 15.
(4) mean trials of recalled nonsense syllables in serial order.

*In the third experiment of anagram solution the comparison of means for correct responses (out of 15) for the two groups of personality and gender indicates the better performance of introverts and females with mean values being 12.48 and 9.54 as compared to extraverts and males with mean values being 6.14 and 9.08. But, the difference between males and females is not significant due to the fact that females are equally introverted and extraverted as males are.

*In the fourth experiment of serial positioning effect, the comparison of means of trials taken in recalling nonsense syllables in serial order for the two groups of personality and sex indicates the better performance of introverts and females i.e. take less trials in learning and recalling the nonsense syllables in serial order with means being 6.68 and 8.32 as compared to extraverts and males—means being 10.08 and 8.44. But, there is a marginal difference between the males and females again due to the fact that females are equally introverted and extraverted as males are (For details see Table 6 and Figure 40).

Analysis of data (ANOVA) for Sherif's Autokinesis using repeated measure i.e. 2 × 2 × (5)

The analysis of variance (see Table 7) reveals that the F-ratio on the variables of personality, sex and stages and for the interaction in Sherif's autokinesis are significant at .01 level and this significantly reflects the lesser movement of the patch of light, better retention of and adherence to norms after a week in the 5th stage by introverts and females as compared to extraverts and males F-ratios being 1081.98** for personality, 691.30** for sex, 79.39** for stages, 27.21** for personally and sex, 103.67** for sex and stages, 131.14** for sex and stages and 42.17** for personality X sex x stages all significant at .01 level.

Interaction effect of Personality and Sex (A × B)

In Sherif's autokinetic effect, the interaction of A × B i.e. personality and sex in 'Error a' in the collated score is significant at .01 level with F-being 27.21**. The Figure 41a and b parts and contingency Table 8 (a and b part) clearly depicts that movement in inches for that of extraverts and males is significantly greater than for the introverts and females with t-values being 8.24** P <.01 for males and females at introverted end and 11.95** P < .01 for males and females at extraverted end; 15.26** P < .01 for introverts vs. extraverts at the males end; and 9.12** p < .01 for introverts vs extraverts at the females end.

Table 7: Summary of ANOVA for Sherif's experiment of autokinesis using repeated measures (2 × 2 × 5)

Sv	*Ss*	*df*	*Ms*	*F*	*Sig. level*
A (Pers.)	703.29	1	703.29	1081.98**	at .01, .05
B (Sex)	449.35	1	449.35	691.30**	at .01, .05
A.B. (Pers. × Sex)	17.68	1	17.68	27.21**	at .01, .05
Error a	62.56	96	0.65		
C (Stages)	88.95	4	22.23	79.39**	at .01, .05
A.C. (Pers. × Stages)	116.12	4	29.03	103.67**	at .01, .05
B.C. (Sex × Stages)	146.88	4	36.72	131.14**	at .01, .05
A.B.C. (Pers. × Sex × Stages)	47.26	4	11.81	42.17**	at .01, .05
Error b	107.59	384	0.28		
Total	**1739.68**	**499**			

Table 8: Means Contingency table for Personality (A) and Sex (B) in Sherif's autokinesis

a part	*Males*	*Females*	*t-value*
Introverts	3.2	1.76	8.24**
Extraverts	5.948	3.67	11.95**
b part	*Introverts*	*Extraverts*	*t-value*
Males	3.2	5.94	15.26**
Females	1.76	3.67	9.12**

t-value ** denotes significant difference at .01 and .05 levels.

Figure 41 (a and b Parts): Showing the interaction effect of Personality × Sex (A × B)in Sherif's autokinesis.

(a part)

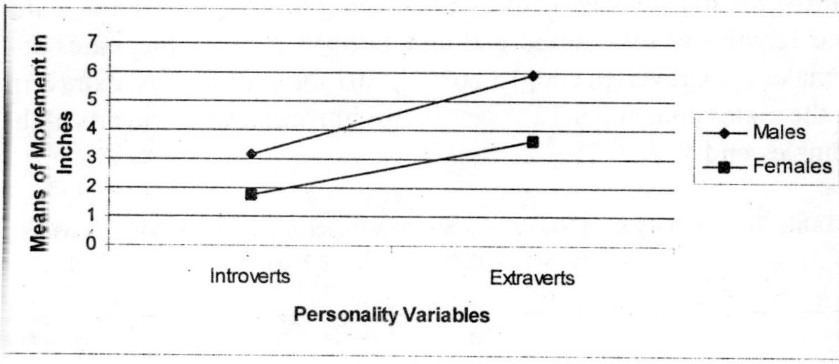

(b part)

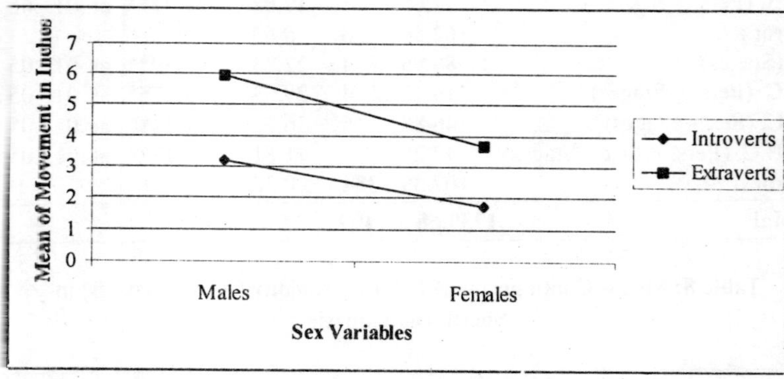

Interaction effect of Personality and Stages (A × C)

Interaction effect of Personality and Stages (A × C) has been found to be significant at .01 level with F-ratio being 103.67** under 'Error b' Readings were taken at 1, 2, 3, 4 stages to know the convergence effect and then after one week, the 5th (final) reading was taken in Sherif's autokinesis to know the retention of norms formed at the 4th stage. Table 9 clearly demonstrates the significant differences at all the stages between introverts and extraverts with extraverts showing more movement of patch of light having the significant t-values of 17.343** for first, 9.251** for second 8.665** for third, 6.637** for fourth and 18.576** for fifth stage. The convergence has almost taken place at the fourth stage (see Figure 42 for interaction and convergence effect) and the norm was retained significantly better by the introverts after one week who showed lesser movement in comparison to the 4th stage than the extraverts who showed more movement than before.

Table 9: Means Contingency table of two levels of Personality and five stages in Sherif's autokinesis

	Stages				
Personality	1	2	3	4	5
Introverts	1.70	2.20	2.77	3.27	2.48
Extraverts	5.01	4.05	4.26	4.53	6.21
t– value	17.343**	9.251**	8.665**	6.637**	18.576**

t– value ** significant at .01 and .05 level.

Figure 42: Showing the interaction effect of Personality × Stages in Sherif's Autokinesis (A × C).

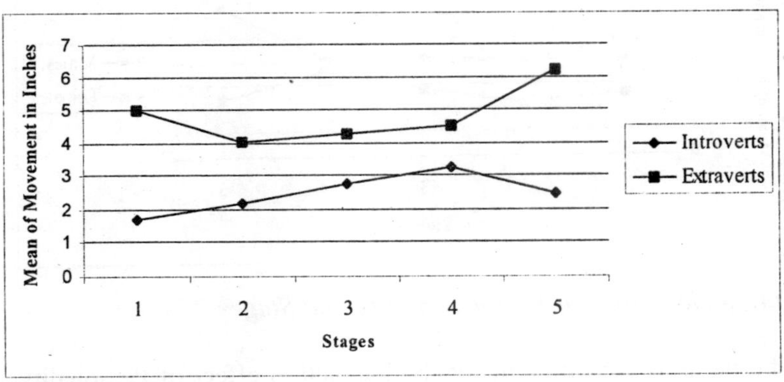

The Interaction effect of Sex and Stages (B × C)

Here also readings were taken to know the convergence effect and 5th, the final reading was taken after one week to know the retention of norms formed at the 4th stage of convergence. An inspection of Table 10 reveals that at all the stages, the differences are found to be significant i.e. males showed greater movement than the females regarding the patch of light. The t-values being significant at .01 level which are 4.138**, 9.384**, 8.057**, 2.632** and 12.343** for five stages.

The convergence has taken place almost at 4th stage and when after one week retention test regarding the norm was taken, females showed better retention by showing lesser movement than the males who showed greater movement of the patch of light in comparison to the 4th stage. For convergence effect and retention of norms see Figure 43.

Table 10: Means Contingency table of sex and stages in Sherif's autokinesis.

	Stages				
Sex	1	2	3	4	5
Males	4.09	4.07	4.21	4.20	6.32
Females	2.62	2.18	2.82	3.60	2.37
t– value	4.138**	9.384**	8.057**	2.632**	12.343**

Figure 43: Showing the interaction effect of Sex × Stages (B × C) in Sherif's Autokinesis

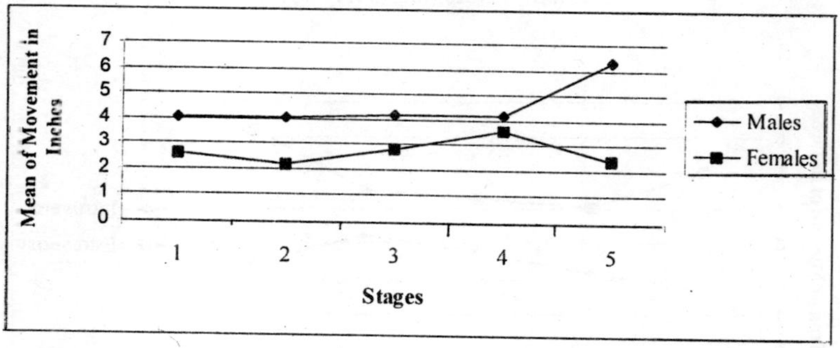

Interaction effect of Personality, Sex and Stages

The patterns are different for the interaction effect of Personality, Sex and Stages. The males and females at the introverted end show lesser difference though significant. The t-values are significant for all the five stages at .01 level which are 9.029**, 12.394**, 7.943**, 3.324** and 14.940** [for details see Table 11(a) and Figure 44a part]. But at the extraverted level, the males and females drift more and especially at the 5th stage they drift much more having the significant t-values for all the five stages at .01 level which are 8.183**, 21.473**, 12.716**, 2.736** and 28.85** [for details see

Table 11(a) and Figure 44b part]. When the interaction was plotted the other way, it depicts that at the males level introverts and extraverts showed greater difference having the significant t-values at .01 level which are 14.704**, 18.817**, 18.691**, 8.796** and 22.899** [see Table 11(b) and Figure 44c part] and at the females' level, introverts and extraverts showed lesser difference though significant having the significant t-values at .01 level which are 36.369**, 19.202**, 9.303**, 8.318**, 7.514** [for details see contingency Table 11(b) part and Figure 44d part]. In short the patterns and t-values show that introverts and females are trying to converge for developing the norms and extraverts and males are oblivious of it. After one week extraverts and males do not retain the norms as good as, introverts and females who retain the group judgement by showing the movement closer to the 4th (convergence) stage (for details see Table 11 and Figure 44a, b, c, d parts).

Table 11: Means Contingency table for A.B.C. (Personality × Sex × Stages in Sherif's Autokinesis).

(a Part)

Groups		*Stages*				
		1	*2*	*3*	*4*	*5*
Introverts	Males	2.44	3.00	3.34	3.58	3.68
	Females	.96	1.40	2.20	2.96	1.28
t– value		9.029**	12.394**	7.943**	3.324**	14.940**
Extraverts	Males	5.74	5.14	5.08	4.82	8.96
	Females	4.28	2.96	3.44	4.24	3.46
t-value		8.183**	21.473**	12.716**	2.736**	28.85**

(b Part)

Males	Introverts	2.44	3.00	3.34	3.58	3.68
	Extraverts	5.74	5.14	5.08	4.82	8.96
	t-values	14.704**	18.817**	18.691**	8.796**	22.899**
Females	Introverts	.96	1.4	2.20	2.96	1.28
	Extraverts	4.28	2.96	3.44	4.24	3.46
	t-value	36.369**	19.202**	9.303**	8.318**	7.514**

Figure 44 (a, b, c, d): Showing the interaction effect of personality × Sex × Stages in Sherif's Autokinesis.

(a Part)

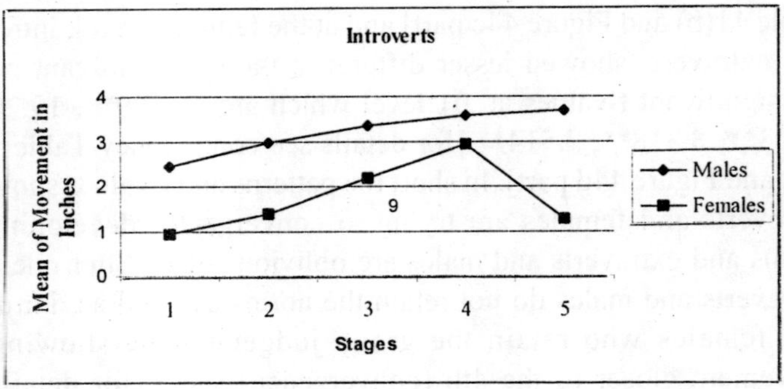

(b Part)

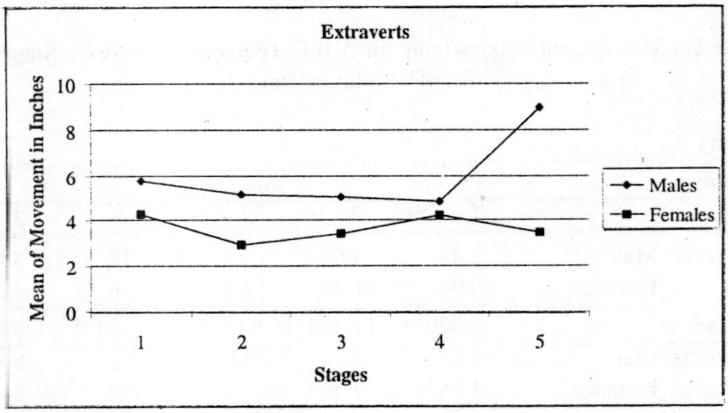

(c Part)

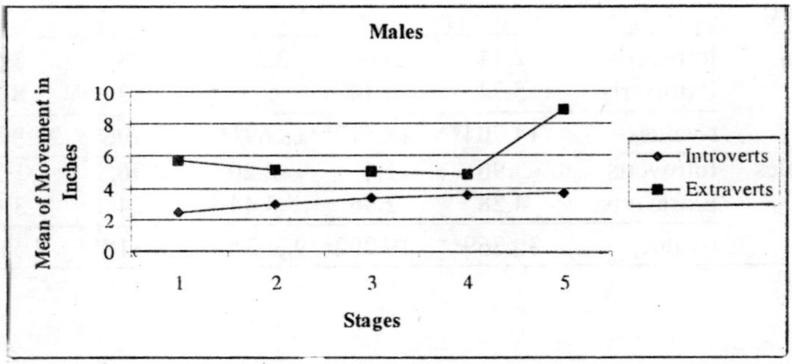

(d Part)

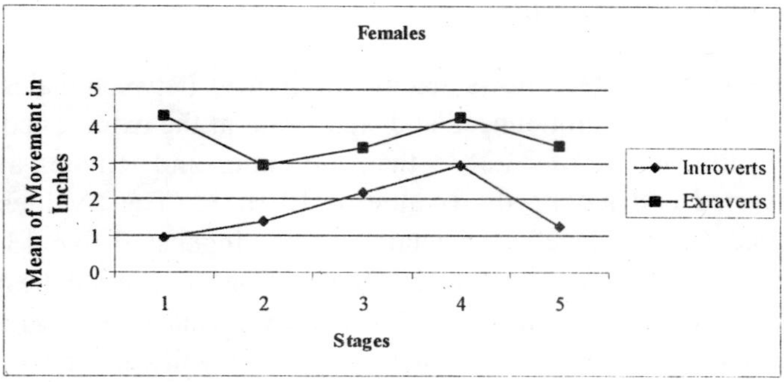

ANOVA for the final reading i.e., after one week in Sherif's autokinetic effect experiment

The analysis of variance for the 5th stage yielded a highly significant F-ratio of 386.46** at .01 level for the variable of personality as the mean difference for introverts and extraverts are quite large in males and females. The F-ratio for the variable of sex is also significant at .01 level which is 433.40**. Similarly the interaction between personality X sex yielded a significant F-ratio of 66.73** at .01 level. This indicates that on the variable of personality, introverts retain the norms formed at the convergence level at 4th stage but the extraverts drift from the norms as they do not remember the norms. Similarly, on the variable of sex, males show more movement and drift at the 5th stage from the norm than the females who retain the norms and show lesser movement more closely to the previous stages. (For details see Table 12 and Figure 45 a and b part).

Table 12: Summary of ANOVA for 5th stage.

Sv	*Ss*	*df*	*Ms*	*F*	*Sig. Level*
A	347.82	1	347.82	386.46**	.01, .05
B	390.06	1	390.06	433.40**	.01, .05
A.B.	60.06	1	60.06	66.73**	.01, .05
With in error	86.4	96	0.9		
Total	**884.34**	**99**			

Interaction Effect of Personality × Sex (A × B) in Sherif's Autokinesis for 5th stage

The interaction effect shows that the differences between males and females are more pronounced and significant at the extraverted end having the t-value of 23.38** than the males and females at the introverted end having the t-value of 10.16**. (The t-values are significant at .01 level) (for details see contingency Table 13 and Figure 45 a part). Likewise when the interaction was plotted the other way, it depicted that at the males' level introverts and extraverts show more difference having the t-value of 22.26** significant at .01 level than the introverts and extraverts at the females' level having the t-value of 8.43**. This shows that introverted males show better retention of norms. Then comes the females who show lesser movement and retain the group judgement more closely (see Table 13 and Figure 45 b part).

In short this shows that introverted males and especially the females show better retention of norms in terms of retaining the group judgement more closely by showing lesser movement.

Table 13: Means Contingency table for Personality (A) and Sex (B) in Sherif's Autokinesis for 5th stage.

(a)

Group	*Males*	*Females*	*t– value*
Introverts	3.68	1.28	10.16**
Extraverts	8.96	3.46	23.38**

(b)

Group	*Introverts*	*Extraverts*	*t-value*
Males	3.68	8.96	22.26**
Females	1.28	3.46	8.43**

Analysis of combined t-values for the difference between 4th and 5th stage in Sherif's Autokinesis for Personality and Sex groups

Table 14 clearly shows the significant differences between personality and gender groups by giving the significant t-values at .01 level for the difference between 4th and 5th stage which are 3.59** for introverts and extraverts and 7.82** for males and females. This concludes that introverts and especially females retain the group judgement by showing the lesser movement much similar to the previous stage i.e. the 4th stage of convergence as compared to the extraverts and males who drift much more from the existing norms of convergence.

Figure 45: Showing the Interaction effect of personality and sex in Sherif's Autokinesis for fifth stage.

(a Part)

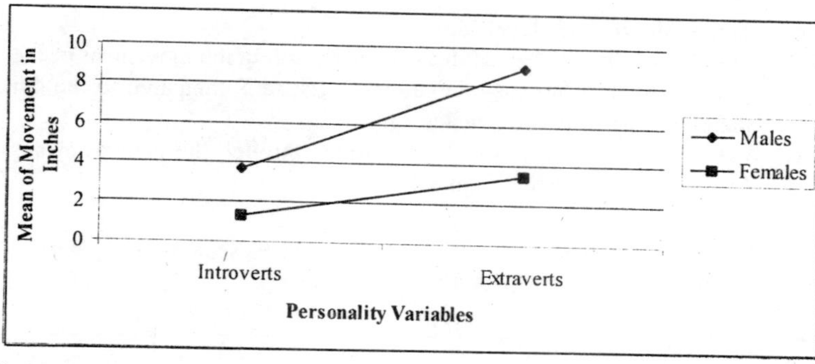

(b Part)

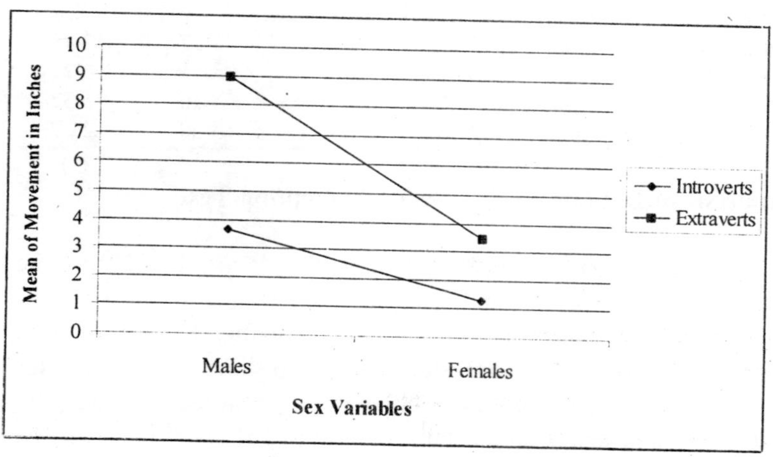

Table 14: Showing the difference between 4th and 5th stage for personality and sex group.

Groups	*4th stage (Mean)*	*5th stage (Mean)*	*5th-4th (Difference)*	t-value
Personality Group				
Introverts	3.27	2.48	–0.79	3.59**
Extraverts	4.53	6.21	1.68	
Sex Group				
Males	4.20	6.32	2.12	7.82**
Females	3.60	2.37	–1.23	

** depicts significance level at .01

– sign depicts the decrement in readings regarding the movement of the patch of light in 5th stage i.e. after a week as 5 compared to the 4th stage for introverts and females.

Note: The above results can also be confirmed through the general means Table (see Table 15 and Figure 46).

Table 15: Showing the general means for all the stages separately in Sherifs Autokinetic Effect Experiment.

Groups	*Stages*				
	1	2	3	4	5
Introverts	1.70	2.2	2.77	3.27	2.48
Extraverts	5.01	4.05	4.26	4.53	6.21
Males	4.09	4.07	4.21	4.20	6.32
Females	2.62	2.38	2.82	3.60	2.37

Analysis of Data on Asch's Visual Perception Test

Analysis of variance yielded F-ratios of 20.89** and 13.79** for the variables of personality and sex which are significant at .01 level respectively. The interaction between personality X sex yielded a significant F-ratio of 8.16** significant at .01 level. This indicates that the introverts and females yield to pressure more as compared to extraverts and males (for details see Table 16). This may also be confirmed through means (see Table 17).

Figure 46: Showing the general means for all the stages separately in Sherifs Autokinetic Effect Experiment.

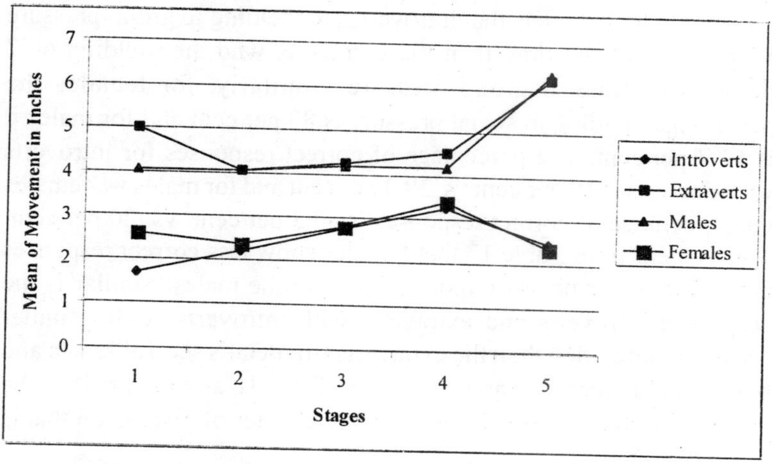

Table 16: Summary of ANOVA for Asch's Visual Perception Test.

Sv	*Ss*	*df*	*Ms*	*F*	*Sig. level*
A (Personality)	10.24	1	10.24	20.89**	.01, .05
B (Sex)	6.76	1	6.76	13.79**	.01, .05
A.B. (P x Sex)	4.00	1	4.00	8.16**	.01, .05
Within error	47.04	96	0.49		
Total	**68.04**	**99**			

Interaction effect of Personality × Sex (A × B) in Asch's Visual Perception Test

An inspection of Table 17 (a part) reveals that males and females do not differ at the introverted end significantly with t-being .81 but at the extraverted end, the sex differences are clearly perceived in yielding to group pressure with t-being significant at .01 level (4.72** $P < .01$). This can be better understood by looking at the interaction curves (see 47a part) when the interaction was inspected from the other angle (see Table 17b part and Fig. 47b part) it shows that at males' end, introverts and extraverts differ significantly in yielding to group pressure with t-being 5.91** at .01 level as compared to introverts and extraverts at the females level with t-being insignificant.

This may also be confirmed through the percentage yielding to social pressure and the percentage of correct responses given in Table 18 which depicts that introverts are yielding to group pressure 82 per cent of the time than the extraverts who are yielding 60.7 per cent of time to group pressure. Similarly, for females the percentage yielding to social pressure is 80 per cent and for males it is 62.7 per cent. The percentage of correct responses for introverts vs. extraverts is 18 per cent vs. 39.3 per cent and for males vs. females the percentage of correct responses is 37.3 per cent vs. 20 per cent. This is clear from Table 17 that females show less correct responses and come under pressure more often than the males. Similar is the case with introverts and extraverts with introverts coming under pressure more often than the extraverts (for details see Table 17a and b parts and Figure 47 a and b parts and Table 18 and Figure 48). The reasons for this will be discussed in the chapter of discussion that is next chapter.

Table 17: Means Contingerncy table for Personality (A) and Sex (B) in Asch's Visual Perception Test.

(a)

Groups	*Males*	*Females*	*t– value*
Introverts	2.4	2.52	.81 (N.S.)
Extraverts	1.36	2.28	4.72**

(b)

Groups	*Introverts*	*Extraverts*	*t-value*
Males	2.4	1.36	5.91**
Females	2.52	2.28	1.12 (N.S.)

Table 18: Depicting the percentage yielding to social pressure and percentage of correct responses by two personality groups two levels of sex in Asch's line drawing test.

	Introverts	*Extraverts*	*Males*	*Females*
% yielding to social pressure	82%	60.7%	62.7%	80%
% of correct responses	18%	39.3%	37.3%	20%

Figure 47: Showing the interaction effect of Personality × Sex in Asch's Visual Perception Test.

(a Part)

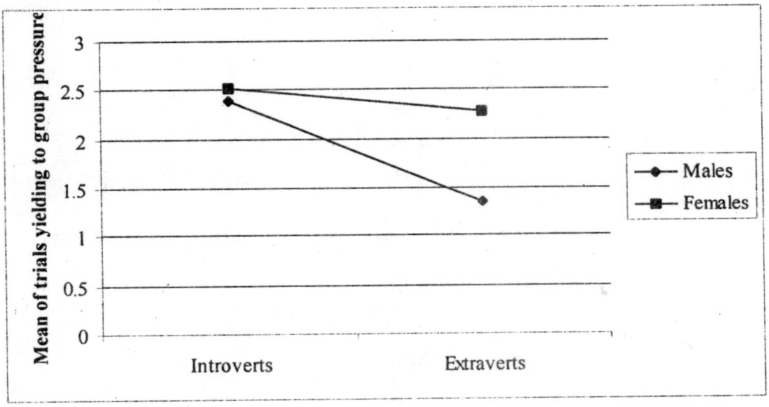

(b Part)

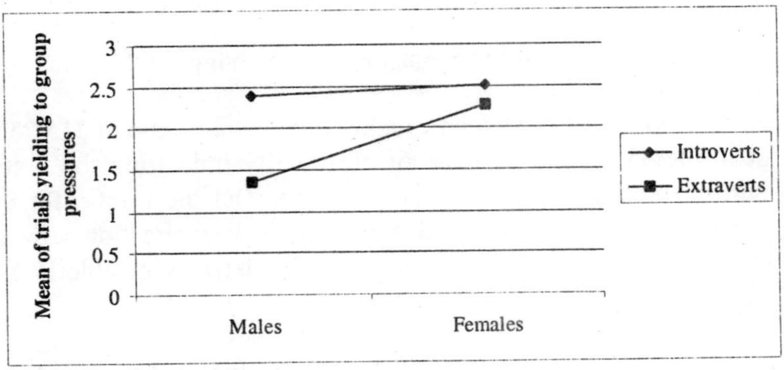

Figure 48: Depicting the % yielding to social pressure and % of correct responses by 2 personality groups and 2 levels of sex in Asch's line drawing test.

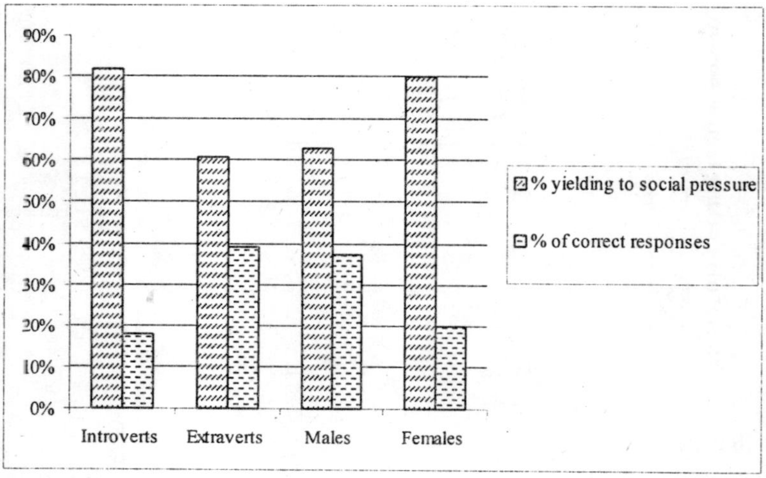

Analysis of Data on Anagram Problem Solving Task

Analysis of variance yielded a highly significant F-ratio of 215.75** at .01 level for the variable of personality indicating the better performance of introverts over extraverts. But the F-ratio for the variable of sex is not significant and similarly the interaction between Personality × Sex is also not significant (for details see Table 19 and for means see Table 6).

Table 19: Summary of ANOVA for Anagram Problem Solving Test

Sv	*Ss*	*df*	*Ms*	*F*	*Significance*
A	1004.89	1	1004.89	215.75**	.01, .05
B	5.29	1	5.29	1.13	N.S.
A.B.	0.09	1	0.09	0.019	N.S.
Within error	447.12	96	4.6575		
Total	**1457.39**	**99**			

Analysis of Data on Serial Positioning Effect

The analysis of variance yielded a highly significant F-ratio of 111.79** at .01 level for the variable of personality indicating the significant difference between the means of the two groups of personality viz. Introverts and Extraverts. The F-ratio for the variable of sex is not significant and similarly the interaction between personality × sex is not significant (for details see Table 20 and for means see Table 6).

The results can also be confirmed through the Table 21 showing the percentage of correct responses for 15 nonsense syllables in serial positioning effect by personality groups and gender groups. For clarity also see Figure 49a, b, c and d parts.

Table 20: Summary of ANOVA of Serial Positioning Effect

Sv	*Ss*	*df*	*Ms*	*F*	*Significance*
A	289	1	289	111.79**	.01, .05
B	0.36	1	0.36	0.13	N.S.
A.B.	0.04	1	0.04	0.01	N.S.
Within error	248.16	96	2.585		
Total	**537.56**	**99**			

Table 21: Table showing the percentage of correct responses for 15 nonsense syllables in Serial Positioning Effect by two personality groups and two sexes.

N.S	*1*	*2*	*3*	*4*	*5*	*6*	*7*	*8*	*9*	*10*	*11*	*12*	*13*	*14*	*15*
M	100	90	72	52	28	8	0	0	0	18	42	57	74	94	100
F	100	96	76	60	42	16	0	0	0	22	50	66	78	98	100
Int	100	100	82	60	42	18	0	0	0	22	48	62	78	100	100
Ext.	100	86	66	42	18	6	0	0	0	18	44	58	74	92	100
Com	**100**	**93**	**74**	**53**	**35**	**12**	**0**	**0**	**0**	**20**	**46**	**60**	**76**	**96**	**100**

Abbreviations used in the above table: N.S. Nonsense Syllables, M : Males, F : Females, Int. Introverts, Ext. : Extraverts, Com. : Combined

Figure 49 (a, b, c, d and e parts) showing the serial positioning curves for the two personality groups viz. introverts and extraverts and two sexes i.e. males and females and (e part) showing the combined serial positioning curve for personality and Sex in serial positioning effect.

Figure 49 (a, b, c, d, e): Showing the Serial Positioning Curves for Two Personality Groups, Two Sexes, and for Combined Scores

(a Part)

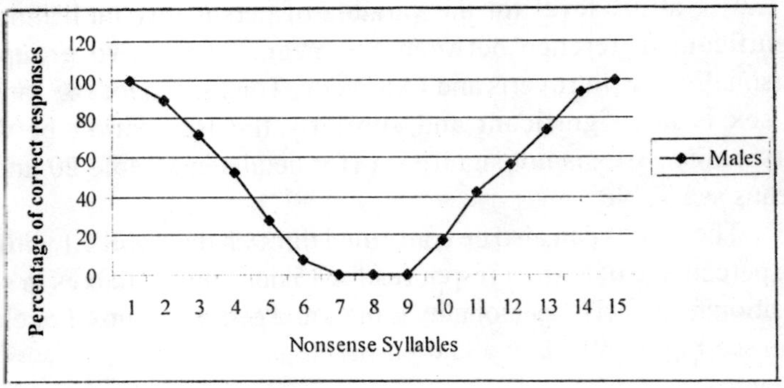

(b Part)

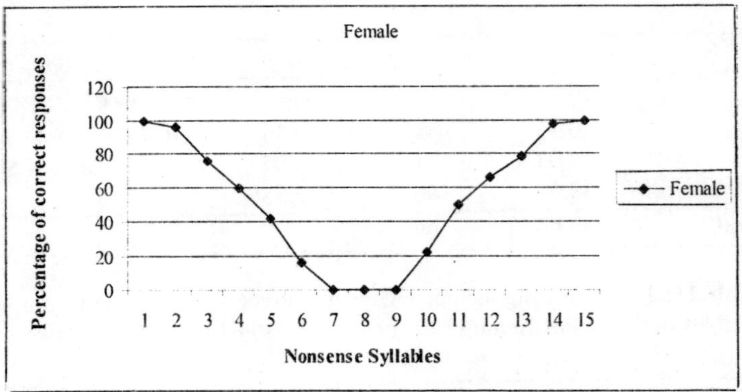

(c Part)

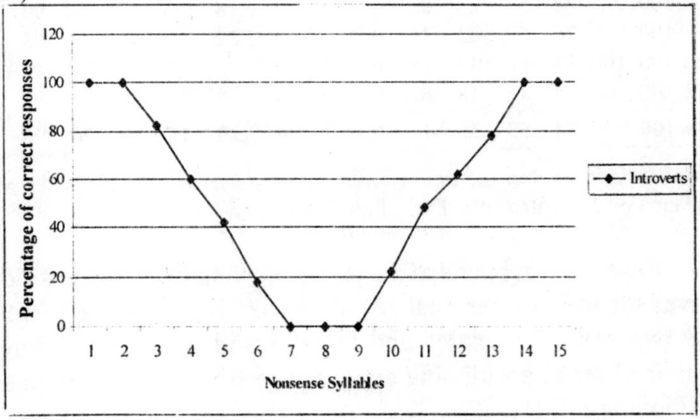

(d Part)

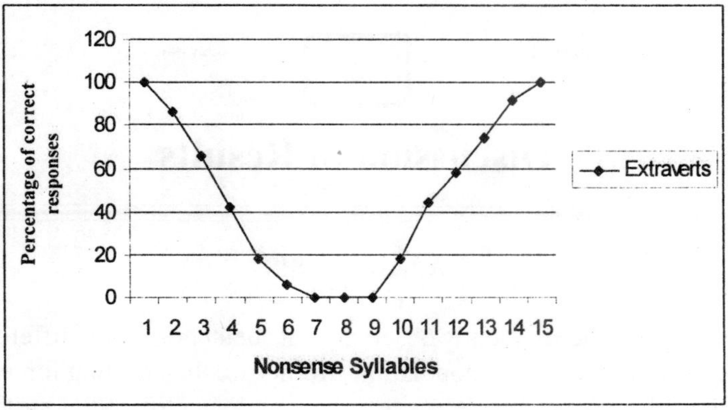
120
100
80
60
40
20
0
Percentage of correct responses
1 2 3 4 5 6 7 8 9 10 11 12 13 14 15
Nonsense Syllables
Extraverts

(e Part)

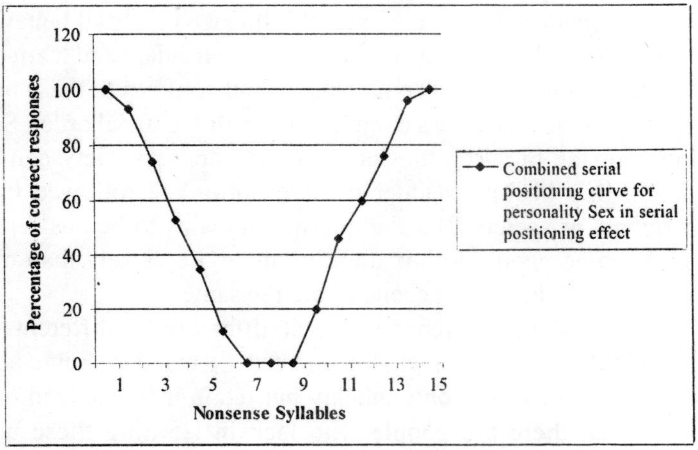
120
100
80
60
40
20
0
Percentage of correct responses
1 3 5 7 9 11 13 15
Nonsense Syllables
Combined serial positioning curve for personality Sex in serial positioning effect

6

Discussion of Results

A. ANALYSIS

It has been quite frequently observed that social norms are differently followed in the general population. Norms are the building force and social fabric of any society since the emergence of social systems. Social norms play an important role in the regulation of social behaviour. They are standards of behaviour that are agreed upon by group members and exert a powerful influence on social behaviour. In the framework of society, individuals have to adapt and learn these norms and values. If they do not adhere and conform to these norms of society, there would be a complete decay of the social order. Social norms are the building blocks of society and a society can only function in a healthy manner if these norms are followed by the inhabitants of society. But the question remains to be answered as why do some people follow these norms more closely than others even when the imparting agencies are the same.

Social norms are generally learnt differently by different kinds of people due to their personality and genetic makeup. Some people learn social norms not only quickly but retain them too and on the other hand, there are people who lack in learning these norms adequately and do not adhere to these norms but rather deviate due to which they become anti-social. Why does this happen? This is mainly due to genetic makeup and environmental influences.

In this regard, Eysenck in 1947, observed that introverts learn the social norms and expectations faster than their counterparts. Eysenck while casting his personality theory traces the origin of differences to Pavlov's conditioning that not all dogs condition alike. i.e., some organisms learn faster and others are slower. Thus, conditioning is the main force which aids in learning of social norms. Socialization is mediated by conditioning. Thus, who condition faster are likely to adhere to norms and behave in accordance with the expected standards of behaviour than those who condition slowly. According to Eysenck (1947, 1957) introverts condition better and learn the norms faster and show more retention than their counterparts.

Similarly, introverts are likely to yield to social pressure more because they believe that yielding to social pressure direct or indirect is desirable even if erroneous than extraverts who withstand the social pressure quite often not subscribing to the expected standards of behaviour.

Earlier some Russian contemporaries of Pavlov viz., Sokolov and Teplov observed that organisms are born with strong and weak nervous systems. Organisms with weak nervous system respond at the lower threshold of stimulation and organisms with strong nervous system respond at the higher threshold of stimulation. These analysis and Wundt's observation cleared the decks for his personality theory. In his personality analysis, Eysenck contended that introverts excite quickly, accumulate Ir slowly and dissipate it faster and converse is true for extraverts. Gales, Coles and Blaydon (1969) vindicated the stance of Eysenck wherein they revealed in their EEG studies that introverts are characterized by higher states of arousal. Eysenck had predicted that on the basis of these physiological differences, introverts have a weak nervous system and are marked by the higher arousal of cortical activity due to which they should learn faster. This has been borne out by sufficient evidence (Eysenck 1957, 1967; Kumar, D., 1974; Kumar, D., Kumari, Malhotra and Jerath, 1986; Kapila, A., 1981, 1987, 1992 and Handa, V., 1994).

But ironically, so far the main stress has been on lab tasks e.g. learning, memory and problem solving tasks and some pharmacological studies, whereas no emphasis has been laid on the differences in learning of social norms and expectations. The present investigation has been primarily designed to study the (1) development of social norms in introverts and extraverts and (2) second to see who retains it better and longer.

Not only this, the present investigation has also been designed to study the percentage yielding to social pressure among introverts and extraverts.

Similarly, gender differences in learning of social norms are due to socialization practices at the very onset of life. According to the process of social learning theory, males and females are taught differently and are rewarded for performing behaviour that are thought by society to be appropriate for men and women respectively. Females are expected to abide by the norms and show the retention of norms more as compared to males who deviate from these norms very often not only for the sake of fun but also because they consider breaching the norms as being their prerogative. Thus, females due to their expected standards of behaviour and social expectation follow social norms seriously as compared to males.

In short, two variables were taken into account for the present study (1) Personality and (2) Gender for the development of social norms. Thus, the present investigation was designed to study the development of social norms among different personality groups viz. introverts and extraverts and gender groups viz. males and females.

A factorial design or 2 × 2 was employed for the present study consisting of 2 groups of personality viz. introverts and extraverts and the sexes (males and females). In all there were 4 conditions or 4 cells, each consisting of 25 subjects who were tested on perceptual and behavioural norm tasks of Sherif's autokinesis and Asch's line drawing test alongwith anagrams and serial positioning effect. Thus, 100 subjects were taken for final individual experimentation. The data were analyzed through analysis of variance (ANOVA) of order of 2 × 2. For Sherif's autokinesis a repeated measure ANOVA of the order of 2 × 2 × (5) was used and for rest of the experiments, ANOVA of the order of 2 × 2 was used (Edwards, 1968).

The results of the present investigation are manifold and varied. Most of the findings support the hypothesis framed earlier. The discussion of the obtained results would follow the pattern in which the present problem was envisaged in the form of hypothesis and each feature would be opened one by one. The main purpose of our study was to see whether or not there are personality and gender differences in learning of social norms. The ensuing discussion will revolve primarily around the two personality dimensions of Extraversion and Introversion and their combined effect on the development of social norms and performance on problem solving (anagrams) and serial positioning effect. Alongwith sex is also taken to know its effect on the development of social norms and problem solving and learning tasks.

Personality and Sherif's Autokinetic Effect Experiment

The results on the autokinetic effect experiment upon the variable of personality indicate that introverts are showing lesser movement and less variation regarding the patch of light in autokinesis as compared to extraverts who are showing more movement and more variation in terms of judgement of movement in autokinesis. The said results are found to be significant, F-ratio being significant at .01 level (for F-ratio see ANOVA Table 7 and for comparison of means see Table 6). The present results are in accordance with the hypothesis framed earlier wherein it was hypothesized that introverts would show lesser movement than extraverts regarding the patch of light in autokinesis. The rationale for the present results could be offered through the following indirect experimental findings and observations. Eysenck (1947) had originally contended that extraverts opt for speed and introverts for accuracy and later Brebner and Cooper (1974) and Kumari, Malhotra and Jerath (1986, 1989) proposed a simple model of Introversion-Extroversion which contended that extraverts are geared to respond than introverts who are geared to inspect. Since extraverts who are response hungry as is clear from Eysenck's descriptive analysis (1957, 1967) that extraverts are casual and do not like to inspect rather drift from one topic to another because of their wandering tendency and seeking behaviour and as a result that the pupil of the eye does not remain stationary coupled with the total absence of frame of reference, as a result of that patch of the light seems to be moving more for extraverts as compared to introverts who are geared to inspect and for them the patch of light seems to be moving less and late. Eysenck in his descriptive analysis further contends that introverts like to pay close attention to anything whereas, extraverts do not like to concentrate, hence the patch of light does not move or move less and late for introverted individuals because of the lesser movement of the pupils and converse is true for extraverts.

Not only this, introverts because of their higher cortical arousal (Eysenck, 1957, 1967; Malhotra, 1974; Kumari, Malhotra and Jerath, 1986) and serious predisposition in general show lesser movement of the patch of light in the autokinetic experiment.

Personality, Stages and Convergence Effect

The interaction effect of personality and stages is significant at .01 level with F-ratio being 103.67** P < .01 (See Table 7). The Figure 42 and means contingency Table 9 clearly demonstrates the convergence effect which almost takes place at 4th stage with mean values for introverts in first four stages being 1.70, 2.20, 2.77 and 3.27 and for extraverts the mean values being 5.01, 4.05, 4.26 and 4.53. The mean values clearly show that introverts initially show lesser movement but gradually indicate an increase in their movement due to interaction with others and move toward the formation of norms and convergence almost takes place at the 4th stage. Whereas, on the contrary, extraverts in the 2nd stage show lesser movement but again steadily climb towards the initial stage i.e. from where they had started. On the whole extraverts have shown significantly greater movement of the patch of light at all the stages. The results clearly indicate that the convergence is taking place at the 4th stage roughly as the mean difference between introverts and extraverts is lesser and so does the magnitude of significance the t-being 6.637** P < .01 as compared to the rest of the stages i.e. I, II, III and V wherein the mean differences are much greater by giving the significant t-values being 17.343**, 9.251**, 8.665** and 18.76** all at .01 level.

When the final reading was taken after one week to know the retention of norms formed at the 4th stage among introverts and extraverts, it was found that introverts had retained the norms more strongly by showing the movement closer to the 4th stage of convergence with mean being 2.48. Whereas, extraverts had drifted from the norms by showing an appreciable increase in the movement of the patch of light with mean value being 6.21 which is much more than the initial movement. The reason for the personality difference in adherence to social norms in the autokinetic effect is that introverts like to pay close attention to their tasks as revealed by Eysenck (1957, 1967) in the descriptive analysis, whereas, extraverts shift from one topic to another because of their wandering tendency and seeking behaviour and as a result, the pupil of the eye does not remain stationary, hence the patch of light seems to be moving more for extraverts as compared to introverts. In addition, the introverts are supposed to form conditioned responses more rapidly than the

Extraverts because of their higher cortical arousal which facilitates the formation of connections (Eysenck 1957, 1967). Not only this, introverts are better in long-term retention (Tanwar and Kumar, 1986) and at the same time inspect, while extraverts show excitement and respond before inspecting (Brebner and Cooper, 1974; Kumar, Malhotra and Jerath, 1986; Shackleton and Fletcher 1984, and Eysenck and Gudjonsson, 1989).

To support the above contention it can be argued in the form of some indirect evidence that Wundt in the 19th century had suggested that extraverts (Sanguines and Cholerics) are changeable and introverts (Melancholics and Phlegmatics) are unchangeable i.e. are subject to lesser variation. This could also be explained through the following:

Eysenck and Franks (1956, 1957) and other researchers e.g. Brebner (1957) and Symonds (1958) have revealed that introverts are easily conditionable and extraverts form conditioned responses slowly as compared to introverts. On the basis of Eysenck's theory that introverts condition better, it may be deduced that they would show a greater degree of socialization because they learn the social norms and expectations faster. Eysenck (1958) later used a verbal conditioning technique and again found that introverts formed verbal conditioned responses quicker than extraverts. Introverts excite quickly, accumulate reactive inhibition (Ir) slowly and dissipate it faster. Eysenck (1956) has confirmed with a group of normal subjects that extraverted subjects generate Ir more quickly and dissipate it slowly, there by accumulating more inhibition (Eysenck, 1962). The implications of these relationships is that extraverts show more of work decrement in comparison with the introverts due to the accumulation of Ir.

On the basis of excitation-inhibition balance (Eysenck, 1957) and higher cortical arousal (Eysenck, 1967; Gale, Coles and Blaydon, 1969; and Shagaas and Canter, 1971), more efficient consolidation (Walker, 1958 and Eysenck, 1963) and better conditionability (Eysenck and Levey, 1963) and fairly better in learning coupled with better long-term retention (Tanwar and Malhotra, 1990, 1992), it can be inferred that their significantly better retention regarding the social norm was expected (hypothesis-I) and not out of place.

Personality and Social Pressure in Asch's Visual Perception Test of Line Drawing

The results on the line drawing experiment upon the variable of personality indicates that introverts yield to indirect group pressure more as compared to extraverts. The said results are found to be significant, F-ratio being significant at .01 level. For F-ratio (see ANOVA Table 16) and for comparison of means (see Table 6). The results have been also confirmed through the percentage of correct responses (see Table 18 and Figure 48) which depicts that there are significant differences between introverts and extraverts with introverts coming under pressure more and showing less correct responses than the extraverts who are not coming under pressure and giving more accurate perception. Introverts are yielding to group/ social pressure more because they believe that yielding is desirable to social pressure even if erroneous, secondly, introverts are susceptible to punishment and hence find it difficult to withstand the social pressure as compared to extraverts who breach the norms very often and do not come under pressure. The present results are in accordance with the hypothesis framed earlier that introverts would come under pressure more than the extraverts. In line with the present results, the review of scientific literature on Eysenck's personality theory has sufficient experimentally substantiated evidence that socialization is more or less positively related to introversion as compared to extraversion (Eysenck, 1956, 1957). The results have been also confirmed through the findings of Gray (1972-73) which show that introverts yield to social pressure more than extraverts due to high susceptibility of punishment in the form of rejection by the group and conditioning of fear is good in introverts as compared to extraverts. An interesting finding of this experiment is that after the experiment, almost all the introverts revealed that line A was equal to B and not C (standard line was equal to the one of the correct size than the other lines in the card), but they yielded to group pressure in the face of erroneous majority because they i.e. introverts did what was called for in the situation. In this society most of the administrative orders are carried out because of pressure from the group and from the top, because people generally believe that (1) majority is right, (2) whatever the norm, has to be followed. Hence, that is how, the society and social order and writ of the group runs.

Personality and Verbal Tasks

The results on the anagram of problem solving task on the variable of personality indicates that introverts are performing better than extraverts by solving more anagrams. The said results are found to be significant, F-ratio being significant at .01 level (see ANOVA Table 9) and for comparison of means (see Table 6). The present results are in accordance with the hypothesis framed earlier wherein it was hypothesized that introverts would perform better and would show greater proficiency in solving the anagrams.

In line with the present results, the review of scientific literature on Eysenck's personality theory has sufficient experimentally substantiated evidence that learning is more or less related positively to introversion especially in learning higher order mental tasks (Problem solving). Eysenck (1959) conducted a study on problem solving by administering Morrisby Compound Series Test to extraverts and introverts and found that extraverts took proportionately longer to obtain correct solution towards the end of the test and attempted less items as compared to introverts. Earlier, Furneaux (1956) demonstrated that on Nufferno Intelligence test extraverts took longer time to obtain correct solution in the later items of the test. Mohan and Kumar (1976) conducted a study on the qualitative difference of the performance of introverts and extraverts on the Standard Progressive Matrices (SPM), (Raven, 1960). The results of the study showed that on the difficult sets of SPM, i.e. C, D and E introverts did significantly better than extraverts. The same was observed by Antonin (1983) i.e. introverts did significantly better and superior to that of extraverts on RSPM. In a study explicitly designed to test performance differences between problem solving ability and Extroversion, Kumar (1974) has clearly demonstrated that on the five insightful problem solving tasks, introverts were significantly superior to extraverts on both the number of trials and time taken.

In a study, Kumar and Kapila (1987) have reported that introverts were significantly better and superior to extraverts on the insightful problem-solving tasks. Kumar and Kumari (1988) on the problem of set found the same results i.e., introverts were superior to that of extraverts. The results were explained through the arousal and inhibition-excitation hypothesis of Eysenck (1967) and Gray

(1972). Introverts (dysthemics) perform better in verbal tasks due to their better vocabulary and hysterics have a bad vocabulary as proposed by Himmelweit (1946), and evidenced by Kumari (1987), Ohri and Malhotra (1989), Kapila (1992) and Monika (1998).

Eysenck (1955, 1957) has hypothesized time and again that learning and performance are related to the level of cortical excitation and inhibition. He traces this differentiation of Pavlov's (1927) experiment with dogs who found that in some dogs the excitation was quicker, built up of inhibition slower and as such they could be conditioned better. Eysenck (1955) explained the concept of inhibition in terms of Hullian concept of reactive inhibition based on Hull's (1943) first submolar principle, "all responses leave in the physical structure a state which acts directly to inhibit the evocation of activity. This inhibitory substance manifests itself through reactive potentials. This negative reaction is called reactive inhibition (Ir). Eysenck (1957, 1967) maintains that Ir is generated more quickly in extraverts than in introverts. The present results that introverts are performing better in anagram solution of problem solving tasks, can be attributed to the slower build up of Ir and its faster dissipation in introverts. Further, level of arousal is the second major construct in Eysenck's theory to explain better learning of introverts. Eysenck (1967) and Gray (1972) agree that introverts are characterized by higher states of arousal. At the same time EEG studies have provided evidence that there is lower level of cortical arousal in extraverts (Gale, Coles and Blaydon, 1969 and Shagaas and Canter, 1971).

Similarly, the results on serial positioning effect on the variable of personality indicates that introverts are performing better than extraverts by learning the nonsense syllables in serial order significantly in lesser number of trials than extraverts. The said results are found to be significant by giving the significant F-ratio at .01 level (see ANOVA Table 20) and for the comparison of means (see Table 6). The results are in line with the hypothesis framed earlier that introverts would learn the nonsense syllables in serial order in lesser number of trials than the extraverts.

Sex and Sherif's Autokinetic Effect

The results of the autokinetic effect upon the variable of sex indicates that females are showing lesser movement regarding the patch of light in autokinesis as compared to males who are showing more in terms of judgement of movement in autokinesis. The said results are found to be significant, F-ratio being significant at .01 level. For F-ratio see ANOVA (Table 7) and for comparison of means (see Table 6). The present results are in line with the hypothesis framed earlier wherein it was assumed that females would show lesser movement of the patch of light in Sherif's autokinesis than males. The results have been confirmed through the early research done by Kapila Malhotra and Sharma (2001) in the article named 'gender' differences in social norms which stated that females retain social norms better and show lesser variation than the males in the retention of social norm. This is due to the expected behaviour from males and females that they differ in terms of adherence to social norms. This all is a result of socialization practices. According to Sandra Bem (1987) socialization produces a gender schema, a cognitive framework that organizes and guides a child's understanding of information relevant to gender. On the basis of what their schemas are regarding what is or is not appropriate for being a male or female, children begin to behave in ways that reflect society's gender roles. Socialization leads to gender discrimination. Females are discriminated against males in terms of education because it is considered as granting them undesirable liberty which would prove quite harmful to the society. Females are made dependent upon males throughout the life whereas, males are given full freedom and are encouraged to be independent. Not only this, religion relegate women to the secondary position curbing their individuality and growth. They are taken less seriously by their counterparts even in the areas in which they outdo men (Malhotra, 1974). All this lowers the status of women which makes them submissive and thereby conform to the norms (Kapila Malhotra and Sharma, 2001).

Thus, the present results are in line with the hypothesis and the earlier researches that females would show lesser movement of the patch of light and better retention of norms than the males due to two main reasons:

(1) Their dependency on males is higher as can be predicted through the process of socialization.

(2) Females take their tasks more seriously as shown through earlier readings, then start conforming to the movement in line with males.

Sex, Stages and Convergence Effect

Here also 5 stages are taken to know the convergence effect and the retention of norms formed at the 4th stage. The results on the variable of stages clearly demonstrate the convergence effect at the 4th stage. The results clearly show that females are showing lesser movement initially but gradually they are showing adjustment by steadily moving towards forming the norms and at the 4th stage convergence takes place. On the other hand, males are showing more movement of the patch of light throughout but the movement remains almost the same. But after a week, females show the movement close by that is to the initial movement by retaining the norms formed at the convergence effect at 4th stage, whereas, the males drift from the norms by showing more movement. Thus, the results of the present study show that the females show better adjustment and make an all effort for convergence than the males. For details (see ANOVA Tables 7 and 12 for F-ratios for main and final reading. F-ratio 131.04** ($P < .01$) for main and F-ratio 433.40** ($P < .01$) for final reading (Fifth stage). This can further be confirmed through Table 10 (means contingency Table with t-values) and Figure 43 which shows that at all the stages t-values are significant at .01 which are 4.138**, 9.384**, 8.057**, 2.632**, 12.343**. This shows that males show significantly more movement of the patch of light in all the stages and drift at the 5th stage after an interval of one week from the norm than females who show lesser movement by retaining the norms formed at the 4th stage of convergence, thus, explaining the main effect of gender.

The results can be explained through the contentions of Baron and Byrne (1988) who contended that females due to their subservient role are yielding more than males. Once they start interacting with other group members they start converging more. One interesting aspect of the present results regarding differences is that females throughout the course of experiment failed to assert their independence and rather yield more, whereas, males show their independence by drifting from the norms. Thus, males show more movement than the females regarding the patch of light due to their wandering and impulsive tendencies. Not only this, expected behaviour from males and females are differently viewed i.e. when females digress from norms, they are looked down upon and when men break the norms, it is viewed as it being their prerogative (Kapila Malhotra and Sharma, 2001). Thus, it may be inferred that females due to their submissive nature and expected behaviour do not challenge the norms and adhere to them in order to win social approval.

Sex and Social Influence in Asch's Visual Perception Test of Line Drawing

The results on the line drawing experiment upon the variable of sex indicates that females yield to indirect group pressure more as compared to males. The said results are found to be significant, F-ratio being 13.79** significant at .01 level. For F-ratio (see ANOVA Table 16) and for comparison of means (see Table 6). The results have been also confirmed through the percentage yielding to group pressure and the percentage of correct responses (see Table 18 and Figure 48) which depicts that there are significant differences between males and females with females coming under pressure more and showing less correct responses as compared to males. Females yield to social pressure significantly more due to the fact that they consider influence as conforming to social norms. This is due to the expected behaviour from males and females that they differ in terms of adherence and yielding to social pressure. This is mainly due to the socialization practices (Kapila Malhotra and Sharma, 2001). The sex roles are taught by the culture to the children at a very early stage starting from the moment of birth, with blue blankets for boys and pink ones for girls. Most parents and adults provide environments that differ in important respects. Such differences in behaviour produce different socialization experiences for men and women. Young children know that their parents want their sons and daughters to act differently. As children grow older, sex differences become even more pervasive, males are motivated toward achievement and power, females are motivated toward affiliation and dependency. Men are more competitive and women are more cooperative (Oetzel, 1966 and Kapila, 1992). Males are given freedom to do anything whereas, females are restricted of such freedom. Socialization practices lead to gender discrimination. Females are taken less seriously by their counterparts even in the areas in which they outdo men

(Malhotra, 1974). Male is considered superior to female as he is the head of the family, whereas, female is confined to the four walls of the house and is neglected of her privileges (Kaushik and Kapila Malhotra, 1997). The human personality according to Milton (1957) is formed on sex lines. Thus, aggression, intelligence and efficacy characterize the male; passivity and ignorance characterize the female. She is supposed to be affectionate, sympathetic, understanding, compassionate, soft-spoken, warm, tender etc., (Buchholz, 1978; Herzog and Bachman, 1982; Maguire, *et al.,* 1982; Feather, 1984; Maxwel and Cumming, 1988; and Kapila, 1992). Though the level of intelligence of females is equal to males but even then they play second fiddle to men because of their lack of independence developed and indirectly taught due to sex roles, fear of success and socialization practices. This is why most women have motive to avoid success because they expect negative consequences such as social rejection and a feeling of being unfaminine as a result of succeeding. Woman with high fear of success maintain self-defeating strategy (Horner, 1968, 1972; Kumar and Kapila, 1987; Kapila, 1992; and Ohri and Malhotra, 1993). The fear of success ingrained by the females during the early years of life leads to lack of will to withstand the social pressure and this is the reason why the females generally do not challenge the norms and adhere to them in order to win social approval. Not only this, they are deprived of education also (Kaushik and Kapila Malhotra, 1997).

Thus, to conclude socialization practices and gender discrimination lowers the status of women and they develop inferiority complex and on the top of it females' lack of educational opportunities put additional pressure on them to conform to the regulated behaviour and secondly in order to win the approval of the social group formal or informal, they are required to be more and more obedient even if it is wrong. Thus, it is due to the aforesaid reasons that females yield to social pressure more as compared to males.

In the present study, most of the interactions reached the desirable level of significance between personality and sex, personality and stages, sex and stages and three level interaction between personality, sex and stages in both Sherif's autokinesis and Asch's line drawing experiments. But no interaction is reportedly significant in anagram and serial positioning task.

B. INTERACTIONS

Interaction Effect of Personality and Sex (A × B) in Sherif's Autokinesis

The interaction effect of personality and sex under A (Error A) in the collated scores is significant at .01 level with F-ratio being 27.21** (See ANOVA Table 7). The means contingency Table alongwith t-values are also provided for the said interaction (See Table 8 a and b parts) which clearly demonstrates that movement in inches for extraverts and males is significantly greater than for the introverts and females with t-values being 8.24** $P < .01$ for males vs. Females at introverted end and 11.95** $P < .01$ for males vs. females at the extraverted end and 15.26** $P < .01$ for introverts vs. extraverts at the males' end and 9.12** $P < .01$ for introverts vs. extraverts at the females' end. The interaction between (A × B) personality and sex may be further confirmed through the curves (See Figure 41 a and b parts given in results section) but the interaction can best be depicted through the curve b of Figure 41 which is once again presented here for convenience. On the whole, it can be said that females and especially introverted females show lesser movement of the patch of light in Sherif's autokinesis as compared to the males and especially extraverted males but at both the levels the differences have been found to be significant as discussed above.

Fig. 41a: Showing the Interaction Effect of Personality and Sex (A x B) in Sherif's Autokinesis (for total).

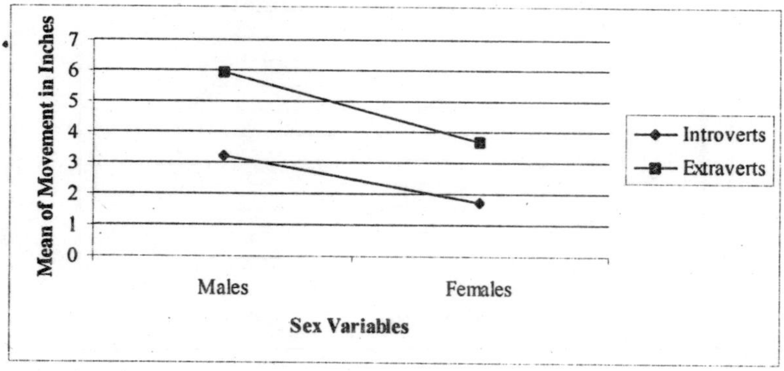

Interaction Effect of Personality and Sex for Final Reading i.e. for 5th stage in Sherif's Autokinetic Effect.

The interaction effect of personality and sex (A x B) for final reading i.e. 5th stage is significant at .01 level with F-ratio being 66.73** (See Table 12). This can be better understood by the means contingency Table 13 (a and b parts) alongwith curves (Figure 45 a and b parts) which clearly show that extraverted males have given the maximum movement (reading) of the patch of light and the introverted females have given the minimum movement. But at the same time the mean differences between males vs. females are significant at both the levels i.e. at introverted and extraverted ends with t-values being 10.16** P < .01 and 23.38** P < .01. Similarly, the differences between introverts Vs extraverts at the males' and females' level are significant with t-values being 22.26** P < .01 and 8.43** P < .01.

In nutshell, the interaction depicts that generally introverts and females show better retention of norms from stage 4 to 5 than their counterparts (See Figure 45b part which is once again presented here for convenience) which may be explain due to the fact that introverts and females take their tasks seriously even in the absence of frame of references and that is how the pupil of the eye move steadily as compared to the extraverts and males whose pupil moves rapidly as presumed earlier (Eysenck, 1957, 1967 and Kapila Malhotra and Sharma 2001).

Fig. 45b: Showing the Interaction Effect of Personality and Sex (A × B) in Sherif's autokinesis for final reading.

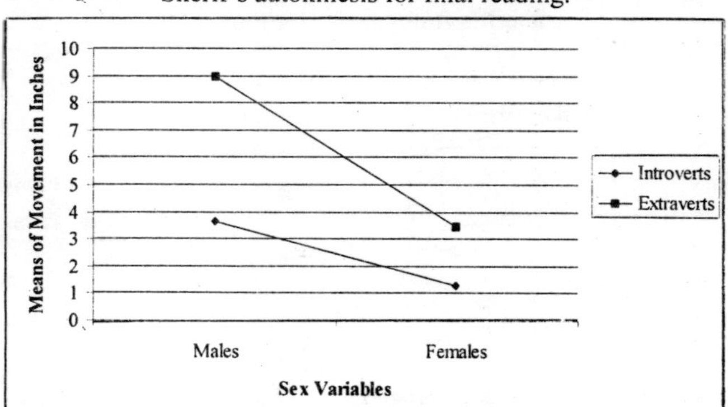

Personality and Stages

The interaction effect of personality and stages is significant at .01 level with F-ratio being 103.67** (see Table 7). The means contingency Table alongwith t-values is also provided for the said interaction which shows that t-values are significant at .01 level for all the stages which are 17.343**, 9.251**, 8.665**, 6.637** and 18.576** (see Table 9). The interaction between personality and stages may be confirmed through the curves (see Figure 42) which reveal that at all the stages the differences are significant that is introverts show less movement and better retention of the norms formed at the 4th stage of convergence than the extraverts who show more movement throughout and the drift is more at the 5th stage by showing exceptionally more movement of the patch of light. The details and reasons for this interaction have been already given in the section of personality and convergence effect of this chapter.

Sex and Stages

The interaction between sex and stages is significant at .01 level with F-ratio being 131.14** (see Table 7). The means contingency Table alongwith t-values is also provided for the said interaction which shows that the t-values are significant at all the stages at .01 level which are 4.138**, 9.384**, 8.057**, 2.632** and 12.343** (see Table 10). The interaction between sex and stages can also be confirmed through the curves (Figure 43) which reveal that at all the stages differences are significant with convergence taking at the 4th stage with the efforts of females who show more adjustment by steadily moving towards forming the norms and after a week they show more adherence and better retention of norms than the males who drift from the norms by showing more movement of the patch of light.

The said interaction clearly suggests that females maintain balance in the society and save it from chaos. Since they are important and primary source of socialization of the child, hence lead the way by example rather than precept preached by males.

Interaction Effect of Personality, Sex and Stages (A ×B × C)

The three order interaction between personality, sex and stages is significant at .01 level with F-ratio being 42.17** (see Table 7). The means contingency Tables with their t-values are also provided which shows that at all the stages the t-values are significant at .01 level for males and females at the introverted and extraverted ends which are 9.029**, 12.394**, 7.943**, 3.324** and 14.940** (at the introverted end) and 8.183**, 21.473**, 12.716**, 2.736** and 28.85** (at the extraverted end) (see Table 11 a part).

When the interaction was plotted the other way round, again the t-values were found to be significant at all the stages at .01 level between introverts and extraverts at males and females ends which are 14.704**, 18.817**, 18.691**, 8.796** and 22.899** (at the males end) and 36.369**, 19.202**, 9.303**, 8.318** and 7.514** (at the females end) (see Table 11 b part). The results for the said interaction can further be confirmed through the (Figure 44 a, b, c, d parts given in the results section), but the interactions can best be depicted through the curves of C and D which are once again presented here for convenience. The curves reveal that at the males' level the differences are significant between introverts and extraverts at all the stages indicating that extraverts show more movement of the patch of light and drift from the norms after a week than the introverts who show lesser movement and retain the norms after a week expectedly as discussed earlier.

Figure 44: Showing the Interaction Effect of Personality × Sex × Stages in Sherif's Autokinesis

(c part) Males

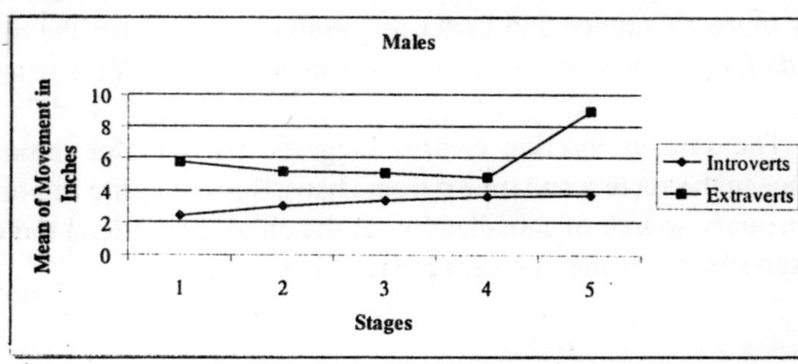

(d part)

Females

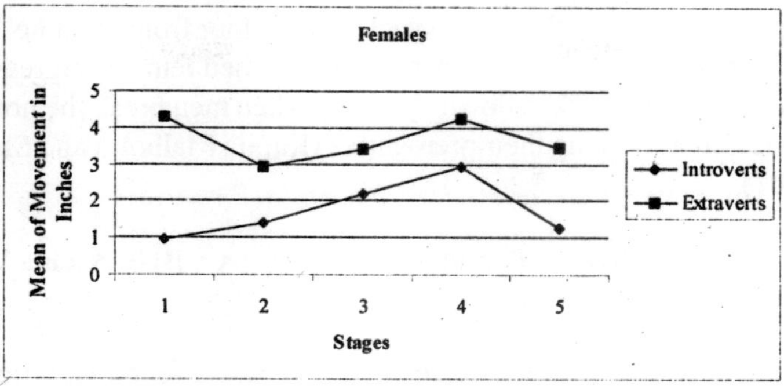

Similarly, at the females end, introverts and extraverts show lesser difference but significant indicating that extraverts show more movement of the patch of light than the introverts who are showing lesser movement and show convergence by steadily rising towards the formation of norms and after a week both show the retention of norms but introverted females show better retention of social norms by showing the movement closer to the initial stages.

Thus, the said interaction suggest that introverts and especially females show lesser movement of the patch of light than their counterparts because they take their tasks seriously even in the absence of frame of reference and hence the pupil of the eye moves steadily.

The reason being that introverts form strong conscience, are wracked by guilt and anxiety whenever they think about violating the rules. Whereas, extraverts condition less readily and so experience less inhibition about anti-social behaviour. It is the impulsivity part of the extraversion that is related to criminality, sociopathy and not the sociability part. Hence extraverts condition more slowly and thus are undersocialized. The component of impulsivity in the overall extraversion seems to come as a stumbling block in learning and is mainly responsible for build-up of inhibition and free responding without stopping to think. That is how they see greater movements in autokinesis and do not come under social pressure. Not only this, introverts' effective social conditioning makes them more conformist and cautious than the extraverts (Shackleton and Fletcher, 1984) who become non-conformist to the extent of being a deviant due to poor conditioning (Eysenck, 1994).

Thus, introverts and females do not challenge the norms and hence adhere to them in order to avoid punishment and to win social approval. Not only this, the expected behaviour from them i.e. males and females are differently viewed that is when females digress from norms, they are looked down upon and when men break the norms, it is viewed as it being their prerogative (Kapila Mälhotra and Sharma, 2001)

Interaction Effect of Personality and Sex (A x B) in Asch's Visual Perception Test

The interaction between personality and sex is found significant at .01 level in Asch's line drawing experiment with F-ratio being 8.16** (see Table 16). The means contingency Table alongwith t-values is also provided for the said interactions (see Table 17 a and b parts). The interaction between personality and sex may be confirmed through the curves (see Figure 47 a and b parts). The interaction curves depict that the difference between males and females at the extraverted end is more pronounced than at the introverted end where the difference is not significant. Similarly, the difference between introverts and extraverts at the males' end is more renounced than at the females' end where the difference failed to reach the level significance.

Thus, the said interaction show that introverts and especially females irrespective of their personality dimensions come under group pressure significantly more directly or indirectly. This can also be confirmed through the tables and graph of percentage yielding to social pressure and percentage of correct responses (see Table 18 and Figure 48).

Despite the ease of the task, the confederates' wrong answers had a considerable impact on the real subjects responses and they also produced a good deal of anxiety. The question arises why did so many subjects yield? When questioned/interviewed later, some subjects especially introverts and females who went along with the group told the investigator that they felt bewildered and were concerned about looking ridiculous. Others said that they quite literally could not believe their eyes and assumed that the group was correct. Even those who remained independent reported discomfort and were still looking for ways to reconcile their judgements with those of the majority when the experiment ended (this is true for independent introverts and females). Whereas, most of the extraverts remained independent, did not come under pressure and also did not report any sort of discomfort. The reason being that introverts are highly susceptible to punishment and conditioning of fear is good in them and to avoid any sort of rejection by the group, do not withstand the pressure (Gray 1971, 1972). Similarly, females come under group pressure significantly more as compared to males due to the reasons being that they are socialized in such a way that they become dependent, submissive and yielding. They do not resist the group pressure to avoid any kind of conflicts and disagreements with others in the interests of group harmony and thereby avoid the negative consequences such as social rejection (Oetzel, 1966; Horner, 1972 and 1974; Sharma, 1979; William and Best, 1990; Duex, 1993; Unger, 1994 and Sharma and Dalip Malhotra, 2003).

In short, the delicate balance in the society is maintained as norms are not always based on logic and reasoning. The basic purpose of social norms is to weave the society together and females and introverts play a pivotal role in preserving the norms of society. The present results throw light on the dynamic thinking of women/females (Kapila Malhotra and Sharma, 2001).

In nutshell, the assumptions and objectives with which the present study was designed have been squarely met.

7

Summary

The present investigation was designed to study the development of social norms among different personality and gender groups alongwith their learning and memory performance. A factorial design of 2 × 2 (Edwards, 1968) was employed in the present study. There were two conditions of personality, i.e. introverts and extraverts and two conditions of sex viz. males and females. In all there were 4 conditions/ cells each consisting of 25 subjects, thereby yielding a total sample of 100 subjects who were tested on perceptual and behavioural norm tasks alongwith anagrams and serial positioning.

Selection of Sample

(1) Initial Sample: A sample of 500 students (250 males and 250 females) of university level was drawn randomly from Himachal Pradesh University, Shimla for the present study.

The subjects were taken in a group of 10-15. First of all, they were administered the Eysenck's Personality Inventory (Eysenck and Eysenck, 1968) to obtain their personality scores on Extraversion/ Introversion dimension. Instructions written on the top of the forms were read out loudly and clearly. They were told to start with the inventory after the administration of instructions. There was no time limit for EPI. On the average, subjects took 20 minutes to answer 57 questions. 24 questions, each were keyed for extraversion and neuroticism and rest of the nine questions constituted the lie scale.

(2) Final Sample: The final sample of 100 subjects were selected on the basis of their scores on personality inventory. Students scoring between 8 to 12 on neuroticism were considered as medium neurotics and at the same time Students scoring either 12+ or –8 were termed

as extraverts and introverts respectively consisting of half males and half females.

Thus, the design came out to be having 100 subjects with 4 groups. The layout of which i.e. 2 × 2 factorial design is presented in Table 5 (stages were only for social influence under Sherif's study for convergence effect).

Tools used

Eysenck Personality Inventory (EPI)

Eysenck and Eysenck (1968). EPI was used to select personality groups. Scoring was done with the help of scoring stencil. The psychometric properties of EPI in terms of its reliability and validity has been established in number of investigations carried out in India e.g. (Kumar, 1974; Kapila, 1992). For Indian samples reliability and validity has been reported by various studies (Kumar, 1974) between .80 to .90.

Autokinesis (Sherif, 1935)

It is an instrument which is placed in a darkened room. The walls were not visible, nor were there any other physical frames of reference for the subjects. In this experiment, subjects were made to sit comfortably in a completely darkened room in a group of 4 i.e. 2 males and 2 females comprising of introverts and extraverts, looking at the patch of light moving/waving up and down. Their task was to judge how far the patch of light approximately moved as it followed its erratic course in the darkness. Readings were taken in 4 stages, then, after a week another reading was taken to see how the convergence effect is retained in introverts and extraverts and two sexes viz. males and females. On the whole, 5 stages were taken.

Asch's Line Drawing Cards: (Asch, 1951)

Asch's line drawing cards (Figure 20) were used with one card containing the standard line and the other three cards containing the comparison lines. In all 4 cards were used. In this test of visual perception, the naive subjects were made to sit with other six confederates of the experimenter around a Table (see Figure 20). Subjects in this experiment were first shown the standard card and then the comparison cards and they were asked to identify which of the three comparison lines best matched the standard line. This procedure was repeated three times with different stimulus cards involving comparison lines. First, the confederates stated their judgements publicly one after another and in the last, the naive subject stated his/her judgement. This experiment was done with all the 100 subjects to know the percentage yielding to group pressure among two sexes i.e., males and females and two personality groups viz. introverts and extraverts.

Anagrams—"Problem Solving Task" (Dominowski, 1966)

An anagram consists of several letters which are jumbled up and subject has to rearrange them to form a meaningful word. In anagram's problem, 15 jumbled up words with single, double and tripple shifts were given to the subjects to make them into meaningful words in 10 minutes. The standardized anagrams have been taken from Dominowski (1966) and adapted for Indian conditions by Sehgal (1990) and Kapila (1992).

Serial Positioning Effect (use of four letter nonsense syllables) (Gamble, 1909 and 1927)

Herman Ebbinghaus (1885) developed this method of studying learning and memory. Here we have used diphthongs following the recommendations of Gamble. In the diphthong generally between initial and final consonants two or a single vowel is used to avoid the anagram to look repulsive and in order to facilitate subject to pronounce it better, the nonsense syllables are the best source and material of learning as these do not have preestablished associations (Hull, 1943).

A list of 15 four letter nonsense syllables were made and arranged and then written down in series and the subjects were asked to memorize the list in the same order, as it appeared in the series. This list was shown through the memory drum apparatus. After the list was exposed to the subjects, they were asked to recall the syllables in the same order as it appeared in the series. Trials were repeated until the subjects were able to recall the nonsense syllables correctly and in the same order.

Objectives

The present study has been undertaken to fulfil certain aims as given below:

(1) The major aim of the investigation undertaken currently was to observe the variation in movement and perceptual relations (initial and final) in the two personality groups and sexes due to social pressure and interaction.

(2) Another aim of the present investigation was to study the differences between two personality groups and sexes on anagram solution of problem solving and serial positioning effect to know their vocabulary and performance based on social norms and empirical research.

The present problem was designed and in the light of meagre evidence and some indirect and presumed sources the main hypotheses for the main effects and their interactions were formed as given below. (The details of aims and hypotheses are already presented in chapter 3).

(1) In Sherif's Autokinesis, on the variable of personality, Introverts would show lesser movement and strong retention of social norms because at the descriptive level according to Eysenck they show more restrain in temperament, whereas, extraverts show more excitement. The principle of autokinesis is that in the absence of frame of reference, the patch of light seems moving as the pupil of the eye moves and the light's movement for extraverts would be more than introverts because extraverts due to their outward and casual disposition cannot pay close attention to most of the things, whereas, the introverts are on the opposite extreme, hence the movement would be lesser for them (Handa, 1994).

(2) On the variable of sex, it can be presumed that females would show lesser movement of the patch of light and would show stronger retention of social norms because females are very sensitive and come to take their tasks seriously even in the absence of frame of reference and thus the pupil of the eye moves steadily thereby showing lesser movement and after a week they i.e. females, would retain the norms

better than males because of the expected behaviour i.e. when females digress from norms they are looked down upon and when males breach the norms, it is viewed as it being their prerogative, hence, females would show better retention of group norm than males (Kapila Malhotra and Sharma, 2000).

(3) In Asch's visual perception task, on the variable of personality, Introverts would yield to social pressure more than the extraverts due to the fact that they i.e. introverts believe that going with the erroneous majority is called for in the situation and thus can avoid the punishment in the form of rejection by the groups (Gray, 1972).

(4) On the variable of sex, females would yield to social pressure more in visual perception of Asch's line drawing experiment than males because they believe that it is in conformity with the norm which is due to the fact of socialization practices and upbringing available to the two sexes. They are required to be obedient, submissive and thus yield more to avoid disagreement or conflict with others in the interests of group harmony, to win social approval and to ensure smooth interpersonal relations (Kapila Malhotra and Sharma, 2000).

(5) On Anagram problem solving, introverts would show superiority to extraverts due to their better vocabulary (Himmelweit, 1946).

(6) Females would perform better than males in anagram problem solving task due to their serious articulation, better vocabulary and better verbal facility (Kumar and Kapila, 1992).

(7) In serial positioning effect, on the variable of personality, introverts would learn the nonsense syllables in serial order in serial positioning effect significantly in lesser number of trials than extraverts because of their higher cortical arousal (Eysenck, 1967 and Kumar, 1974).

(8) On the variable of sex, females would learn the nonsense syllables in serial order in serial positioning effect significantly in lesser number of trials than males because of their higher learning capacity due to their serious disposition towards the task (Kumar, 1974; Kapila, 1992 and Kapoor, 1997).

Means were calculated for the various conditions i.e. for two groups of personality and two groups of sex for each of the four experiments (see Table 6).

To find out the significance of difference between the said means, ANOVA of the order of 2 × 2 was employed (Edwards, 1969), but for Sherif's autokinetic effect ANOVA of the order of 2 × 2 × (5) was employed and for the final reading i.e. for the 5th stage ANOVA of the order of 2 × 2 was employed.

Thus, in this way 5 analysis of variance i.e. 2 for Sherif's Autokinesis (1 for total readings and 1 for final reading i.e. 5th stage in terms of movement of the patch of light in inches), 1 for Asch's visual perception test, (in terms of trials yielding to group pressure), 1 for right responses in Anagrams Problem Solving task and 1 for trials taken in Serial Positioning Effect (for details see the section of results with ANOVA Tables 7, 12, 14, 19, 20).

Results and Discussion

In the present investigation, the results on the variables of personality in Sherif's autokinesis are very much in accordance with the hypothesis framed earlier, the F-ratios being significant at .01 level (see ANOVA Tables 7 and 12). On this variable, it was hypothesized that introverts would show lesser movement of the patch of light in Sherif's autokinesis than the extraverts and after a week would retain the norms significantly better than the extraverts because of their serious disposition and their higher cortical arousal which helps in warming up and also helps in paying close attention to inspect and thus show lesser movement of the patch of light than the extraverts who are response hungry and show more variation in the judgement of movement.

On this variable in Asch's visual perception of line drawing experiment, the results are very much in accordance with the hypothesis wherein it was stated that introverts would come under pressure significantly more as compared to extraverts (see ANOVA Table 16). They i.e. introverts, go along with the erroneous majority because this is what they consider as called for in the situation and secondly Eysenck (1947) and Gray (1972) contends that introverts learn the social norms and expectations faster than extraverts.

Not only this, on the variable of anagram solution and serial positioning effect, it was hypothesized that introverts would do better than extraverts because of their better vocabulary and serious disposition and the results are very much in accordance with the hypothesis stated above (see ANOVA Tables 19 and 20). This is due to the fact that introverts excite quickly, accumulate (Ir) reaction inhibition slowly and dissipate it faster. On the top of it, introverts have higher cortical arousal and hence learn faster than extraverts.

The above said results are very much in line with the earlier investigations (Eysenck, 1959, 1967, 1970; Gray, 1972; Brebner and Cooper, 1974; Malhotra and Jerath, 1986; Kumar and Kapila, 1987; Kumar and Kumari, 1988; Handa, V., 1994 and Eysenck, 1994).

On the variable of sex in Sherif's Autokinesis also, the results are very much in accordance with the hypothesis framed earlier (see ANOVA Tables 7 and 10). On this variable, it was hypothesized that females would show lesser movement of the patch of light and better retention of social norms than their counterparts i.e. males in Sherif's Autokinesis. This is due to the fact that females fail to assert their independence and yield more whereas, males are given freedom throughout their life from the very beginning and that is why when females break the norms they are looked down upon and when males breach the norms, it is viewed as being their prerogative. Thus, this is the reason why females show convergence and retention of social norms more than males. These results are in line with the earlier studies (Crutchfield, 1955; Sistrunk and Mcdavid, 1971, Baron and Byrne, 1988; Handa, V., 1994 and Kapila Malhotra and Sharma, 2001).

In Asch's visual perception of line drawing experiment, it was hypothesized that females would yield to group pressure significantly more than the males because they believe that yielding to pressure is in conformity with the norms. Not only this, this is also due to the fact of socialization practices and upbringing available to the two sexes. Socialization practices lead to gender discrimination and gender schemas. They are deprived of education, medical treatment etc. Thus, females' lack of educational opportunities puts additional pressure on them to conform to the regulated to be more and more obedient even if it is wrong. This is also due to fear of success because young women who succeed in school and in their jobs may feel torn between the rewards of success and the cultural norm that devaluates achievement for females. If they want a career, they may fear success because they will loose friends or be unable to marry. Thus, fearing social rejection as a result of achievement, females may not perform as well as they can and thus avoid dealing with the conflict by yielding to social pressure than their counterparts i.e. males. These results do find the support from earlier studies (Crutchfield, 1955; Horner, 1968, 1972, 1974; Sistrunk and Mcdavid, 1971; Bern, 1987; Baron and Byrne, 1988; Kumar and Kapila, 1987; Ohri and Malhotra, 1989; Kapila, 1992; Handa, V., 1994; and Kapila Malhotra and Sharma, 2001).

On this variable in anagram solution and serial positioning effect, the results are not in accordance with the hypothesis framed earlier wherein it was stated that females would do better than males due to their serious articulation and better vocabulary. This is clear from F-ratios which are not significant and the hypothesis stand disproved (see ANOVA Tables 19 and 20), but trend of means show that females perform better than males.

The three order interaction between Personality × Sex × Stages is significant at .01 level (for F-ratios see Table 7 and for t- values see Table 11. The two level interaction between Personality × Sex, Personality × Stages and Sex × Stages could be taken care by the three factor interaction of Personality × Sex × Stages. The three order interaction show that from stage I to V, introverts and females are moving towards conformity behaviour that is they show more conformity by showing comparatively more movement by moving towards convergence for the formation of norms whereas, extraverts and males in the second stage show lesser movement but again steadily rise towards the initial stage i.e. from where they started and this is further borne out by the fact that after a week extraverts and males drift more and introverts and females show more retention of group norms.

The interaction between Personality × Sex in Asch's visual perception of line drawing experiment is also significant at .01 level (see ANOVA-Table 16 for F-ratio). The interaction depicts that at the level of introversion, the difference between males and females is not significant whereas, at the level of extraversion, the difference between males and females is more pronounced. Similarly, the difference between introverts and extraverts at the males end is more marked and sharp than at the females end where the difference is not significant. Thus, the said interaction reveals that introverts and especially females irrespective of their personality dimension come under group pressure significantly more directly or indirectly (see Table 16 and Figure 47 a and b parts).

Qualitatively how much you are an introvert or extravert, a basic issue in question is specific situation that what it matters. So extraverts will abide at one point and drift from that on the other. Whereas, introverts show their convergence at all the points. Extraverts do not come under group pressure because they do not consider it to be a norm that is why they do not abide by the norm. Whereas, for introvert whether if it is right or wrong or rain or shine, they carry it out in letter and spirit.

The delicate balance in the society is maintained as norms are not always based on logic and reasoning. The basic purpose of social norm is to weave the society together and females play a pivotal role in preserving the norms of society and save it from chaos and great disorder. The present results throw light on the dynamic thinking of women/females.

Bibliography

Adams, H.F., (1912). Autokinetic sensations, Psychological Monographs, No. 59: 32-44.

Adey, W.R. Segundo, J.P. and Livingston, R.B., (1957). Corticifugal influence on intrinsic brainstem conduction in cat and monkey. Journal of Neurophysiology, 20: 1-16.

Adler, A., (1927). Practice and Theory of Individual Psychology. New York: Harcourt Brace and World.

Allen, V.L., (1965) "Conformity and the Role of Deviant", Personality, 33. New York: Academic Press.

Allen, V.L. (1975). Social support for non conformity. In Berkovitz (ed.), Advances in Experimental Social Psychology, (Vol. 2), New York: Academic Press.

Allen, V.L., Levin, J.M., (1971). Social support and conformity: The role of independent assessment of reality. Journal of Experimental Social Psychology, 4, 48-58.

Allport, F.H., (1924). Social Psychology. Boston: Houghton Mifflin.

Allport, G.W., (1937). Personality: A Psychological Interpretation. New York: Holt, Rinehart and Winston.

Allport, G.W. (1961). Pattern and Growth in Personality. New York: Holt, Rinehart and Winston.

Alper, J. (1993, April 16). The pipeline is leaking women—all the women all the way along. Science, 260: 409-411.

Altman, I., (1975). The Environment and Social Behaviour. Monterey, CD: Brooks/Cole.

Antonin, M., (1983). Relationship between Eysenck's dimension and pubescents performance on Raven's progressive matrices. (Crez). Psychologia a Pato Psychologia Dietas, 18(2): 113-122.

Asbury, H., (1927). The Gangs of New York. New York: Knopf.

Asch, S.E., (1951). Effects of Group Pressure on the Modification and Distortion of Judgement. In H. Guetzkow (ed.), Groups, Leadership and Men. Pittsburgh, Pa.: Carnegie Press, 177-190.

Asch, S.E., (1952). Social Psychology, Prentice-Hall.

Asch, S.E., (1956). Studies of independence and submission to group pressure: A minority of one against a unanimous majority. Psychological Monographs, 7: 416.

Atkinson, J.W. and Feather, N.T., (1966). Review and Appraisal. In J.W. Atkinson and N.T. Feather (eds.), A Theory of Achievement Motivation. New York: Wiley

Atkinson, J.W. and Litwin, G.H., (1960). Achievement motive and test anxiety conceived as motive to approach success and to avoid failure. Journal of Abnormal and Social Psychology, 60: 52-63.

Baken, D., (1966). The Duality of Human Existence: Chicago, Rand McNally.

Baker, G.W., and Chapman, D.W., (1962). Man and Society in Disaster. New York: Basic Books.

Bandura, A., (1969). Principles of Behaviour Modification. New York: Holt, Rinehart and Winston.

Bannister, D., (1977). New Perspective in Personal Construct Theory. New York: Academic Press.

Baringer, H.R., Blankstein, G.I., and Mack, R.W., (eds.) (1965). Social Change in Developing Areas. Cambridge, Mass.: Schenkman.

Barlett, F.C., (1951). The Mind at Work and Play. London: Allen.

Barnett, H.G., (1953). Innovation: The Basis of Cultural Change. New York: McGraw-Hill.

Baron, R.A., (1988). Social Psychology. New Delhi: Prentice Hall of India Private Limited.

Baron, R.A. and Byrne, D., (1988). Social Psychology: Understanding human interaction (5th ed.). Boston: Allyn and Bacon.

Barron, M.L., (1974). The Criminogenic Society: Social Values and Deviance, in Abraham, S. Blumberg, ed., Current Perspectives on Criminal Behaviour. New York: Knopf.

Barry, H., Bacon, M.K. and Child, I.L., (1957). A cross cultural survey of some sex-differences in socialization. Journal of Abnormal and Social Psychology, 55, 327-332.

Bartholomew, A.A., (1959). Extraversion, introversion and neuroticism in first offenders and recidivists. British Journal of Delinquency, 10: 120-129.

Becker, E., (1962). "Socialization, Command of Performance, and Mental Illness". American Journal of Sociology, 67: 494-501.

Becker, W.C., (1960). Cortical inhibition and extraversion-introversion. Journal of Abnormal and Social Psychology, 61: 52-56.

Bedell, R.C., (1934). The relationship between the ability to recall and the ability to infer in specific learning situations. Science Education, 18, 158-162.

Bem, S.L., (1974). The measurement of Psychological androgyny. Journal of Consulting and Clinical Psychology 42: 155-162.

Bem, S.L., (1975). Sex-role adaptability: One consequence of Psychological androgyny. Journal of Personality and Social Psychology, 31: 634-643.

Bem, S.L., (1977). On the utility of alternative procedures for assessing Psychology of androgyny. Journal of Consulting and Clinical Psychology.

Bem, S.L., (1987). Gender Schema Theory and its Implications for Child Development. Raising Gender—Aschematic Children in a Gender—Schematic Society. In M.R. Walsh (ed.), The Psychology of Women: Ongoing Debates. New Haven, C.T.: Yale University Press.

Bem, S.L., (1993). Lenses of Gender. New Haven, C.T.: Yale University Press.

Bem, S.L. and Lenney E., (1976). Sex-typing and the avoidance in cross-sex behaviour. Journal of Personality and Social Psychology, 33: 48-54.

Bem, S.L., Martyna, W. and Watson, C., (1976). Sex-typing and androgyny. Further explorations of the expressive domain. Journal of Personality and Social Psychology: 34: 1016-1023.

Benbow, C.P. and Stanley, J.C., (1980). Sex differences in mathematical ability: Fact or artificat? Science, (Dec.), 210 (4475): 1262-1264.

Bending, A.W., (1957). Extraversion, neuroticism and manifest anxiety. Journal of Consulting Psychology, 21: 398

Benedict, R., (1934). Anthropology and the Abnormal. Journal of General Psychology, 10: 59-82.

Benedict, R., (1942). Race and cultural relations, Problems in American life. No. 5. Washington: Natural Education Association.

Benedict, R., (1946). The Chrysanthemum and the Sword, Boston: Houghton Mifflin.

Bennet, E.M. and Cohen, L.R., (1959). Men and Women Personality Patterns and Contrasts. Genetic Psychology Monographs 1959.

Berg, I.A., and Bass, B.M., (eds.) (1961). Conformity and Deviation. New York: Harper and Row.

Bergin, D.J. and Williams, J.E., (1991). Sex Stereotypes in the United States revisited: 1972-1988. Sex Roles, 24: 413-423.

Berkovitz, L., (1954). Group Standards, Cohesiveness and Productivity. Human Relations, 7: 509-519.

Berkovitz, L., (1975). A Survey of Social Psychology. Hillsdale, Illinois.

Berzins, J.I., (1975). New perspectives on sex-role and personality dimensions. In sex-roles: Masculine, Feminine, Androgynous or None of the above. Symposium presented at the meeting of American Psychological Association, Chicago.

Billings, M.L., (1934). Problem-solving in different fields of endeavour. American Journal of Psychology, 46: 259-272.

Block, J.H., (1973). Conception of sex-role. Some cross-cultural and longitudinal perspectives. American Psychologist. 28: 512-526.

Bond, M.H., (1988). Finding universal dimensions of individual variation in multi-cultural studies of values: the Rokeach and Chinese value surveys. Journal of Personality and Social Psychology, 55: 1009-1015.

Bovard, E.W., Jr., (1948). Social norms and the individual. Journal of Abnormal and Social Psychology, 43, 62-69.

Bovard, E.W., Jr., (1953). Conformity to social norms in stable and temporary groups. Science, 117: 361-363.

Brebner, J.M., (1957). An experimental investigation of the relationship between conditioning and introversion/extraversion in normal subjects. Master's thesis, Abderdeen University.

Brebner, J.M., and Cooper, C., (1974). The effect of a low rate of regular signals upon the RT of introverts and extraverts. Journal of Research in Personality, 4: 263-276.

Brierley, H., (1961). The speed and accuracy characteristics of neurotics. British Journal of Psychology, 52: 273-280.

Broadbent, D.E., (1958). Perception and Communication. Newyork: Pergamon Press.

Brody, N., (1972). Personality Research and Theory. London: Academic Press.

Broom, L. and Selznick, P., (1963). Sociology: A text book with adaptive readings.

Broota K.D., Misra, G. Sibia, A. and Srivastava, A.K., (2002). Introduction to Psychology. National Council of Educational Research and Training, Sri Aurobindo Marg, New Delhi, 76-74.

Brown, S.R., and Hendrick, C., (1971). Introversion-extraversion, and social perception. British Journal of Social and Clinical Psychology, 10: 313-319.

Buchanan, J.S., and Dale, E.C.A., (1924). History of Oklahoma Evanston, III: Row, Peterson.

Buchholz, R.A., (1978). An empirical study of contemporary beliefs about work in American Society. Journal of Applied Psychology, 63: 219-227.

Bull, R.H.C., and Strongman, K.T., (1971). Anxiety neuroticism and extraversion. Psychology of Reports, 29: 1101-1102.

Burger, J.M., (1987). Desire for control and conformity to a perceived norm. Journal of Personality and Social Psychology, 53: 355-360.

Cameron, W.B., (1966). Modern Social Movements. New York: Random House.

Campbell, E.Q., (1975). Socialization: Culture and Personality. Dubuge, Ia: William C. Brown.

Carey, G.L., (1958). Sex differences in problem solving performance as a function of attitude difference. Journal of Abnormal and Social Psychology, 56: 256-266.

Carment, D.W., Miles, C.G., and Cervin, V.B., (1965). Persuasiveness and persuasibility as related to intelligence and extraversion. British Journal of Social and Clinical Psychology, 4: 1-7.

Carrigan, F.M., (1960). Extraversion-introversion as a dimension of personality: A Reapraisal. Psychological Bulletin, 57: 329-360.

Carter, B., (1991, May 1). Children's TV, where boys are king. New York Times. AI, C. 18.

Castelfranchi, C., Conte, R. and Paolucci, M., (1998). Normative reputation and the costs of compliance. Journal of Artificial Societies and Social Stimulation. 1(3).

Cattell, R.B., (1950). Personality a Systematic Theoretical and Factual Study. New York: McGraw Hill.

Cattell, R.B., (1956). Second order personality factors in the "Questionnaire Realm". Journal of Consulting Psychology, 20: 411-418.

Child, D., (1964). The relationship between introversion, extraversion, neuroticism and performance in school examination. British Journal of Educational Psychology, 34: 187-196.

Child, D., (1966). Personality and Social Status. British Journal of Social and Clinical Psychology, 5: 196-199.

C aldini, R.B., Reno, R.R. and Kallgren, C.A., (1990). A focus theory of normative conduct: Recycling the concept of norms to reduce littering in public places. Journal of Personality and Social Psychology, 58: 1015-1026.

Clansen, J.A., (ed.) (1968). Socialization and Society. Boston: Little Bronen.

Claridge, G., (1960). The excitation-inhibition balance in neurotics. In Experiments in Personality. Vol. 2 (Ed. by Eysenck, H.J.): 107-154.

Clinard, M.B., (1965). "The Relation of Urbanization to Criminal Behaviour." Chicago: Chicago University Press.

Clinard, M.B., (1973). Crime in Developing Countries: A Comparitive Perspective. New York: Wiley.

Clinard, M.B., (1978). Cities with Little Crime. Cambridge: Cambridge University Press.

Cohen, Albert, K., (1966). Deviance and Control. Englewood Cliff, N.J.: Prentice Hall.

Condry, J. and Dyer, S., (1974). Fear of Seven: Attribution of cause to the victim: Unpublished Manuscript, Cornell University.

Conolley, E.S., (1964). Social influence on visual discrimination judgement. Unpublished Master's Thesis, San Diego State College.

Constantinople, A., (1973). A masculinity femininity: An exception to a famous dictum? Psychological Bulletin, 80: 389-407.

Constantinople, A., (1974). Analytical ability and perceived similarity to parents. Psychological Reports, 35: 1335-1345.

Conte, R. and Castelfranchi, C., (1993). Norms as mental objects: From normative beliefs to normative goals. In Proceedings of MAAMAW'93 Neuchatel: Switzerland.

Conte, R. and Castelfranchi, C., (1995a). Understanding the functions of norms in social groups through stimulation. In Gilbert N. and Conte R., (eds.) Artificial Societies. The computer stimulation of social life. London: UCL Press. pp. 252-267.

Conte, R. and Castelfranchi, C., (1995b). Cognitive and social action. London UCL Press. pp. 74-118.

Corson, D., (1955). World view cultural values and discourse norms. International Journal of Intercultural Relations, 19(2): 183-195.

Cosmides, L., (1989). The Logic of Social Exchange: Has natural selection shaped how humans reason? Studies with the Wason selection task. Cognition, 31: 187-276.

Cousins, L. and Mabrey, T., (1998). Re-gendering social work practice and education. The case for African American girls. Journal of Human Behaviour in the Social Environment, 1 (2/3): 91-104.

Crabb, P.B. and Pristash, D., (1992, June). Gender typing of material culture in children's books. 1937-1989: Paper presented at the annual meeting of the American Psychological Society, San Diego, C.A.

Crandall, C.S., (1988). Social Contagion of binge eating. Journal of Personality and Social Psychology, 55: 588-598.

Crutchfield, R.S., (1955). Conformity and Character. American Psychology, 10: 191-198.

Dahrendorf, R., (1962). On the Origin of Social Inequality. In Laslett P. and Runciman, W.G., (Eds.) Philosophy, Politics and Society. Oxford: Basil Blackwell.

Dashiell, J.F., (1939). Some Rapproachments in Contemporary Psychology. Psychological Bulletin, 36: 1-24.

Davis, K., (1966). Social Norms, Reprinted in C-I. Biddle and E.J. Thomas (eds.) (1966). Role Theory Concepts and Research. New York: Wiley.

De'Ameto, M.R., (1970). Experimental Psychology, New York: McGraw Hill Book Company.

Deaux, K., (1982). Sex as a Social Category: Evidence of gender stereotypes. Invited address, American Psychological Association, Washington, D.C.

Deaux, K., (1993). Commentary: Sorry, wrong number—a reply to Gentiles call. Psychological Science, 4: 125-126.

Deci, E.L. and Ryan, R.M., (1985). Intrinsic Motivation and Self-Determinaton in Human Behaviour. New York: Plenum Press.

DeNuoy, L., (1947). Human Destiny, New York: Mckay.

Divesta, F.J., (1958). Susceptibility to pressures toward uniformity of behaviour in social situations: A study of taste motivational and personality factors in conformity behaviour. Syracuse University.

Dollard, J. and Miller, N.E., (1950). Personality and Psychotherapy. New York: McGraw-Hill.

Dominowski, R.L., (1966). Anagram solving as a function of letter moves. Journal of Verbal Learning and Verbal Behaviour, 5: 107-11.

Driskell, J.E. and Mullen, B., (1990). Status, expectations and behaviour: A meta-analytic review and test of the theory. Personality and Social Psychology Bulletin, 16: 541-553.

Druckman, D., Broome, B.J., and Korper, S. H., (1988). Value differences and conflict resolution. Journal of Conflict Resolution, 32(3), 489-510.

Durkheim, E., (1915). Elementary Forms of Religious Life. New York: Macmillan.

Durkheim, E., (1965). Regeln der sozialogischen Methode. (2nd edition). Nevwich: Luchterhand.

Durkheim, E., (1966). The division of labour in society. 3rd edition. New York Free Press.

Eagly, A.H., (1987). Sex Differences in Social Behaviours: A Social-Role Interpretation. Hillsdale, NJ: Erlbaum.

Eagly, A.H., and Wood, W., (1985). Gender and Influenceability: Stereotype versus behaviour. In V.E. O'Leary, R.K. Unger, and B.S. Wallston (eds.), Women, Gender and Social Psychology. Hillsdale, N.J.: Erlbaum. (p. 261).

Eaves, L.J., and Eysenck, H.J., (1975). The nature of extraversion: A genetical analysis. Journal of Personality and Social Psychology, 32: 102-112.

Ebbinghaus, H., (1885). Memory: A Contribution to Experimental Psychology. New York: Dover.

Eccles, J.S., Jacobs, J.E. and Harold, R.D., (1990). Gender role stereotypes, expectancy effects and parents' socialization of gender differences. Journal of Social Issues, 46: 183-201.

Edwards, A.L., (1969). Statistical Analysis (3rd ed.). New York: Holt.

Edwin M. L., (1951). Social Pathology. New York: McGraw-Hill.

Ellickson, Robert C., (2001). The market of social norms. 3 American Law and Economics Review.

English, H.B. and English, A.C., (1974). A comprehensive dictionary of psychological and psychoanalytical terms, New York: McKay.

Epperson, S.E., (1988). Studies link subtle sex bias in schools with women's behaviour in the workplace. Wall Street Journal, 19.

Erikson, E., (1964). Inner and outer space: reflections on Womenhood. In R.J. Lifton (ed.), The Women in America. Boston: 1-26.

Eron, L.D., (1982). Parent-child interaction, television violence, and aggression of children. American Psychologist, 37: 197-211

Erving, G., (1959). The Presentation of Self in Every day Life. New York: Doubleday Anchor Books, especially Chap. 1.

Eysenck, H.J., (1947). Dimensions of Personality. London: Routledge and Kegan Paul.

Eysenck, H.J., (1952). Scientific Study of Personality. New York: Macmillan.

Eysenck, H.J., (1953). Structure of Human Personality. New York: John Wiley.

Eysenck, H.J., (1955a). Cortical inhibition, figural after-effect, and theory of personality. Journal of Abnormal and Social Psychology, 51: 94-106.

Eysenck, H.J., (1955b). A dynamic theory of anxiety and hysteria. Journal of Mental Science, 101: 28-51.

Eysenck, H.J., (1956a). Reminiscence, drive and personality theory. Journal of Abnormal and Social Psychology, 53: 328-333.

Eysenck, H.J., (1956b). The questionnaire measurement of Neuroticism and Extraversion, Psychological Review, 554: 113-140.

Eysenck, H.J., (1957). The Dynamics of Anxiety and Hysteria: an experimental application of modern learning theory to psychiatry. New York: Frederic A., Prager.

Eysenck, H.J., (1959a). Manual of Maudsley Personality Inventory. London: Routledge and Kegan Paul.

Eysenck, H.J., (1959b). Personality and problem solving. Psychological Reports, 5: 592.

Eysenck, H.J., (1960a). Structure of Human Personality. London: Routledge and Kegan Paul.

Eysenck, H.J., (1960b). Experiments in Personality. Vol. I and II. London: Routledge and Kegan Paul.

Eysenck, H.J., (1961). Personality and Social Attitudes. Journal of Social Psychology, 53: 243-248

Eysenck, H.J., (1962a). Reminiscence, drive and personality revision and extension of a theory. British Journal of Social and Clinical Psychology, 1: 127-140.

Eysenck, H.J., (1962b). Conditioning and Personality. Br. J. Psychological., 53: 299-305.

Eysenck, H.J., (1963a). The biological basis of personality. Nature 199: 1031-1034.

Eysenck, H.J., (1963b). Comments on the relation of neuroticism and extraversion to intelligence and educational attainment.

Eysenck, H.J., (1964). Biological factors in neurosis and crime. Scientia.

Eysenck, H.J., (1965). Extraversion and the acquisition of eye blink and GSR conditioned responses. Psychological Bulletin, 663: 258-270.

Eysenck, H.J., (1966a). On the dual function of consolidation. Perceptual and Motor Skills, 22: 273-274.

Eysenck, H.J., (1966b). Personality and Experimental Psychology. British Bulletin of Psychology and Society, 1962.

Eysenck, H.J., (1966c). Conditioning, introversion, extraversion and the strength of the nervous system. Proceedings of the International Congress of Psychology. 18, Symposium 9, 33-43.

Eysenck, H.J., (1967). The Biological Basis of Personality. Vol. I, II and III. Springfield. Illinois.

Eysenck, H.J., (1970). Structure and Measurement of Human Personality. London Metheun.

Eysenck, H.J., (1971). Readings in Extraversion-Introversion, 3 Staples Press London.

Eysenck, H.J., (1977). Crime and Personality (Second Edition). London: Routledge and Kegan Paul.

Eysenck, H.J., (1981). A model for personality. Berlin: Springler Verlag.

Eysenck, H.J., (1985). Personality and Individual Differences. London: Methuen.

Eysenck, H.J., (1991). Dimensions of Personality: 16, 5 or 3 .... Criteria for a taxonomic paradigm. Personality and Individual Differences. 12: 773-790.

Eysenck, H.J., (1992). Four ways five factors are not basic. Personality and Individual differences. 13: 667-773.

Esyenck, H.J., (1994). The Big Five or Giant Three: Criteria for a paradigm. In C.F. Halverson Jr., A. Kohnstamm and R.P. Martin (Eds.). The developing structure of temperament and personality from infancy to adulthood. Hillsdale: Lawrence Erlbaum Associates, inc.

Eysenck, H.J., (1997). Personality and Experimental Psychology. The Unification of Psychology and the possibility of a paradigm. Journal of Personality and Social Psychology, 73: 1224-1237.

Eysenck, H.J., and Cookson, D., (1969). Personality in primary school children: I. Ability and Achievement. British Journal of Educational Psychology, 39: 109-122.

Eysenck, H.J. and Gudjonsson, G., (1989). The causes and cures of criminality. New York: Plenum Press.

Eysenck, H.J. and Levey, A., (1972). Conditioning, introversion-extraversion and the strength of the nervous system. In Nebylitson, V.D., Gray J.A. (eds.), Biological Basis of Individual Behaviour. Academic Press, New York and London, 206-220.

Eysenck, H.J. and Rachman, S., (1965). "The Causes and Cures of Neurosis". R.R. Knapp. San Diego.

Eysenck, H.J. and Esysenck, S.B.G., (1968). The manual to the Eysenck Personality inventory. San Diego: California.

Eysenck, H.J., and Wilson, G.D., (1976). Know Your Own Personality. New York: Penguin.

Eysenck, S.B.G. and Eysenck, H.J. (1963). The validity of questionnaire and rating assessments of extraversion and neuroticism and their factorial stability. British Journal of Psychology. 54: 51-62.

Eysenck, S.B.G., (1965). A new scale for personality measurement in children, British Journal of Educational Psychology, 35: 362-367.

Eysenck, S.B.G. and Eysenck, H.J., (1970). Crime and Personality: An empirical study of the 3-factor theory. British Journal of Criminology. 10: 225-239.

Eysenck, S.B.G., and Eysenck, H.J., (1974). Personality and recidivism in Borstal. British Journal of Criminology, 14: 385-387.

Fagot, B.I. and Patterson G.R., (1969). An in vivo analysis of reinforcing contingencies for sex-role behaviour in the preschool. Child Developmental Psychology, 1: 563-568.

Farley, G.H., (1966). Individual differences in solution time in error-free problem-solving. British Journal of Social and Clinical Psychology, 5: 306-309.

Feather, N.T., (1984). Masculinity, Femininity, Psychological androgyny and the structure of values. Journal of Personality and Social Psychology. 47(3): 604-620.

Feldman, M.P., (1964a). Drive level and stimulus input: an optimal stimulation approach. In Experiments in Motivation (Ed. by H.J. Eysenck) Pergamon Press.

Feldman, M.P., (1964b). The experimental measurement of motivation and reminiscence. Ph.D. Thesis, London University.

Feldman, S., (1962). Neurophysiological mechanisms of modifying afferent hypothalamo-hippocampal condition. Journal of Experimental Neurology, 5: 269-291.

Felen, B.K., (1975). An analysis of science problem solving among Male and Female Students in Grade One Through Twelve. Dissertation Abstract, 27: 2508.

Field, J.G. and Branglemann, J.C., (1961). Eyelid conditioning and their personality parameters. Journal of Abnormal and Social Psychology, 63: 517-523.

Fine, B.J., and Danforth, A.V., (1975). Field-dependence, extraversion and perception of the vertical: empirical and theoretical perspectives of the Rod and Frame Test. Perceptual and Motor Skills, 40: 683-693.

Fischer, Claude, S., (1975). "The effect of urban life on traditional values", Social Forces, 53: 420-432.

Ford, C.S. and Beach, F.A., (1951). Patterns of Sexual Behaviour. New York: Harper and Row.

Fordham, F., (1991). An Introduction to Jung's Psychology, (Ch. 1-8).

Fordham, S., (1993). Those loud black girls (Black) women, silence and gender "passing" in the academy. Anthropology and Education. Quarterly, 2(1): 3-32.

Forsyth, D.R., (1983). An Introduction to Group Dynamics. Monterey, C.A: Brooks/Cole.

Foulds, C.A., (1961). The logical impossibility of using hysterics and dysthymics and criterion groups in the British Journal of Psychology, 52: 385-387.

Franks, C.M., (1954). An experimental study of conditioning as related to mental abnormality. Unpublished Ph.D. Thesis, London University.

Franks, C.M., (1956). Conditioning and Personality: A study of normal and neurotic subjects. Journal of Abnormal and Social Psychology, 52: 143-150.

Franks, C.M., (1957). Personality factors and the rate of conditioning. British Journal of Psychology, 47: 119-126.

Freud. S., (1922). Group Psychology and Analysis of the Ego. London, Hogarth.

Friedan, B., (1964). The Feminine Mystique, New York: Dell.

Furneaux, W.D., (1956). Report of Imperial College of Science and Technology.

Furneaux, W.D., (1961). Neuroticism, Extraversion and Drive and Suggestibility. Introduction to Journal of Clinical and Experimental Psychology 9: 195-215.

Gagnon, J.H., (1968). Sexual deviation: Social aspect. International Encyclopedia of the Social Sciences. New York: Crowell-Collier and Macmillan, 14: 216.

Gale, A., (1973). Individual Differences: Studies of extraversion and the EEG. In P. Kline (ed.), New Approaches in Psychological Measurement, London: Wiley.

Gale, A., Coles, M., and Blaydon, J., (1969). Extraversion-Introversion and the EEG. British Journal of Psychology, 60: 209-223.

Gamble, E.A., (1909). A study of memorizing various materials by the reconstruction method. Psychological Monographs, 43.

Gamble, E.A., (1927). A study of three variables in memorizing. American Journal of Psychology, 39: 223-234.

Garfinkel, H., (1967). Studies in Ethnomethodology. Englewood Cliffs, N.J.: Prentice-Hall.

Garnets, L. and Pleck, J.H. (1979). Sex-role identity, androgyny and sex-role transcedence: A sex-role strain analysis Psychology of Women Quaterly. 3(3), 270-283.

Garrett, H. E., (1961). Statistics in Psychology and Education. Bombay, Vikils, Fegger and Simons Ltd., Bombay.

Gerard, H.B.,Wilhelmy, R.A. and Conolley, E.S., (1968). "Conformity and Group Size", Journal of Personality and Social Psychology, 79-82.

Gibbs, J.C., and Schnell, S.V., (1994). Moral Development *versus* Socialization. Garland Publishing, Inc: New York, 235-244.

Gibbs, J.P., (1972). 'Issues in Defining Deviant' Behaviour in Robert A. Scott and Jack D. Douglas (eds.), Theoretical Perspectives on Deviance. New York: Basic Books.

Gibson, H.B., and Corcoran, M.B., (1975). Personality and differential susceptibility to hypnosis: Further replication and sex differences. Unpublished Paper, Hatfield Polytechnic, England.

Gibson, H.B., and Curran, J.D., (1974). Hypnotic susceptibility and personality: A replication study. British Journal of Psychology, 65: 283-291.

Gieger, T., (1962). Arbriten zur Soziologie. Neuwied: Luchterhand.

Gilbert, Geis, (1977). White Collar Crime: Offences in Business, Politics and the Professions. New York: Free Press.

Goldfrank, E.S., (1945). "Socialization, personality and the structure of pueblo society with particular reference to Hopi and Zuni. American Anthropology, 47: 516-539.

Goldman, I., (1937). "The Zuni Indian of New Mexico", in M. Mead, ed., Cooperation and competition among primitive peoples. New York: McGraw Hill, 1937, p. 324.

Gorer, G., (1948). The American People: A Study in National Character, New York: Norton.

Gough, H.G., (1960). Theory and Measurement of Socialization. Journal of Consulting Psychology, 24: 23-30.

Gray, J.A., (1965). Pavlov's Typology. Oxford Pergamon Press.

Gray, J.A., (1967). Strength of the Nervous system, introversion-extraversion, conditionability and arousal behaviour. Clinical Research Therapy, 5: 151-169.

Gray, J.A., (1970a). Sodium amobarbital, the hippocampal theta rythm and the partial reinforcement extinction effect. Psychological Review, 77: 465-480.

Gray, J.A., (1970b). The psychophysiological basis of introversion-extraversion. Behavioural Research Therapy, 8: 249-266.

Gray, J.A., (1971). Medial septal lesions, hippocampal theta rhythm and the control of vibrissal movement in the freely moving rat. Accepted in Electroencephalographic and Clinical Study in Neurobiology.

Gray, J.A., (1972). The psychophysiological nature of Introversion-Extraversion: A Modification of Eysenck's Theory. In V.D. Nebylitsyn and J.A. Gray (eds.), Biological Basis of Individual Behaviour. New York: Academic Press.

Gray, J.A., (1973). Causal theories of personality and how to test them. In J.R. Royce (ed.), Multivariate Analysis and Psychological Theory. London: Academic Press.

Grossman, S.P., (1967). A Text Book of Physiological Psychology. London, New York: John Willey.

Guilford, J.P., (1934). Introversion-extraversion Psychological Bulletin, 31: 331-334.

Guilford, J.P., (1959). Personality McGraw Hill and Company. New York.

Guthrie, E.R., (1944). Personality in terms of associative learning in J. Mc.V. Hunt, Personality and the Behaviour Disorders. New York: Ronald. 6: 160.

Haferkamp, H., (1980). Herrschaft and Strafrecht. Opladen: Westdt. Verlag.

Haferkamp, H., (1984). Herrschaftsverlust and Sanktionsverzicht. Kritische Bemerkungen zur Theories des starken Staates, der neuen sozialen Kontrolle und des ideellen Abolitionismus. Kriminologisches Journal 15. 112-131.

Haferkamp, H., (1987). Zur Kunftigen Neuorientierung der kriminologischen Forschung. Kriminologisches Journal 18. 171-192.

Hall C.S. and Lindzey, G., (1962). Theories of Personality. New York: John Wiley.

Hamilton, V., (1959). Eysenck's theories of anxiety and hysteria: A Methodological Critique. British Journal of Psychology, 50: 48-65.

Hampson, J.L., (1965). Determinants of Psychosexual Orientation. In F. Beach (ed.), Sex and Behaviour. New York: Wiley, 108-132.

Handa, V., (1994). Effect of social influence in different personality groups. Unpublished M.Phil. Dissertation Himachal Pradesh University, Shimla (India).

Hanson, A. and Jessor, S.L., (1968). Society, Personality and Deviant Behaviour. A Study of Tri-ethnic Community. New York: Holt, Rinehart and Winston, Inc.

Hart, H.L.A., (1961). The Concept of Law. Oxford University Press.

Hartley, R.E., (1960). Norm Compatibility, norm preference and the acceptance of new reference groups. Journal of Social Psychology, 52: 87-95.

Hasija, S., Malhotra, D., Punia, R.K. and Hasija, R.C., (1989). Problem solving as a function of extraversion, sex and induced stress. Paper presented at XIX All India Sociological Conference held at H.A.U. Hissar (India) from March 3-5, 1989.

Hayes, N., (1994). Foundation of Psychology, (Ch. 7). www.google.com.

Hayes, T.R., (1978). Interpersonal and non-personal problem solving: A comparison with respect to subject's sex, sex-role orientation and Problem orientation. Dissertation Abstract, 38: 6155.

Herzog, R.A. and Bachman, J.G., (1982). Sex-role attitude among high school seniors-views about work and family roles. Michigan University, Ann Arbor, M.I.

Hilderbrand, H.P., (1958). A factorial study and introversion/extraversion. British Journal of Psychology, 49: 1-11.

Hilgard, E.R., (1962). Theories of Learning. Appleton Century Corofts., New York.

Hilgard, E.R., and Bentler, P.M., (1963). Predicting Hypnotizability from the Maudsley Personality Inventory. British Journal of Psychology, 54: 63-69.

Hilgard, E.R., Jones, L.V. and Kaplan, S.J., (1951). Conditioned discrimination as related to anxiety. Journal of Experimental Psychology, 42: 994-99.

Himmelweit, H.T., (1946). Speed and accuracy of work as related to temperament. British Journal of Psychology, 36: 132-144.

Hoffman, E.L., Swander, D., Baron, S.H., and Roher, J.H., (1953). Generalisation and exposure time as related to autokinetic movements. Journal of Experimental Psychology, 46: 171-177.

Hoffman, L.R., and Maier, N.R.F., (1961). Quality and acceptance of problem solution by members of homogenous and heterogeneous groups. Journal of Abnormal and Social Psychology, 62: 401-407.

Hoffman, L.R. and Maier, N.R.F., (1966). Social factors influencing problem-solving in women. Journal of Personality and Social Psychology, 4: 382-390.

Hoffman, L.W., (1974) Fear of success in males and females. Journal of Consulting and Clinical Psychology. 42: 353-358.

Hoffman, M.L., (1953). Some psychodynamic factors in compulsive conformity, Journal of Abnormal and Social Psychology, 48: 383-393.

Hollander, E.P., (1958). Confirmity, status and indiosyncrasy credit. Psychological Review 65: 117-127.

Horner, M.S., (1968). Sex differences in achievement motivation and performance in competitive and non-competitive situations. Unpublished Ph.D Thesis, Michigan University.

Horner, M.S., (1972). Towards an understanding of achievement related conflicts in women. Journal of Social Issues, 28: 157-176.

Horner, M.S., (1974). Towards an understanding of achievement related conflicts in women. In J. Stacey, S. Bereand and Daniels (eds.), and Hill came Tumbling After; Sexism in American Education. New York: Dell., pp. 43-63.

Hovland, C.I., and Janis, I.L., (1959). Personality and Persuasibility. New Haven, Community: Yale University Press, 1959.

Howard, S.B., (1963). Outsiders' studies in the sociology of Deviance. Glencoe, 111: The Free Press.

Hull, C.L., (1943). Principles of Behaviour. New York: Appleton-Century-Crafts.

Hunt, B.J., (1970). The effects of massed and distributed practice on problem solving. Dissertation Abstract Int., 30: 3408-B.

Jacklin, C.N. and Reynolds, C., (1993). Gender and Childhood Socialization. In A.E. Beall and R.J. Sternberg (eds.). The Psychology of India. New York. Guilford.

Jackson, J., (1965). Structural characteristics of norms. In I.D., Steiner and M. Fishbein (eds.), Current Studies in Social Psychology. New York: Holt, Rinehart and Winston, 3001-3009.

Jacobs, M.K. and Dominowski, R.C., (1981). Learning to solve the insight problems. Social Psychological Bulletin, 17: 171-174.

Janis, I.L., (1954). Personality correlates of susceptibility to persuasion, Journal of Personality, 22: 504-518.

Jennings, J., Geis, F.K., and Brown, V., (1980). Influence of television commercials on women's self-confidence and independent judgement. Journal of Personality and Social Psychology, 38: 203-210.

Jensen, A.R., (1962). Extraversion-neuroticism and serial learning. Acta Psychologica., 20: 69-77.

Johnson J.M., and Jack D.D., (1978). Crime at the Top Deviance in Business and the Professions. Philadelphia: Loppincott.

Johnson, B.T., and Eagly, A.H., (1989). Effects of involvement on persuasion. Psychological Bulletin, 106(2) 290-314.

Johnson, D.M., (1966). Solution of Anagrams. Psychological Bulletin, 66: 371-384.

Johnson, D.M., (1984). Sex differences in problem solving. Journal of Educational Psychology, 76: 1359-1371.

Jung, C.G., (1923). Psychological Types. Harcourt Brace and Company: New York.

Kagan, J., (1964). Acquisition and significance of sex-typing and sex-role identity. In M.L. Hoffman and L.W. Hoffman (eds.) Review of Child Development Research. Vol. 1. New York. Russell Sage Foundation, pp. 137-167.

Kapila, A., (1992). Effect of personality variables on problem solving among women. Unpublished Ph.D. Thesis, Himachal Pradesh University, Shimla.

Kapila, M. and Sharma A., (2001). The Influence of Social Norms and Gender in learning. Journal of Community Guidance and Research. Vol. 18 (2): 247-256

Kapoor, M., (1997). Field-dependennce, field independence, cognitive styles and imagery variables in memory and problem solving. Unpublished Ph.D Thesis, Himachal Pradesh University, Shimla.

Kardiner, A., (1939). The Individual and His Society, with a forward and two ethnological reports by R. Linton. New York: Columbia University Press.

Kaushik, S. and Malhotra Kapila, A., (1997). "Girl Child and Family" and Education. Sponsored by the department of women and child development, Government of India, New Delhi.

Kelley, H.H., and Shapiro, M.M., (1954). Conformity to group norms. American Sociological Review, 19: 667-677.

Kelman, H., (1958). "Compliance, Identification and Internalization," Journal of Conflict Resolution, 2.

Kempf, E.J., (1919). Automatic Functions and the Personality. Nervous Mental Disorder. Monographs, 28: 373.

Klausmeier, H.J. and Longlilin, L.T., (1961). Behaviours during problem solving among children of low, average and high intelligence. Journal of Educational Psychology, 52: 148-152.

Klienmuntz, B., (1966). Problem solving: Research, Method and Theory (ed.). New York: John Wiley.

Klienmuntz, B., (1967). Personality Measurement: An Introduction. H. Wood, J.A. Dossey.

Kohlberg, L., (1966). A cognitive development analysis of childrens sex role concepts and attitudes. In E.E. Maccoby (ed.) The Development of Sex-Differences. Stanford, California Stanford University Press.

Kohlberg, L. (1969). Stage and Sequence: The Cognitive Development Approach to Socializaton. In D. Goslin (ed.). Handbook of Socialization Theory and Research. Chicago: Rand McNelly.

Kohlberg, L., (1971). From is to ought. In Mischel Th (ed.) Cognitive development and epistemology. New York: Academic Press.

Krauss, R.M., Freedman, J.L. and Whitcup, M., (1978). Field and Laboratory studies of littering. Journal of Experimental Social Psychology, 14: 109-122.

Krech, D., Crutchfield, R.S., and Ballachhey, E.L., (1962). Individual in Society. New York: McGraw-Hill.

Kumar, D., (1974). An experimental study of problem-solving behaviour as a function of personality, drive and practice. Unpublished Ph.D. Thesis, Panjab University, Chandigarh.

Kumar, D., (1983). The role of motivating instructions in insightful problem solving in males and females. Psychological Studies, 27: 36-40.

Kumar, D. and Kapila, A., (1987). Problem solving as a function of extraversion and masculinity. Personality and Individual Differences, 8: 129-132.

Kumar, D. and Kumari, S., (1988). Problem solving as a function of creativity and personality. Psychological Studies, 33: 157-161.

Kumar, D. Malhotra, L., and Jerath, J., (1986). Speed and accuracy in learning as a function of personality. Psychologica Belgica. 25: 227-233.

Kumar, D., Malhotra, L. and Jerath, J., (1989). Speed and accuracy in learning as a function of personality. Personality and Clinical Studies. 5: 5-9.

Kumari, S., (1987). Problem solving as a function of extraversion, intelligence and induced stress. Unpublished Ph.D. Thesis, Himachal Pradesh University, Shimla.

Lalancette, M.F. and Standing, L., (1990). Asch fails again. Social Behaviour and Personality, 18: 7-12.

Lang, P.J., and Lazovik, A.D., (1962). Personality and hypnotic susceptibility. Journal of Consulting Psychology, 26: 317-322.

Larsen, K.S., (1974). Conformity in the Asch experiment. Journal of Social Psychology, 94: 303-304.

Larsen, K.S., (1990). The Asch conformity experiment: Replication and transhistorical comparisons. Journal of Social Behaviour and Personality, 5: 163-168.

Laski, H.J., (1948). The American Democracy. New York: Viking.

Leibert, R.M. and Morris, L.W., (1967). Cognitive and emotional components of test anxiety: A distinction and some initial data. Psychological Reports, 20: 975-978.

Leith, G.O.M., (1974). Individual differences in learning: interactions of personality and teaching methods. Association of Educational Psychologists Conference, London.

Lewin, K., (1943). Forces behind food habits and methods of change. Bulletin of the National Research Council, 108: 35-65.

Levey, A., (1967). Eyelid Conditioning, extraversion and drive. An experimental test of two theories. Unpublished Ph.D. Thesis, University of London.

Lewin, K., Dembo, T., Festinger, L. and Sears, P., (1944). Level of aspiration. In Personlaity and Behaviour Disorders (ed. by J.Mc.V. Hunt). New York: Ronald.

Lewis, D., (1969). Convention. Cambridge, M.A: Harvard University Press.

Liebert, R.M. and Sprafkin, J., (1988). The early window. Effects of television on children and youth (3rd ed.). New York: Pergamon.

Linton, R., (1945). The Cultural Background of Personality. New York Appleton. Century – Crofts, Inc.

Linton, R., (1957). The Tree of Culture, P. 29, Alfred A Knopf, New York. Reprinted by permission.

Little, A., (1963). Professor Eysenck's theory of crime: an empirical test on adolescent offenders. British Journal of Criminology, 4: 152-163.

Lombrosso, C., (1876). Criminal Man in L'Uomo Delinquente, Milan., Hoepli. Reuter, E.B., "Book Review of Earnest A. Hooton's Crime and the Man," The American Journal of Sociology, 45: 1939.

Lott, A.J. and Lott, B.E., (1961). Group cohesiveness, communication level and conformity, Journal of Abnormal and Social Psychology, 62: 408-412.

Lott, A.J., and Lott, B.C., (1965). Group cohesiveness as interpersonal attraction: A review of relationships with antecedent and consequent variables. Psychological Bulletin, 64: 259-309.

Lowell, E.L., (1952). The effect of need for achievement on learning and speed of performance. Journal of Psychology, 33: 3-40.

Luchins, A.S., and Luchins, E. H., (1955). On conformity with true and false communications. Journal of Social Psychology, 42: 283-305.

Luchins, A.S., and Luchins, E. H., (1961). On conformity with judgement of a majority or an authority. Journal of Social Psychology, 53: 303-316.

Luchins, A.S., and Luchins, E. H., (1963a). Effects of order or evidence on social influences on judgement. Journal of Social Psychology, 61: 345-363.

Luchins, A.S., and Luchins, E. H., (1963b). Half views and the autokinetic effect. Psychological Review, 13: 4, 415-444

Luchins, A.S., and Luchins, E.H., (1984). Sex differences in reasons given for responses to the water jar problems. Journal of Psychology, 118: 207-220.

Lynn, R., (1960a). Extraversion, reminiscence and satiation effects. British Journal of Psychology, 51: 319-325.

Lynn, R., (1960b). Individual differences in introversion-extraversion, reactive inhibition and reading attainment. Journal of Educational Psychology, 51: 318-321.

Lynn, R., (1962). Comments on the articles by J.B. Biggs. British Journal of Educational Psychology, 32: 196-199.

Lynn, R. and Gordan, I., (1961). The relation of neuroticism and extraversion to intelligence and educational attainment. British Journal of Educational Psychology, 31: 194-203.

Maccoby, E.E., (1966). Sex-differences in intellectual functioning: In E.E. Maccoby (ed.). The Development of Sex-differences, Stanford, Stanford University Press.

Maccoby, E.E., (1965). The choice of variables in the study of socialization. In I.D., Steiner and M. Fishbein (eds.), Current Studies in Social Psychology. New York: Holt, Rinehart and Winston, 56-68.

Macionis, J.J., (1987). Sociology. Prenctice Hall, Englewood Cliffs, New Jersey.

MacNeil, M.K., (1965). Norm change over subject generations as a function of arbitrariness of prescribed norms. Master's thesis, Oklahoma University. One of the series directed by M. Sherif with N.S.F. support.

MacNeil, M.K., (1967). Power of status in norm formation under differing conditions of group solidarity. Ph.D. Thesis, Oklahoma University.

Madan, V., (1967). The relation of neuroticism and extraversion to intelligence and educational attainment at different levels. Unpublished. Ph.D. Thesis, Panjab University, Chandigarh.

Maddi, S.R., (1972). Personality theories: A comparative assessment, Homewood Illinois: Dorsey.

Maguire, T.O., Romaniuk, E.W. and MacRury, K.A., (1982) The Development and Validation of an instrument to assess student attitudes towards work. Education and Psychological Measurement., 42: 643-649.

Maier, N.R.F., (1930). Reasoning a Humans: I. On Direction. Journal of Comparative Psychology, 10: 115-143.

Maier, N.R.F., (1930). Reasoning in human II. The solution of a problem and its appearance in consciousness. Journal of Comparative Psychology, 12: 184-194.

Maier, N.R.F., (1933). An aspect of human reasoning. British Journal of Psychology, 24: 144-155.

Maier, N.R.F., (1945). Reasoning in humans III. The mechanism of equivalent stimuli and of reasoning. Journal of Experimental Psychology, 35: 349-360.

Maier, N.R.F., (1970). Problem solving and Creativity in individual and Groups. Belmont Books.

Maier, N.R.F., and Burke, R.J., (1967). Response availability as a factor in the problem solving performance of males and females. Journal of Personality and Social Psychology, 5: 304-310.

Maier, N.R.F., and Cassellmann, G.G., (1970). Locating the difficulty in insight problems: Individual and sex differences. Psychological Reports, 26: 103-117.

Makkar, M. and Malhotra, D.K., (2000). Imagery variables in problem-solving. Journal of Community Guidance and Research, 17(1), 31-37.

Malhotra, D.K., (1974). An experimental study of problem solving behaviour as a function of personality, drive and practice, Ph.D Thesis. Panjab University, Chandigarh.

Malhotra, D.K. and Sharma, A., (2001). Social Norms and Gender Differences. Journal of Community Guidance and Research, 18: 247-256.

Malinowski, B., (1945). The Dynamics of Social Change: An Inquiry Into Race Relations in Africa. Africa. New Haven: Yale University Press.

Mantell, D.M., (1991). The Potential for Violence of Germany. Journal of Social Issues, 27(4): 101-112.

March, J.G., (1954). Group norms and the active minority. American Social Review, 19: 733-740.

Martin, C.L., (1987). A ratio measure of sex stereotyping. Journal of Personality and Social Psychology, 52: 489-499.

Martin, C.L. and Parker, S., (1995). Folk theories about sex and race differences. Personality and Social Psychology Bulletin, 21: 45-57.

Marx, K., (1936). Capital, a critique of political economy. The process of capitalist production, translated from the third German edition by S Moore and E Aveling. Edited by F Engels, revised and amplified edition by E Untermann. New York: The Modern Library.

Maxwell, A.A., (1975). Exploratory study of secondary school geometry students. Problem-solving related to convergent, divergent productivity. Dissertation Abstract, 35: 4987.

Maxwell, G.S. and Cumming, J.J., (1988). Measuring occupation aspiration in research on sex-differences an overview and analysis of issues. Journal of Vocational Behaviour, 32: 60-73.

May, M., (1929). The adult in the community. In C. Murchison. Foundations of Experimental Psychology. Worcester, Mass: Clark University.

McAdams, Richard H., (2001). Signaling Discount Rates: Law, Norms and Economic Methodology. 110 Yale Law Journal, 625.

McCauley, C., (1989). The nature of social influence in group thing: Compliance and internalization. Journal of Personality and Social Psychology, 57: 250-260.

McClelland, D.C., (1951). Personality. New York: Sloane.

McCord, F., (1948). The formation of group norms. Journal of Social Psychology, 27: 3-15.

McDavid, J. JR., (1959). Personality and situational determinants of conformity. Journal of Abnormal and Social Psychology, 58: 241-246.

McDonald, S.M., (1989). Sex bias in the representation of male and female characters in children's picture books. Journal of Genetic Psychology, 150: 389-402.

McNeil, J.C., (1975). Feminism, femininity and the television series. A content analysis. Journal of Broadcast, 19: 259-271.

McNemar, O.W., (1955). An attempt to differentiate between individuals with high and low reasoning ability. American Journal of Psychology, 68: 20-36.

McWay, J.D., (1975). The relation of sex-role identification to Psychological differentiation. Dissertation Abstract, 37: 1916.

McWay, J.D., (1976). The relationship of sex-role identification to Psychological differentiation. Dissertation Abstract, 37: 1916.

Mead, M., (1935). Sex and Temperament in three Primitive Societies. New York, Morrow.

Mead, M., (1939). Coming of Age in Samoa. In From the South Seas: Studies of Adolescence and Sex in Primitive Societies. New York: Morrow.

Mead, M., (1949). Male and Female. New York: Dell.

Mead, M., (1959). Quoted in La difference Time, September, 1959, 28: 53.

Meeus, W.H.J. and Raaijmakers, Q.A.W., (1986). Administrative Obedience: Carrying out orders to use Psychological-Administrative Violence. European Journal of Social Psychology, 16: 311-324.

Mehta, P. and Kumar, D., (1985). Relationship of an acdemic achievement to personality, study habits academic motivation and adjustment. Personality and Clinical Studies. Vol. 11: 57-68.

Mehta, P., Kumar, D. and Jerath. J., (1990). Psychological predictors of academic achievement at school level. Journal of Educational Psychology, 47: 26-33.

Meier, M .J., (1961). Inter-relationship among personality variables, kinesthetic figure after effects and reminiscence in motor lerning. Journal of Abnormal and Social Psychology, 63: 87-94.

Merton, R.K., (1938). Social Structure and Anomie. American Sociological Review, 3: 672-682.

Milgram, S., (1961, December). Nationality and Conformity Scientific American, December, pp. 45-51.

Milgram, S., (1963). The behavioural study of obedience. Journal of Abnormal and Social Psychology. (67), 467-472.

Milgram, S., (1965). Some conditions of obedience and disobedience to authority. Human Relations, 18: 56-57.

Milgram, S., (1974). Obedience to Authority. New York: Harper and Row.

Miller, J.B., (1976). Towards a new psychology of women. Allen Lane, Penguin Books Ltd., London.

Miller, N.E., and Dollard, J., (1941). Social Learning and Imitation. New Haven: Yale University Press.

Millett, K., (1970). Sexual Politics. Garden City, New York: Doubleday.

Milton, G.A., (1957). The effects of sex-role identification upon problem-solving skills. Journal of Abnormal and Social Psychology, 55: 208-12.

Milton, G.A., (1959). Sex-differences in problem solving as a function of role appropriateness of the problem content. Psychological Reports, 5: 705-708.

Mischell, W., (1968) Personality and Assessment, Wiley, London.

Mischell, W., (1976). Introduction to Personality (2nd ed.). New York: Holt, Rinehart and Winston.

Mischell, W., (1977). On the future of personality measurement American Psychologist 32: 246-254.

Mohan, V. and Deol, R., (1970). Effect of personality and frequency in time estimation. Proceedings of Indian Science Congress.

Mohan, V. and Gupta, V.K., (1972). Effect of personality, induced motivation and frequency of KR on the acquisition of efficiency in weight estimation. Indian Journal of Psychology, 47: 29-38.

Mohan, V. and Kumar, D., (1973). Performance of Introverts and Introverts on backward alphabet writing as a function of K.R. Psychological Studies, 18: 61-64.

Mohan, V. and Kumar, D., (1974). Performance on hand steadiness test as a function of personality, magnitude of stimulus figure and duration. Indian Journal and Experimental Psychology, 8: 44-47.

Mohan, V. and Kumar, D., (1975). Sementic differential measurment of the effect of suggestion on aesthetic choice in different personality groups. Studia Psychologica, 17: 244-248.

Mohan, V. and Kumar, D., (1976). Qualitative analysis of the performance of introverts and extraverts on Standard Progressive Matrices. British Journal of Psychology. 67: 391-397.

Mohan, V. and Mohan, J., (1965). Personality and variability in esthetic evaluation. Studia Psychologica, 10: 57-60.

Mohan, V., (1969). Acquisition of efficiency in two psychomotor tasks as a function of knowledge of results. Acta Psychologica, 31: 183-188

Monika, (1997). Field-dependence, field-independence, cognitive styles and imagery variables in memory and problem solving. Unpublished. Ph.D. Thesis, Himachal Pradesh University, Shimla.

Morgan, M., (1982). Television and adolescents' sex-role stereotypes: A longitudinal study. Journal of Personality and Social Psychology, 43: 947-955.

Morris, W.N., and Miller, R.S., (1975). The effect of consensus breaking and concensus pre-empting partners on reduction of conformity. Journal of Personality and Social Psychology, 11: 215-223.

Moscovics, S., (1985). Social influence and conformity. In G. Lindzey and Aronson (eds.), Handbook of Social Psychology, New York: Random House.

Munsterberg, H., (1923). On the witness stand. Essays on Psychology of Crime. New York: Boardman.

Murphy, G., (1947). Personality: A Biosocial Approach to Origin and Structure. New York: Harper and Row.

Murphy, G., and Murphy, Lois B., (1931). Experimental Social Psychology. New York: Harper and Row.

Murphy, G. and Murphy, Lois B., and Newcomb, T.M., (1937). Social Behaviour and Child Personality. New York: Columbia University Press.

Murray, H.A., (1938). Explorations in Personality and Social Change. New York: Holt, Rinehart and Winston.

Mussen, P.H., (1969). Early sex-role development. In D.A. Goslin (ed.), Handbook of Socialization. Theory and Research. Chicago: Ran-McNally.

Nadler, E.B., (1959). Yielding, authoritarianism and authoritarian ideology regarding groups. Journal of Abnormal and Social Psychology, 58: 408-410.

Newell, A., Shaw, J.C. and Simon, H.A., (1958). Elements of a theory of human problem-solving. Psychological Review, 65: 151-166.

Nicholson, N., Cole, S.G., and Rocklin, T., (1985). Conformity in the Asch situation: A comparison between contemporary British and U.S. University Students. British Journal of Social Psychology, 24: 59-63.

Nonner and Winkler, G., (1984). Norman. In Kerber, H. and Schmieder, A. (eds.). Handbuch Soziologie. Zur Theorie und Praxis Sozialer Beziehungen Reinbek: Rowohit, 398-408.

Oetzel, R.M., (1966). Classified summary of research in sex differences. In: E.E. Maccoby (ed.). The Development of Sex Differences. Stanford, California, Stanford University Press, 323-51.

Ogburn, W.F., (1955). Technology and the Changing Family. Boston: Houghton Mifflin, 1955.

Ohri, R. and Malhotra, D.K., (1989). Problem solving as a function of fear of success, induced motivation and residential background among University Women. Psychologia. 32: 260-265.

Ohri, R. and Malhotra, D.K., (1993). The role of fear of success and neuroticism in successful problem solving. Psychologia, 36: 114-118.

Omirsky, M. and Kimble, G.A., (1966). Anxiety and eyelid conditioning. Journal of Experimental Psychology., 71: 471-472.

Organ, D.W., (1975). Extraversion, locus of control and individual differences in conditionability in organisations. Journal of Applied Psychology, 60: 401-404.

Orlofsky, J.L. and Windles, M.T., (1978). Sex-role orientation, behavioural adaptability and personal adjustment Sex-roles. 4(6): 801-811.

Ortner, S., (1996). Making gender: The politics and erotics of culture Boston: Beacon Press.

Panek, R.E., (1962). Relation between autokinesis and introversion-extraversion. Journal of Consulting Psychology, 26: 477.

Parish, T.S. and Nunn, G.D., (1988). The importance of the family informing life values and personal values. Journal of Psychology, 22(5), 519-521.

Park R.E., (1949), Race and Culture. New York: Free Press.

Parsons, T., (1949). The Social System. Glencoe, III: The Free Press, 2nd ed.

Parsons, T., (1960). Structure and Process in Modern Societies. New York: Free Press.

Parsons, T., (1964). The Social System. New York: Routledge and Paul.

Parsons, T., and Bales, R.F., (1955). Family, Socialization and Interaction Process. New York: Free Press.

Patel, A.S., and Gordon, J.E., (1960) Some personal and situational determinants of yielding to influence. Journal of Abnormal and Social Psychology, 61: 411-418.

Pavlov, I.D., (1927). Conditioned Reflexes: An Investigation of the Physiological Activity of Cerebral Cortex. London: Oxford University Press.

Pavlov, I.D., (1941). Lectures on conditioned reflex. Vol. II. Conditional Reflexes and Psychiatry. New York: International Publishers.

Perrin, S. and Spencer, C., (1981). Independence or conformity in the Asch experiment as a reflection of cultural or situational factors. British Journal of Social Psychology, 20: 205-209.

Pesh, H.G., (1985). Sex variation of eighth-grade students' on Piagetian task performance. Journal of Genetic Psychology, 1: 141-142.

Piaget, J., (1932). The Moral Judgement of the Child. London: Kegan Paul, Trench, Trubner.

Power, T. (1981). Sex typing in infancy: The role of the father. Infant Mental Health Journal, 2: 226-240.

Priested, R.E. and Hunskar, P.L., (1969). Compensating for a female's disadvantage in problem-solving. Personality. Journal of Experimental Research, 4: 57-64.

Prince, M., (1924). The Unconscious (2nd ed.). New York: Macmillan.

Pulkkinen, Lea, (1996). Female and male personality types. Journal of Personality and Social Psychology 70(6): 1288-306.

Quay, H.C. and Hunt, M.A., (1965). Psychopathy, neuroticism, and verbal conditioning: A replication and extension. Journal of Consulting Psychology, 29: 283.

Raheim, K., (1963). Sex differences on problem solving tasks. J. Psychological., 29: 283.

Raheim, K. and Kaufman, G., (1974) Sex-role related Behaviour. I.Q. and Problem Solving in 15-16 years olds. Journal of Genetic Psychology, 90: 233-236.

Raven, B.H., and J.R.P., French, JR., (1958). Group support, legitimate power, and social influence. Journal of Personality, 26: 400-409.

Raven, J.C., (1960). Guide to the standard progressive matrices: Sets A, B, C, D and E (Revised) Lewis and Company Limited, London.

Ray, O., (1959). Personality factors in motor learning. Journal of Abnormal and Social Psychology, 59: 199-203.

Rechtschaffen, A., (1958). Neural satiation, reactive inhibition and introversion-extraversion. Journal of Abnormal and Social Psychology, 57: 283-291.

Reed, E.S., (1996). Selves, Values, Cultures. Lawrence Ealbaum Associates, Inc: Marwah, 181: 1-15.

Reinhardt, J.M., (1938). Social Psychology. Chicago: Lippin Cott, 253.

Reiss, A.J. and Roth J.A., (1993). Understanding and Preventing Violence. Washington, D.C.: National Academic Press.

Reynolds, G.S., (1960). The effect of stress on problem solving. Journal of Genetic Psychology, 62: 83-88.

Rhine, R., and Magoun, H.W., (1946). Brainstem facilitation of cortical motor responses, Journal of Neuro Psychology, 9: 219-229.

Rhine, R., and Magoun, H.W., (1947). Spasticity and the Extrapyramidal System II. Springfield, Thomas.

Rim, Y. and Siedenross, H., (1971). Personality and response to pressure from peers versus adults. Personality, 2: 35-43.

Robert, E., (1976). Deviance: A Cross-Cultural Perspective. Mento Park, California: Cummings Publishers.

Roberts, F.J., (1965). Some psychological factors in religious conversion. British Journal of Social and Clinical Psychology, 4, 185-187.

Rokeach, M., (1960). The Open and Closed Mind. New York: Basic Books.

Rokeach, M., (1961). Belief versus race as determinants of social distance. Journal of Abnormal and Social Psychology, 62: 187-188.

Roll, S., (1970). Sex-differences in problem-solving as a function of content and order of presentation, Psychonomic Science, 19: 97.

Rommetveit, R., (1955). Social Norms and Roles: Explorations in the Psychology of Enduring Social Pressures. Minneapolis University Press.

Rosenberg, L.A., (1961). Group size, prior experience and conformity. Journal of Abnormal Social Psychology, 63: 436-437.

Sagarin, E., (1971). Deviants and Deviance: An Introduction to the Study of Disvalued People and Behaviour. New York: Holt, Rinehart and Winston.

Sakurai, M.M., (1975). Small Group Cohesiveness and Detrimental Conformity. Sociometry, 38: 340-357.

Savage, R.D., (1962). Personality factors and academic performance. British Journal of Educational Psychology, 32: 251.

Schelling, T.C., (1960). The strategy of conflict. Oxford: Oxford University Press.

Sears, R.R., (1965). Development of gender role. In: F.A. Beach (ed.) Sex and Behaviour: New York, Wiley, pp. 133-163.

Sears, R.R., Rav, C. and Alpert R., (1965). Identification and Child Rearing. Stanford University Press.

Secord P.F. and Backman, (1965). Interpersonal approach to personality. In B.H. Maher (ed.) Progress in Experimental Personality Research. Vol. 2. New York: Academic Press, Inc. 91-125.

Sehgal, R., (1990). Problem solving as a function of neuroticism and fear of success in university and working women. Unpublished Ph.D. Thesis, Himachal Pradesh University, Shimla.

Shackleton, V.J. and Fletcher, C.A., (1984). Individual Differences—Theories and Applications. London, U.K.: Methuen.

Shagaas, C. and Canter, A., (1971). Cerebral Evoked Responses and Personality. In V.D. Nebylitsyn and J.A. Gray (eds.) Biological Basis of Individual Behaviour. London, New York: Academic Press.

Shapiro, J.P., (1979). "Fear of Success". Imagery as a reaction to sex-role inappropriate behaviour. Journal of Personality Assessment, 43: 33-38.

Sharma, A. and Malhotra, D.K., (2003). Psychological analysis of gender discrimination. Paper presented on March, 21 in National seminar on women at work place, India and Canada at Himachal Pradesh University, India.

Sharma, C., (1979). Perceived sex-typing: Ideal and Actual. In Parameshwaran (ed.).

Sheldon, W.H., (1949). Varieties of Delinquent Youth. New York: Harper.

Sherif, M., (1935). A study of some social factors in perception Arch. Psychology.

Sherif, M., (1936). The Psychology of Social Norms. New York: Harper.

Sherif, M., (1967). Formation of social norms. The experimental paradigm. In Sherif, M., (1967) Social Interaction. Chicago: Aldine.

Sherif, M., and Sherif, Carolyn, W., (1956). An Outline of Social Psychology (rev. ed.). New York: Harper and Row.

Sherif, M., and Sherif, Carolyn, W., (1967). Conformity—Deviation, Norms and Group Relations. In M. Sherif, Social Interaction: Process and Product. Chicago: Aldine.

Shoham, Y. and Tenneholtz, M., (1992a). On the Synthesis of useful social laws for artificial agent societies (preliminary report). In proceedings of the AAAI conference. pp. 276-281.

Shoham, Y. and Tenneholtz, M., (1992b). Emergent conventions in multi agent systems: Initial experimental results and observations. In proceedings of the 3rd International Conference on KR and R. Cambridge, M.A: pp. 225-232.

Sigal, J.J., Star, K.H., and Franks, C.M., (1958a). Hysterics and dysthymics as criterion groups in the study of introversion-extraversion. Journal of Abnormal and Social Psychology, 57: 143-148.

Sigal, J.J., Star, K.H., and Franks, C.M., (1958b). Hysterics and dysthymics as criterion groups in the study of introversion-extraversion: A rejoinder to Eysenck's reply. Journal of Abnormal and Social Psychology, 57: 381-382.

Signorella, M.L. and Janison, W., (1986). Masculinity, femininity, androgyny and cognitive performance: A Meta-Analysis Psychological Bulletin. 100: 207-228.

Singer, J.E., (1975). Sexual Mythology: A social learning approach to the elimination of sex-role stereotyped behaviour in women. Dissertation Abstract, 34: 2484.

Sinha, A.K.P., and Ojha, H., (1963). An experimental study of the operation of prestige suggestions in extraverts and introverts. Journal of Social Psychology, 61: 29-34.

Sistrunk, F., and McDavid, J.W., (1971). Sex variable in conforming behaviour. Journal of Personality and Social Psychology. 17: 200-207.

Smelsor N.J., (1967). Sociology: An Introduction. New York: John Wiley and Sons Inc.

Snyder, A., Mischel, W., and Lott, B.E., (1960). Value, information, and conformity behaviour. Journal of Personality, 28: 333-341.

Sokolov, E.N., (1963). Perception and the Conditioned Reflex. Oxford Pergamon Press. (Brody, 1972).

Spence, J.T. Helmreich, R. and Stapp, J., (1975). Ratings of self and peers on sex-role attributes and their relation to self-esteem and conceptions of masculinity and femininity. Journal of Personality and Social Psychology, 32: 29-39.

Spence, K.W. and Taylor, J.A., (1953). The relation of conditioned response strength to anxiety in normal, neurotic and psychotic subjects. Journal of Experimental Psychology, 45: 265-272.

Spence, K.W., (1956). Behaviour Theory and Conditioning. New Haven, Cornell. Yale University Press.

Spence, K.W., (1958). A theory of emotionality based on drive (D) and its relation to performance in simple learning situations. American Psychologist, 13: 131-141.

Spence, K.W., (1964). Anxiety (Drive) level and performance in eyelid conditioning. Psychological Bulletin, 61: 129-139.

Spence, K.W., and Beecroft, R.S., (1954). Differential conditioning and level of anxiety. Journal of Experimental Psychology, 48: 399-403.

Spence, K.W., and Taylor, J.A., (1951). Anxiety and strength of the UCS as determinants of the amount of eyelid conditioning. Journal of Experimental Psychology, 42: 183-188.

Spencer, H., (1855). Principles of Psychology. London: Williams and Norgate.

Spencer, R.E., (1957). The relationship between personality anxiety and selected problem solving processes. Dissertation Abstract International, 17: 2504-2505.

Spielberger, C.D., and Smith, L.H., (1966). 'Anxiety (Drive) stress and serial position effects in serial verbal learning'. Journal of Experimental Psychology, 72: 589-593.

Spielberger, C.D., Goldstein, L.D., and Dehlstron, W.G., (1958). Complex incidental learning as a function of anxiety and task difficulty. Journal of Experimental Psychology, 56: 158-161.

Sprague, J.M., (1953). Stimulation of the reticular formation in intact., unanestheized and in decerebrated cats. Fed. Proc., 12: 137.

Sprague, J.M., and Chambers, W.W., (1954). Control of the posture by reticular formation and cerebellum in the intact, anestheized and anaestheized and in the decerebrated cats. American Journal of Physiology, 176: 52-64.

Staats. A.W., (1957). Verbal and instrumental response hierarchies and their relationship to problem-solving. American Journal of Psychology, 70: 442-446.

Standish, R.R., and Champion, R.A., (1960). Task difficulty and drive in verbal learning. Journal of Experimental Psychology, 59: 361-365.

Stumpf, C.H., (1965) Drug action on the electrical activity of the hippocampus. International Review of Neurobiology, 8: 77-138.

Sudarshan, K., (1987). Problem solving as a function of extraversion, intelligence and induced stress. Unpublished Ph.D. Thesis, Himachal Pradesh University, Shimla.

Sumner, W. G., (1906). Folkways. New York: New American Library.

Super, D.E., (1995). Values: Their nature, assessment, and practical use. 397, 54-61.

Sweeney, E.J., (1953). Sex-differences in problem-solving. Technical Report, Stanford University. Stanford.

Sweetbaum, H.A., (1963). Comparison of the effects of introversion-extraversion and anxiety on conditioning. Journal of Abnormal and Social Psychology, 66: 249-254.

Symonds, P.M., (1928). The nature of conduct. New York: Macmillan.

Tanford, S., and Penrod, S., (1984). Social Influence Model: A formal interaction of research on majority and minority influence processes. Psychological Bulletin, 95: 189-225.

Tanwar, U., (1988). Short term memory as a function of personality and imagery, Unpublished Ph.D. Thesis, Himachal Pradesh University, Shimla.

Tanwar, U. and Kumar, D., (1986). An experimental study of distractor and probe technique in short-term memory as a function of extraversion and levels of intelligence. Journal of Psychological Research, 30: 105-160.

Tanwar, U., and Malhotra, D.K., (1990). Imagery variables in short term memory. Psychological Studies. 35: 191-196.

Tanwar, U., and Malhotra, D.K., (1992). Short-term memory as a function of personality and imagery. Personality and Individual Differences, 13: 175-180.

Taylor, D.W., and Faust, W.L., 1952. Twenty questions: Efficiency in problem-solving as a function of size group. Journal of Experimental Psychology, 44: 360-368.

Taylor, J.A., (1951). The relationship of anxiety to the conditioned eyelid response. Journal of Experimental Psychology, 41: 81-92.

Taylor, J.A., (1953). A personality scale of manifest anxiety. Journal of Abnormal and Social Psychology, 48: 288-290.

Taylor, J.A., and Spence, K.W., (1954). Conditioning level in behaviour disorders. Journal of Abnormal and Social Psychology, 49: 497-502.

Teplov, B.M., (1963). Typological Features of Higher Nervous Activity in Man. In J.A. Gray (ed.) Pavlov's Typology. Oxford: Pergaman Press.

Terman, L.M., (1956). Concept Mastery Test Manual. New York: Psychological Corporation.

Terman, L.M. and Tyler, L.E., (1954). Psychological Sex Diffrences. In L. Carmicheal (ed.), Manual of Child Psychology (2nd ed.). New York: Wiley.

Thibaut, J.W. and Kelley, H.H., (1959). The Social Psychology of Groups. New York: Wiley.

Thibaut, J.W., and Strickland, L.H., (1956). Psychological set and social conformity. Journal and Personality, 25: 115-129.

Thomas, E.J., and Fink, C.F., (1963). Effects of group size. Psychological Bulletin, 60: 371-384.

Traub, S.H., and Dodder, R.A., (1988). Intergenerational conflict of values and norms. A theoretical model. Adolescence. 23(92), 975-989.

Treurniet, N., (1989). On having and giving values. Sigmund Freud Houst Bulletin, 13(1), 1-14. (Psychological Abstr. 77, No. 4599).

Triandis, H.C., Bontempo, R., Villareal, M.J., Asai, M., and Lucca, N., (1988). Individualism and Collectivism: Cultural perspectives on self-in group relationship. Journal of Personality and Social Psychology, 54, 323-338.

Tylor, E.B., (1924). Primitive Culture. Brentano's (9th ed.), New York.

Ullman-Margalit, E. (1977). The emergence of norms. Oxford: Clarendon Press.

Unger, R.K., (1994). Alternative conceptions of sex (and sex differences). In M. Haug, R. Whalen, C. Aron, and K.L. Olsen (eds.), The development of sex differences and similarities in behaviour. Dordrecht, The Netherlands: Kluwer Academic.

Vogel, M.D., (1961). GSR conditioning and personality factors in alcoholics and normals. Journal of Abnormal and Social Psychology, 63: 417-421.

Walker, A. and Wooldridge, M., (1995). Understanding the emergence of conventions in multi-agent systems. In Proceedings of ICMAS (International Joint Conference on Multi Agent Systems) San Francisco.

Walker, E.L., (1958). Action decrement and its relation to learning. Psychological Review, 65: 124-142.

Wallach, M.A., Kogan, N.K. and Bem, D.J., (1962). Group influence on individual risk taking. Journal of Abnormal and Social Psychology, 65:78-86.

Wallestein, I., (1966). Social change. The Colonial Situation. New York: Wiley.

Warren, R. and Heist, P., (1966). Personality Attributes of gifted college students. Science, (132), 330-337.

Watson, J.B., (1924). Psychology from the Stand Point of a Behaviourist. Philadelphia Lippincott.

Watson, J.B., (1925). Behaviourism. New York: Norton.

Weber, M., (1960). Soziologische Grundbegriffe. In Weber, M., (1960). Wirtschaft und Gesellschaft. Tubingen: Mohr.

Weiss, W., (1969). Effects of the mass media on communication. In C. Lindzey and E. Aronson (eds.), The Handbook of Social Psychology (2nd ed.) Vol. 5. Reading, Mass: Addison Wesley Publishing Company, Inc., 77-195.

Whittaker, J.O. and Mead, R.D., (1967). Social pressure in the modification and distortion of judgement: A cross-cultural study. International Journal of Psychology, 2: 109-113.

Williams, R., (2003). Racial/ethnic discrimination and health: Findings from community studies. American Journal of Public Health. 92(2): 7-15.

Williams, J.E., (1982). An overview of finding from adult stereotypes studies in 25 countries. In: R. Rath, H.S. Asthana, D. Sinha and J.B.H. Sinha (eds.); Diversity and Unity in cross-cultural Psychology. Lisse; Swets and Zelinger.

Williams, J.E. and Best, D.L., (1990). Measuring sex stereotypes: A multinational study. Newbury Park, C.A. Sage.

Wilson, G.D., and Gregson, R.A.M., (1967). Effect of illumination on the perceived intensity of acid tastes. Australian Journal of Psychology, 19: 69-73.

Witkin, H.A., Dyk, R.B., Faterson, H.F., Goodenough, D.R. and Kerp, S.A., (1962) Psychological Differentiation. New York: Wiley.

Woodworth, R.S., and Schlosberg, H., (1954). Experimental Psychology. New York: Holt, Rinehart and Winston.

Wright, O., (1949). Modern technology and the world order, in W.F. Ogburn (ed.), Technology and International Relations. Chicago University Press.

Yinger, J., (1977). Counter cultures and social change. American Sociological Review, 42: 833-853.

Young, K., (1930). Social Psychology: an analysis of social behaviour New York: Appleton Century Crofts.

Zayas, Luis H., (1994). Hispanic family ecology and early childhood socialization: Health care implications. Family Systems Medicine, 12: 315-325.

Index